Sunday Best

Favorite Recipes from
Sunday Dinner with Juanita Garrison

Sunday Best: Favorite Recipes from *Sunday Dinner* with Juanita Garrison

Copyright 2016 Courier Publishing

All Rights Reserved

ISBN: 978-1-940645-33-9

Greenville, South Carolina

PUBLISHED IN THE UNITED STATES

Foreword

Growing up on a farm and later becoming a career full-time farmer, I've had the opportunity to experience many things most folks haven't, particularly the enjoyment of a steady supply of fresh, homegrown foods. From eggs, milk and meat to hand-picked vegetables, we grew up eating the most natural and safest food known to man.

In my younger years, meal time was what we all looked forward to (since our only entertainment was a black-and-white TV with rabbit ears that managed to pull in three hazy channels). Of course, it helped to have great cooks like my mother and my grandmother to prepare those wonderful meals — the likes of which few people today can remember.

My favorite dishes back then were the ones I still enjoy today: fresh fried chicken, chicken and dumplings, cubed steak, pork chops and gravy, homemade biscuits, green beans, squash, tomatoes and sweet corn — not to mention breakfast or the many made-from-scratch desserts from my mom's kitchen. If you enjoy meals like these, you'll love this book.

Farm life is not for everyone; it is a tough way to make a living. But with it comes the pleasure of a simple life, along with a deep sense of gratitude and satisfaction. Of all the joys of farm living, however, one of the most memorable will always be those delicious and nourishing home-cooked meals — prepared with love.

Tom Garrison III
Anderson, South Carolina

Introduction

Welcome to our Baptist Courier cookbook! Doing this column over the years has been a pleasure because I talked to so many good-cooking Baptists. Some of the recipes come from people who send them to the Courier, and many are from church cookbooks that you share with us.* We are grateful for both because I know that the recipe, whichever route it took, will be a good one. It always is! No one attaches his or her name to a dish that isn't good.

Remembering an afternoon from years ago, I was very proud of my 5-year-old self. Mixing a small amount of water with soil from our yard, I pressed it into two canning jar lids from the kitchen. Carefully turning over and emptying the lids, I had two layers for a cake. Taking a bit of flour from the kitchen, I "frosted" the cake, then I cut a serving piece from my creation. Pride goeth before a fall, and my little dirt cake soon collapsed. Still, it was a pretty little thing. I've made a lot of cakes since then, but no others from soil.

Cooking has always been a pleasure for me, ever since my two years of high school home economics. The girls all took "home ec," as it was called, and the boys all took science, but I never really knew what they did in there. In a district 4-H contest, I won an award for my tomato soup and, again, was rather pleased with myself. I still make soup.

Often I carry dishes I have made from your recipes to church suppers, and almost always someone asks, "Will this be in the Courier?" My fellow Baptists don't know I'm using them for my test group!

Sometimes I hear people, mostly women, say, "Oh, I don't ever cook!" as if not cooking is an achievement. Everyone should know how to cook, especially since that unpleasant episode with Eve and the forbidden fruit, the supposed apple. There may not be enough wild-growing "fruit in the garden" to feed us all. Instead, how fortunate we are to have foods from local farmers, from growers around the state, and from other countries.

Remember that home economics class? We learned that a balanced meal should contain a meat or meat-substitute, a carbohydrate and two vegetables. Toss in bread, dessert and a beverage if you wish. This is still a good menu plan, but sometimes our serving portions are larger than they should be, and our weight becomes our enemy. Wasn't it St. Paul who suggested "moderation in all things"?

Paul also talked about being hospitable, and Titus says that the bishops should be lovers of hospitality. Peter says to offer hospitality one to another without grudging. I suppose that means that even if you feel you have to invite someone to your house you don't especially like, you should be nice about it.

I thank Butch Blume, the Courier's managing editor, and the staff for their encouragement over the years. Just as important, I thank all the contributors who have shared their recipes with us to read, cook and enjoy for our next … *Sunday Dinner*.

Juanita Garrison
Denver Downs Farm
Anderson, South Carolina
April 2016

* Editor's note: While acknowledging that some of our recipe contributors have passed away and pastors may have moved or retired, we have chosen to preserve the names and places described herein as they originally appeared in the pages of The Baptist Courier.

Table of Contents

Planning and Serving

Cleaning Cabinets	15
Pantries	17
Summer Party Time	19
Plan for Guests	21
Table Setting	22
Cooking Terms	25

Appetizers and Beverages

Veggie Squares	33
Hot Crab Dip	35
Chicken Rolls	37
Iced Tea	38

Brunch

Brunch with Crabmeat Newberg	45
Quiche	47
Shrimp and Grits	51

Soups and Salads

Acorn/Butternut Squash Soup	57
Catfish Stew	59
Hearty Potato Soup	62
Broccoli-Cheese Soup	64
Gumbo Creole	66
Yum-Yum Chicken Soup with Cornbread	68

Salads and Dressings	71
Frozen Fruit Salad	74
Cabbage Slaw	76
Chinese Slaw	78
Marinated Cukes and Onions	80
Regal Chicken Salad	83
Layered Lettuce Salad	85
Cherry Congealed Salad	88

Vegetables and Side Dishes

Macaroni and Cheese	93
Crock Pot Macaroni	96
Macaroni and Cheese My Way	98
Infallible Rice Casserole	101
One-Pot Potatoes	102
Stuffings and Dressings	104
Zesty Vegetable Casserole	108
Corn Casserole	110
Fresh Corn Pudding	112
Corn Pie	114
Stuffed Tomatoes with Yellow Rice	116
Bacon and Tomato Pie	118
Baked Onions	120
Green Bean Casserole	122
Green Beans	124
Broccoli	126
Okra Casserole	129
Cabbage Casserole	131
Cabbage, Collards and Kale	133
Collards and Cabbages	137

Luncheon Vegetable Dish and Squash Casserole	139
Glorified Squash	142
Squash Casserole	145
Ever Best Eggplant	147
Grated Sweet Potato Bake	149
Sweet Potato Crunch	151

Main Dishes

Julie's Roast Beef	157
Basic Chicken Pie	159
Baked Chicken that Makes Its Own Gravy	161
Sunday Glazed Ham	164
Boiled Ham	166
Pork Chop Casserole	168
Baked Savory Pork Chops	170
Cranberry Pork Chops	173
Cheeseburger Pie	175
Meatloaf and Veggies	177
Neapolitan Casserole	179
Mama's Scalloped Oysters	181
Salmon Loaf	184
Catfish	186
American Chop Suey	189
Toaster Oven Recipes	191
Hay and Straw with Pear Pie	193

Breads and Rolls

Biscuits	199
Spoon Bread	202
Easy Yeast Rolls	205

Refrigerator Rolls — 207
Strawberry Bread — 209
Popovers — 212
Sandwiches — 214

Desserts

Baptist Pound Cake — 219
Pound Cake — 221
Pineapple Pound Cake — 224
Strawberry Pound Cake — 226
$100 Coconut Cake — 229
Pineapple Cake — 231
Blackberry Jam Cake with Caramel Icing — 233
Lemon Berry Cake — 236
Lemon Cheesecake — 238
Eclair Cake — 240
Honey Bun Cake — 242
The Best Fruitcake — 244
White Fruitcake — 246
Japanese Fruitcake — 247
Pie Crusts — 250
Fresh Apple Pie — 253
Fresh Strawberry Pie — 255
Coconut Pies — 258
Coconut Peach Pie — 261
Peanut Butter Pie — 263
Apple Dumpling Bake — 266
Warm Apple Crisp — 268
Applesauce Soufflé — 270

Peach (or Apple) Strudel	272
Denver Downs Delight	274
Chocolate Lust	276
Sour Cream Banana Pudding	278
German Chocolate Brownies	280
Lonesome Cowboy Bars	282
Baked Caramel Corn	284
Pecan Candy and Sugar Peanuts	286

Miscellaneous Goodies

Pear Honey	291
Pear Relish	293
Pickled Peaches	296
Chowchow	298
Crisp Pickle Slices	300

Index   305

Planning and Serving

Cleaning Cabinets
(Published October 9, 2003)

"You are forbidden to go to the supermarket for six months," commanded daughter Lee with mock bossiness, standing two steps up on the ladder and attacking the kitchen cabinets.

It was a job that had needed doing for a long time, and Lee, who inherited her grandmother's clean gene, could bear it no longer. She went through my kitchen like Sherman through Georgia.

She took down, cleaned and put back. I was supposed to be making decisions about what to keep, but she edited a lot of the things before I got my hands on them, tossing left and right.

There were some interesting discoveries. "What's this?" (an ice crusher); "And this?" (a food grinder).

We also found 20-plus boxes of gelatin of assorted flavors and brands; seven cans of cranberry sauce; six cans of small, early green peas; five little containers of poppy seeds; four quarts of mayonnaise; and five boxes of Band Aids in various sizes, totaling 285 bandages. During the entire year of 2003, I have used three.

There were toothpicks: two boxes of 750 each and one box of 1,000. Scarcely anyone here uses toothpicks, but if the need ever arises …

There were enough Tupperware tops to satisfy any Tupperware rep. I don't know what happened to the bowls and boxes to which the tops had been married; only the tops remained. And I don't even want to tell you the number of canning jar rings; both Ball and Kerr would be envious.

In the end, we put things — what there was left of them — back in the same areas, because my kitchen was already arranged for easy use. Time and management people use the phrase, "Store things at the point of use." I call it putting things where they ought to be.

All baking supplies — including flours, salt, baking powder, sugar, sifter, scales, mixer and mixing utensils — are together. Canned vegetables, soups, fruit and meat products are all in their allocated areas. Cereals are together. Mixes — and I don't use many of these — are together. Spices and seasonings, including the poppy seeds, are arranged alphabetically. (The latter arrangement may not survive the first three meals.)

One change we did make was that I discarded 30 years of unmatched socks. I have been living in the constant, confident hope that one day, by whatever means, all the strayed matches would return home. We washed the plastic basket and now use it as a depository for paper products. If one day — from behind the washer, under the bed and beneath sofa cushions — socks begin to appear, seeking their now-dispatched mates, it may be more than I can handle.

This season was a good time to do this, because most families do more cooking in fall and winter than in summer, when we say, "Out with the light cuisine and in with rich pies, robust stews, hearty soups, etc." This cleaning is not only a time for the actual cleaning and discarding of outdated items, but also for checking equipment and food items. I discovered I need two more pie plates to replace two that I thought had been "put somewhere." To keep the basic food items current, I keep a pad and pencil in the kitchen and make a list of things I need to replace as I use the item.

We lack only a couple of places to complete the kitchen attack, and then we will work a bit on the laundry side of the room. I haven't even mentioned to her the shelves that hold my cookbook collection.

A kitchen that is orderly is much easier to cook in than a cluttered one. Equipment and food items are easier and faster to locate, and it looks better. I'm glad she pushed into the job. Lee is an inspiration to us all, but once every 10 years is often enough.

Pantries
(Published October 20, 2005)

We had had no rain during September, and the temperatures were above 90 much of the time. On the first day that we had the tiniest little tinge of crispness in the air, I decided to make chili. I thawed ground beef from the freezer and went through the whole thing, then looked for a can of red kidney beans. No beans. I ended the dish by adding a can of chili-with-beans to my pot. It was good, but I was still put out with myself for not having the beans. Therefore, today's column is to help you avoid being without beans.

We should keep our pantries stocked with basics. This doesn't mean that you run to the grocery and spend a couple of hundred dollars. Add a few of these each week until they are in place. Even more important, when you use an item, replace it during the next shopping trip. You never know when (a) you'll be sick, (b) the car will be in the shop, or (c) the bridge will be washed out.

Your list will be different from mine, but with the things listed here you can make a number of dishes for all the meals at your house:

- Canned vegetables: red kidney beans, black beans, green beans, baked beans, stewed tomatoes, diced tomatoes, whole kernel corn, asparagus, sweet potatoes, peas
- Baking needs: all-purpose flour, self-rising flour, self-rising corn meal, granulated sugar, brown sugar, 5x or 10x confectioners' sugar, yeast, baking powder, non-sugar sweetener packs, cocoa, cornstarch
- Starches and pastas: grits, rice, noodles, spaghetti, macaroni, fettuccine, tomato-herb/tomato-meat sauce
- Oils: vegetable, canola, olive, spray-on, shortening or lard

- Canned meats: salmon, tuna, crabmeat, corned beef hash, corned beef, ready-to-eat chili
- Condiments: mayonnaise, honey, horseradish, ketchup, prepared mustard, dry mustard, hot sauce, corn syrup, honey, maple or other syrup, tomato paste, Worcestershire sauce, soy sauce, chicken and beef bouillon cubes or broth, minced garlic
- Canned fruit: pears, peaches, pineapple, coconut, blueberries
- Packaged foods: pancake mix, baking mix, cake mix, macaroni and cheese, creamed potatoes
- Beverages: regular, decaffeinated or instant coffee and tea; lemon, orange, cranberry and apple juices
- Seasonings/spices: salt, black pepper, chili, cumin, oregano, thyme, cinnamon, nutmeg, onion salt, garlic powder, bay leaves
- Miscellaneous: evaporated milk, sweetened condensed milk, pimientos, ripe olives, peanut butter, gelatin, vinegar
- Crackers: saltine, butter-flavored, graham, vanilla wafers
- Soups: vegetable, cream of chicken, mushroom, tomato
- Cereals: oatmeal, cream of wheat, ready-to-eat favorites
- Vegetables: white potatoes, onions, green pepper, carrots
- In refrigerator: milk, yogurt, cheese, eggs, butter, sour cream, cottage cheese
- In freezer: 5 packs of meat, fish, or poultry; frozen pecans; pie shells; chopped parsley; shredded cheese; packs of vegetables

From these basics, you can make many good meals, especially if Uncle Tom from Tucson or Aunt Susie from Savannah arrives unexpectedly for ... *Sunday Dinner*.

Summer Party Time
(Published June 30, 2005)

June 21 brings us the first day of summer. It also brings flies, gnats, fire ants and yellow jackets, but these are perpetual scourges with which we have to deal. More pleasant things about summer are the longer daylight hours and the outdoor entertaining.

I've talked about this before, but it should be repeated often. The Bible discusses hospitality. Remember Christ telling Zacchaeus He was going to his house for lunch? I hope someone ran ahead to tell Mrs. Zacchaeus. We also learn from the Bible that Abraham dispatched servants to kill a choice, tender calf for the three visitors. I wonder how long they had to make small talk until that meal was ready?

Our guests are not usually so unexpected — or shouldn't be — and we can make preparations for them. Often, hosts will invite their guests to a restaurant for a meal. That is all right, of course, because one usually has good food — but hospitality in one's home is always more gracious than in a restaurant.

Don't worry about your housekeeping beyond normal tidiness. Guests don't look in closets and under beds or open closed doors. The thing they will remember is the pleasant company.

If you are planning a party, may I make seven suggestions:

1) Determine the reason for the party. If it is a national holiday such as July 4, Thanksgiving, etc., or a personal occasion such as a birthday or anniversary, the theme is in place. But maybe you just want to have a party.

2) Give thought to your invitation list. If it is a family event, the list is set. If not, think about it. Invite only a number that you can seat comfortably. Sometimes at a large, informal party, that advice is totally ignored and people sit anywhere they can.

3) Unless he or she is from out of town, every guest should know at least two other people besides the host. There is also the old adage, "The roof is the introduction," meaning that guests can initiate conversations without being formally introduced. Invite people whom you believe will be compatible and congenial. This isn't a high school party, so you don't have to have an equal number of men and women.

4) Make the menu fit the occasion. It's your house and you can serve anything anywhere, but barbecued ribs are better served on a picnic table on the deck than in the dining room. Keep the finger-lickin' foods such as corn on-the-cob and tacos in an informal setting. Try new recipes, but give them a test run at least once before you serve the new dish to your guests.

5) Plan the menu and table decorations early. Buy ahead as many menu items as possible. Meat and vegetables will be purchased the day before or the day of the party. Whether indoors or out, you need to check table coverings, napkins, flower arrangements, etc. Plan and lay out the serving containers and utensils.

6) Prepare ahead as many food items as you can. You don't want to spend the whole day of the party in the kitchen.

7) Have both your family and yourself ready to receive guests a half hour before they are to arrive. Some may arrive early — and if no one does, you'll have a chance to drink a glass of iced tea, catch your breath and prepare to be charming.

Again, your guests will remember you, the laughter, the conversation, the camaraderie and the pleasant evening, so start planning your next party today.

Plan for Guests
(Published January 17, 2013)

Now that the tree is down (or should be) and the church class parties are over (or probably are), we can settle down to some kind of a schedule. I recommend that this schedule include entertaining guests in your home. I usually write about this once a year because I think it is important to bond friendships.

Besides that, the Bible says so.

When Christ was going to and fro preaching, he, in the absence of motels, stayed in the homes of friends. These people are not usually named, but he told his disciples to stay with the same family during the time they were in an area, not to trot from house to house.

You recall that he and his disciples traveled rather lightly — no change of clothes, no money, etc. We are told in Romans 12:13 to "practice hospitality." In 4:9 of his first letter, Peter says, "Be hospitable to one another without grumbling." Of course, it was probably Mrs. Peter who was doing the cooking, the washing of the dishes, and the grumbling. Titus talked a lot about hospitality. In talking about the bishops, he says they should be hospitable, etc.

I especially like the story of the three "men" visiting Abraham unexpectedly and Abraham insisting on "fetching" them a little food. He then went out to the herd, selected a "fine, tender calf and gave it to the servant" to prepare. I wonder how much small talk had to go on while that calf was being slaughtered and barbecued.

The point of this is that we are to show love and friendship to our fellow Christians and to others by entertaining them in our homes, whether "home" is a tent, an apartment or an estate.

Some people you should invite to your home: the pastor and his family, members of your Sunday school class or WMU group, the frequent visitor to your church, the church staff, longtime church members (because you will have a lot to talk about), fellow members that you may not see often because they are in different classes, etc.

Keep the number small enough to handle easily. It is more congenial so everyone can enjoy the conversation to seat everyone at the same table (whether that is six, 10, or whatever) than to have them scattered all over the house. It is all right to do the latter, of course, if the group is a large number such as your Sunday school class.

Keep the menu simple: a main dish (usually a meat dish); one or two vegetables (perhaps a green vegetable and a starchy one); a salad; hot bread; and a good, rich, and highly fattening dessert. Keep this as simple or as busy as you want. You may serve soup or salad, then the main dish, and then the dessert in courses — or you can put it all on the table or buffet at the same time.

The things your guests will remember will be your hospitality, the good food (whatever it is and however it is served), and your friendship and love — not if the curtains have been recently laundered.

Be generous and hospitable. The Bible says so.

Table Setting
(Published December 18, 2003)

Christmas is wonderful, if you don't go crazy.

I love the carols, the churches decorated with poinsettias and greenery, the special music, the nativity plays — all of it. I especially like the Christmas dinners held by Sunday school groups, clubs, etc. Even more, I like having guests in our house.

And I love a beautifully set table. You can offer your guests plastic plates, forks and cups, and sometimes, because of the size of the crowd, this is the most practical. But it isn't nearly as gracious.

There are a few rules for setting the table, whether the food is to be served from a buffet table or put on the table. The first is to allow 24 inches between the center of one place setting to the center of the next place setting. This will give wiggle space for elbows, chairs, etc.

Don't use every piece of flatware — whether sterling or stainless — that you have. Use only those pieces that will be needed for the meal, with two exceptions. One exception is to use a knife in the place setting, even if you are serving a food such as a casserole that doesn't require cutting. The knife makes a balanced setting. The other exception we will see later. This usually means that only a knife and fork are put at the place setting. If you are having a salad course, you need a salad fork. If you are having a soup course, you need a soup spoon. But if you are having only a meat course and a dessert course, you will need only a knife and fork.

The only time a teaspoon is placed on the table is for breakfast, because breakfast is the only time coffee is served with the meal. At lunch, supper or dinner — whatever you call it — coffee is not served during the meal, but is brought in afterwards to be served with the dessert or following it. The coffee spoon — a teaspoon — is brought on the saucer with the coffee cup, lying behind the cup and parallel with the handle.

If you have a salad served on a separate plate along with the meat course, the salad plate should be placed to the left of the dinner plate. You don't need a salad fork unless the salad is served as a separate course. You wouldn't use your dinner fork for the meat and potatoes, lay it down, then pick up the salad for the salad. If the salad is served with the meal, the dinner fork is used for both.

The salad course is served correctly after the meat course, but in this country we are accustomed to restaurants serving the salad immediately after we order. That gives the customer something to nibble on while the main meal is being prepared.

Bread and butter plates are used for lunch or supper, not for a formal dinner. However, it's your house, and you may use them if you wish. If you have individual butter spreaders or knives, these are placed parallel with the edge of the table across the edge of the bread plate. You can put a pat of butter on each plate if you wish, or you can pass the butter. The diner will use the butter server on the butter plate, take a pat of butter, and put it on his bread and butter plate. Don't use a separate salad plate if you are also using the bread and butter plate. It makes the table too crowded.

A serving spoon is never used to put the food served — such as butter, jam, etc. — onto the diner's toast, roll, etc., but instead is put onto the plate. Then the diner uses his knife to spread the butter, etc.

The dessert utensils may be handled two ways. The first is to put the dessert fork and spoon on the table above the plate. The fork is nearest the plate, with the tines on the right and turned downward. The dessert spoon is above it, with the spoon's bowl to the left and turned downward. When the other plate and utensils are removed, these stay in place, waiting for the dessert to be served. The second way is to place the fork and spoon on the dessert plate — one on each side of the food — in the kitchen and carry all together to the table. Both are equally correct — just a matter of preference. I usually put the spoon and fork on the table.

Earlier, I said to include only those utensils you need for eating. The dessert is the exception. It is always served with both a fork and spoon, even if only one is needed.

Here is how your place setting should look for a meat course and dessert course (left to right): the dinner fork, the dinner plate, the dinner knife turned with the sharp part of the blade toward the plate.

If soup is being served, the setting would be like this: dinner fork, dinner plate, dinner knife, soup spoon.

If there is to be a separate salad course, this will be the order: dinner fork, salad fork, dinner plate, dinner knife, soup spoon.

One always starts from the outside of the flatware, working toward the plate.

The napkin may be placed in the center of the plate or on the left side. Sometimes in restaurants, the napkins are tucked into the water glass. You can do that if you wish, but the other methods are more common.

Usually, two glasses are used. The larger goblet (or iced-tea glass) is at the tip of the knife, and the smaller (or water) glass is at the tip of the soup spoon, sitting on a slant. Even if your guest doesn't drink tea, put the glass there anyway. He can leave the tea untouched, and you can refill his water glass as needed.

The dinner plate and flatware should be one inch from the edge of the table.

The centerpiece should be low enough so that diners on each side of the table can see each other. Candles should not be used unless they are needed and are lit. This means they're not used for noon luncheons or dinners. If you have them on the evening dinner table, light them; they make the whole table lovely.

Cooking Terms
(Published May 25 and June 13, 2007)

I once read the little sentence: "The only thing worse than a person who can cook and doesn't is a person who can't cook and does." Whether you cook because of pleasure or necessity and have been doing so for a long time, all these following words will be familiar to you. Perhaps you can share them with a young, inexperienced cook.

Sauté, fry, and deep fry: These are degrees of cooking food — usually meat, but also vegetables and fruits — in fat.

Sauté means to brown quickly in the tiniest bit of fat; fry or pan fry means to cook uncovered in hot fat usually about ½ inch deep in a pan, and deep fry means to cook the food in fat deep enough to cover the food.

To grill is similar, but no fat is used and the food is cooked either under direct heat of a broiler on the range — or over direct heat on an outdoor grill, cooking only one side at a time and turning, usually only once.

Sear: This means to place meat in a very hot skillet, etc., without oil so the meat surface cooks quickly to seal in the juices. It is then turned to sear the other side.

Stir, whisk, whip, cream, beat, fold: To stir means to move the food slowly around in the bowl or pot in a circular motion to keep the food moving while it is cooking or cooling.

To whisk, one beats the food quickly using a wire whisk, as for egg whites, etc. To whip is similar and means to beat quickly to add air to the mix and to increase the volume. When creaming — especially the butter and sugar in cake baking — use either a large spoon or electric mixer to thoroughly combine the two so the resulting mix is light and fluffy. Sometimes powdered sugar and cream cheese are also creamed.

To beat is to stir forcefully and vigorously in an up and over motion, especially for cakes, frostings, and candy.

To fold is to gently lift the food in a bowl up from the bottom with a spoon then turn the spoon upside down so that the lifted food falls on top of the food that is being mixed in this way. This is done with "folding in the flour," "folding in the egg whites," etc.

Glacé, glaze: The first word, glacé, should be written with an accent on the "e" so that the word is pronounce "glaw-say." This means to cover (usually sweet rolls) with a sweet frosting or icing so that it looks like a glacier.

To glaze means to make a smooth, shiny surface such as pouring a sweet mixture over a pound cake. It also means to cover meat with a broth/sauce that will leave a shine and add flavor.

Fricassee, braise: Chicken, and other meats, are often cooked as a fricassee, meaning the meat is cooked and served in its own gravy.

To braise meat is to brown quickly in a small amount of fat, add water, cover, and cook slowly until tender.

Cube, dice, mince, julienne: These are ways of preparing food for cooking. To cube is to cut the food — whether meat, vegetable, or fruit — into cube-shaped, uniform sizes of about an inch or so.

To dice is about the same, but usually the dice is much smaller, about a half inch.

To mince means to chop the food in tiny pieces as one would do with herbs.

To julienne food, cut it into long, narrow strips, as is often done with carrots, zucchini, etc.

Roast, bake: Both mean to cook in the oven with dry heat. Roast usually refers to meats, and bake to cakes, breads, etc. I suppose one could "roast" a cake, but that doesn't sound right to the ear.

Par-boil: This means to cook a food in boiling water until partly tender. The water is usually discarded, and the food goes on to a second step in preparation.

Scalloped, au gratin: A scalloped dish is one made with a sauce and bread crumbs to give the dish firmness or to sprinkle the dish with crumbs.

Au gratin is similar, but the topping is of cheese and crumbs, spread on top of the dish and baked to a lightly browned crust.

Blanch, scald: To blanch a food means to lower the food briefly (a few minutes or less) in boiling water, then remove and drain. This is done frequently before freezing fresh vegetables.

To scald means to bring a liquid (usually milk) to the boiling point. The surface will appear ruffled. Don't allow it to bubble.

Alfresco or al fresco: To dine alfresco is to eat out of doors but in a refined style involving linens, china, etc., and can be on a patio or under the trees — not the porch. It is far removed from having a hot dog in a paper napkin and drinking from a soft-drink bottle.

Cocktail: Although we often think of the word as meaning a beverage, it is an appetizer that is served before the meal and usually in a room other then the dining room. Cocktail food is usually in small, bite-sized pieces. It can also be a beverage.

Canapé: Pronounced CAN-a-pay, it is a cracker or a thin slice of toasted bread on which is placed a piece of highly flavored food such as cheese, shrimp, fish, etc., and is served as a cocktail or an appetizer before the main meal.

Demitasse: This can mean the small cup, about half the size of a normal cup, in which coffee is served after the evening meal. It can also mean the serving itself, such as, "The meal included demitasse."

Mornay: A dressed-up white sauce to which cheese, egg, heavy cream, etc., is added. One of my favorite dishes is Eggs Mornay.

Hollandaise: A sauce of beaten eggs, butter and lemon juice, most often used over vegetables or over Eggs Benedict.

Soufflé: Pronounced sou-FLAY, it is a light, spongy dish, most often cheese soufflé, made fluffy by the addition of beaten egg whites. Soufflés must be served immediately or they will fall flat instead of being light and fluffy.

Tortilla: A thin, flat bread made of either flour or corn meal and used with many Mexican dishes.

Hors d'oeuvre: A French word meaning the light food served before a meal; usually consists of olives, celery, etc., but can include canapés and other light food. Sometimes an invitation will read "heavy hors d'oeuvres," which means the food will be more substantial but not a meal.

Crepes: Very thin pancakes for a luncheon dish or dessert usually served with a filling of either chicken or fruit, folded, and covered with a sauce.

Florentine: If a dish has this word in it, it means that it includes spinach.

Bouquet garni: A mixture of several small dried or fresh herbs tied in a cheesecloth and added to the pot while food is cooking. The bouquet garni is removed before the food is served.

Croutons: Pieces of bread which have been cut into cubes and toasted or fried and served in soups or on salads.

Frappé: Pronounced fra-PAY, this can refer to fruit juice or coffee, etc., sweetened and either frozen or whipped with ice to a thick, frosty consistency.

Charlotte: A dessert held in shape with gelatin and served in a glass bowl lined with lady fingers or cake strips.

Parfait: A dessert, usually ice cream and fruit, layered in the tall, slender glasses of the same name specifically for this dessert.

Puff pastry: A buttery rich pastry used for patty shells or baked and filled with a rich cream.

Try a new recipe this weekend so that the meal at your house will always be an adventure when you have ... *Sunday Dinner.*

Appetizers and Beverages

Veggie Squares
Sandy Schwarz
(Published September 13, 2012)

I have on my desk a drawing made for me from our visiting grandson Tillman of Mt. Pleasant, who is celebrating his fifth birthday this month. Across the bottom is a "mural" of a person (or a Martian, it's hard to tell), a bale of hay (which looks like an upside down "U"), another, smaller upside down "U," and then another smaller upside down "U" with a stem at the top (ergo, a pumpkin).

On the first line at the top are the letters T-I-L-L-M. On the second line one sees "A-N." Then there is a third line consisting of the letters A-P-T-L-M-O-M-A. I asked him what word those letters spelled.

"I don't know, Nannie," he answered. "I thought you would know."

You're going to like this recipe, and it is much easier to understand than Tillman's mystery word. You will use it often and thank Sandy Schwarz of Rhode Island (by way of St. Helena Baptist Church on South Carolina's coast) for sharing it with us. It is from a church cookbook, as are most of the recipes here. Please send us a copy of your book so our other good South Carolina cooks can enjoy dishes prepared your way.

A few weeks back, I used another recipe from St. Helena's book and shared with you that Rev. Richard Spearman is the pastor and that the church, organized in 1966, has a current membership of around 300. It is part of the Savannah River Association.

Mrs. Schwarz lives in Middleton, R.I., and it is appropriate that a Rhode Islander contribute to a South Carolina Baptist church cookbook. Remember your Baptist history that it was Roger Williams (1603-1683) of Providence, R.I., who started the first Baptist congregation on these shores in 1639 (although some claim that it was John Clark in Newport, R.I., who did so in 1638).

When asked by her friend Jean Jones of St. Helena to submit a recipe to the book the church was compiling, Sandy did so. After living in Ohio, she and her late husband, Bill, moved to Middleton, where they lived for many years. A medical secretary, Sandy doesn't recall where she got the recipe, but we thank her for contributing it to the St. Helena cookbook so we can all enjoy it.

Mrs. Schwarz lists this as an appetizer, but it is so good that you may want to have it as a snack any time of day. Because of the cream cheese, it should be kept in the refrigerator. We can't really say it is low-calorie (with all that sour cream, cream cheese, mayo and rolls), but the several vegetables take away some of the guilt. Try making this soon — either for a snack, or to serve as an appetizer while everyone is waiting for you to serve … *Sunday Dinner.*

Veggie Squares

    ½ cup mayonnaise

    ½ cup sour cream

    2 packages crescent rolls

    ½ cup chopped cauliflower

    ½ cup chopped carrots

    ½ cup diced tomatoes

    1 package dry Hidden Valley Ranch dressing

    2 8-ounce packages cream cheese

    ½ cup chopped broccoli

    ½ cup chopped green onions

    ½ cup chopped or sliced black olives

Let cream cheese soften at room temperature. Heat oven according to directions on the package of crescent rolls. Press the rolls into a 15×10-inch jelly roll pan, pressing the seams together and making the dough level. Bake 7-8 minutes. When baked and still hot, press down gently to remove all air pockets.

Cream together the mayonnaise, sour cream, the dry dressing mix and cream cheese. Spread evenly over the cooled crust in pan. Sprinkle the chopped vegetables on the cream cheese mixture. Using fingers or the back of a spoon, press the vegetables very gently into the cream cheese mixture. Chill and cut into squares for serving.

Hot Crab Dip
Elizabeth Chamblee Renedo
(Published December 20, 2012)

Here's the situation: You aren't hungry enough for a meal but you want something, or you don't want to cook, or you want a bite of something to tide you over until dinner. *Voila!* Elizabeth Chamblee Renedo's hot crab dip.

This is a simple, yet really good, recipe to use primarily as a dip for parties, but great also for any of the above situations. Served with crackers or chips, it is a very satisfying dish.

Elizabeth is a twice-removed Baptist now attending a Presbyterian church. Her grandparents are Marian and the late C.D. Chamblee, members of Providence Baptist Church in Anderson.

Elizabeth lives in Columbia, where she grew up, the daughter of Mike and Jenny Chamblee Renedo. She works downtown with the budget and control board as director of one of the divisions. A former editor of South Carolina Wildlife Magazine, she keeps her finger in the writing pie by occasionally doing small writing jobs and web designs.

She is a Clemson graduate and is a busy lady with a lot of interests. She enjoys certain arts and crafts, including jewelry-making and embroidery, as well as writing blogs for an organization she likes. She goes to a gym regularly and also has two dogs who want (demand) daily walks.

As a teenager, Elizabeth stopped eating red meat (although she isn't extreme about it) but enjoys seafood and occasionally chicken.

The recipe, which comes from her mother, Jenny, who got it from her mother, Marian, fits Elizabeth's culinary style. As do many cooks, Elizabeth has tweaked this one a bit, and I think you'll like the result. She usually serves it with Triscuits. We served it with Scoops and potato chips. Both were good. Bake it in a pretty bake-and-serve dish.

Consider making Elizabeth's dish for yourself, or for yourself and others for your next gathering, or to enjoy after church this weekend while waiting until it's time to serve … *Sunday Dinner*.

Hot Crab Dip
- 1 8-ounce package cream cheese, softened
- 1 tablespoon milk
- 2 teaspoons Worcestershire sauce
- 1 7½-ounce can crabmeat, drained and flaked
- 2 tablespoons chopped green onion
- 2 tablespoons toasted, slivered almonds

Thoroughly combine the cream cheese with milk and Worcestershire sauce. Add the crabmeat and onion. Spread into a small, shallow baking dish. Top with the almonds. Bake at 350 degrees for 15 minutes or until heated through. Keep warm, serve with assorted crackers.

Chicken Rolls
Becky Chamblee
(Published January 3, 2013)

Today's recipe is a good one that can be used as an hors d'oeuvre, an addition to a light luncheon plate, or as a snack. The recipe makes a bunch, so ask a friend over.

The recipe is easily put together. If you think your time will be limited, you can make part of it early as indicated or do it all at once.

The recipe is from Dr. Becky Chamblee in Anderson County, formerly a member and pianist at Mountain Creek Baptist Church in Anderson but now a member of Central Presbyterian Church. She is known in education circles, having retired this past May after 48 years with two school systems. Her title was school psychologist for elementary schools. She retired after 30 years with District 5 schools in Anderson, then she trotted over to Hartwell for a one-year stay as an elementary guidance counselor. That one year turned into 18.

Since her retirement, she and her husband, Jones, have traveled a lot, including many trips to visit their only child, Amiee Barwick, and granddaughter, Ashlee, in Georgia.

In her retirement, Becky — whose doctorate is from USC — is enjoying some new things. For many years, she was pianist for Mountain Creek. She has now been taking guitar lessons for a few weeks and mastered "Jingle Bells" just in time for Christmas. She has dusted off her golf clubs. She and Jones live near a nine-hole course, so the playing is convenient. She also enjoys reading.

When Becky and Jones aren't traveling, during their new "free time" schedule they are caring for their dogs, two schnauzers and two Yorkies (Yorkshire terriers). The dogs are usually their traveling companions.

You may find these rolls to be a bit bland, so instead of using the canned chicken, you may use 1½ cups of chopped, left-over turkey or chicken from a holiday dinner or from that package you put in the freezer. This home-cooked chicken or turkey will probably have more flavor than the canned.

If you are looking for quick and tasty food during these winter days, consider making Becky's chicken rolls. They will be a good snack for your family as they wait for you to complete preparing ... *Sunday Dinner*.

Chicken Rolls
- 1 10-ounce can white chicken
- 1 8-ounce package cream cheese, softened
- 1 small onion, finely diced
- 4 tablespoons milk
- Salt, pepper to taste
- 2 tubes of croissant rolls

Mix together the chicken, softened cream cheese, onion, salt and pepper. Refrigerate overnight.
Roll out the croissants. Spread chicken mixture on rolls, slice and place on baking sheet. Bake 12 minutes at 350 degrees.

Iced Tea
(Published July 28, 2005)

Very carefully I unwrapped the cups and saucers. They match the teapot, sugar and creamer I had ordered earlier. Being reared in the South, where iced tea is the drink of both king and commoner, I don't drink much hot tea. I do, however, like tea sets, and this one will sit prettily on the table while I drink my iced tea from a glass.

I buy decaffeinated tea and prefer it without sugar. Our son Tom asked me why I bother to drink it at all. The answer is that I like the tea taste, not the sweet. We all have our ways of making our Southern "national drink." Here is mine:

Into a small saucepan, I put a quart of water and four family-size tea bags. When the water comes to a boil, I remove it from the heat and let it steep for a bit. Meanwhile, into a pitcher, I put a half-cup sugar, then add the tea and stir. I put another quart of cold water on the tea bags and let them sit a few minutes, then add that water to the pitcher of tea.

There are two young men, Eddie and Mike, who help my husband, Ed, with things around the house, and part of the deal is that I make lunch for them every day. So this week we had a tea-testing. I am offering you three recipes we tried. These were the results from the test panel:

Almond Tea: Good. They liked the sweetness (which was too sweet for me).

Spicy Orange: Too much spice. Our daughter Lee, who stopped by during this scientific survey, said this would probably be better served in the afternoon than with a meal.

Lemon Tea: Good, but tastes like the purchased instant lemon tea — and that's good, too.

The Eddie and Mike decision: They liked the "sugar water," as they called it (i.e., the Almond Tea). Try one or all of these and have your own test for the iced tea you serve at … *Sunday Dinner*.

Almond Tea

    4 regular-size tea bags
    2 cups boiling water
    1½ cups sugar
    ⅓ cup lemon juice
    1 teaspoon vanilla extract
    1 teaspoon almond extract
    2 quarts water

Warm teapot by rinsing with small amount of boiling water. Place tea bags in teapot; pour 2 cups boiling water over tea. Cover and steep 3 to 5 minutes. Remove tea bags from teapot. Add sugar, lemon juice and flavorings, stirring until sugar dissolves. Add the 2 quarts of water to the mixture and stir. Refrigerate tea mixture and let chill thoroughly. Serve tea over ice. Yields 2½ quarts.

Spicy Orange Iced Tea

    6 whole cloves
    8 whole allspice
    ½ cup sugar
    1¼ cups water
    1¼ cups orange juice, chilled
    2 teaspoons lemon juice
    1¾ cups tea (your recipe), chilled

In a medium saucepan, combine spices and sugar with 1¼ cups water; bring to a boil. Reduce heat and simmer for 10 minutes.

Cool, then strain the mixture to remove cloves and allspice. Add the juices and tea. Serve over ice cubes in 4 tall glasses. Makes 4 servings.

(Note: Don't use ground spices; they will discolor the tea.)

Lemon Tea

3 quarts water

2 quart-size (family-size) tea bags

½ cup sugar

1 12-ounce can frozen lemonade concentrate, thawed and undiluted

Bring water to a boil and add the tea bags. Remove from heat; cover and let stand 20 minutes. Add sugar and lemonade concentrate, stirring until sugar dissolves.

Serve over ice. Garnish with lemon slices or mint leaves if desired. Yields 3½ quarts.

Brunch

Brunch with Crabmeat Newberg

(Published July 29, 2004)

Brunch. I've always liked the word and the concept.

The word means a meal that comes halfway between breakfast and lunch and has characteristics of each.

The concept is that of a slow, leisurely meal with good food in the company of good friends. People say they grabbed a quick breakfast or a quick lunch. No one ever said he had a quick brunch.

There are many occasions when brunch is the answer to nutritional needs.

Brunch is often the answer for a late vacation morning. Sleeping a bit later than usual, vacationers don't want to have a late breakfast and then lunch at the usual time. The solution: brunch, which will serve for both meals.

A brunch is a good way to have guests on a Saturday, or on any day if one doesn't work away from home. The guests — and the hostess, if she has prepared well — can sleep a bit later and then attend the casual brunch.

Brunches are favorites for entertaining brides or out-of-town guests, or for adult birthday celebrations.

Brunches adapt easily to the change of seasons. In warm weather, a brunch served on a deck or patio in the shade can be relaxing and charming with warm-weather foods. In colder weather, an indoor brunch featuring hot, nourishing foods makes any day a pleasure.

The usual time for brunch is 10:00, 10:30 or 11 a.m. If you plan your brunch for much later, it has become lunch.

This "casual" meal doesn't mean you can be sloppy in your hosting duties. Set your table prettily. If you are eating in the dining room, use your best dishes and stemware for a more "formal" brunch — if there is such a thing. A porch or patio meal calls for more casual dinnerware, and this is the time to be creative with colorful plates, napkins, etc.

Plan to have a slow, relaxed meal, with many refills of the coffee.

The food for a brunch is a combination of breakfast and lunch. The menu always includes a hot dish, and this most often is an egg dish. There should be something fresh and colorful, and fruit fits this need. Add something cheesy, too. Unlike breakfast, brunch includes a dessert — and layer cake, coffee, or fruit cobbler are good choices. The dessert can be more elaborate, but it should be pretty in its presentation so the guests will all say, "Ohhh."

A simple brunch menu that is more like breakfast than lunch could include ham, sausage, or bacon and eggs, sautéed apples or broiled peach halves, cheese grits, hot biscuits, honey and butter, and a blueberry cobbler.

A sample of a more elaborate menu is this: tomato juice served to guests as they arrive, Crabmeat Newberg, stuffed eggs in tomato sauce, grapefruit and orange sections, hot bread with butter, a strawberry layer cake, and lots of coffee (or hot tea, if you prefer). If the weather is warm, you may want to have iced tea.

If you have a large group, you will want — and need — to serve several dishes.

Here is a recipe you will enjoy for your brunch, and if your church has an early service, you can have Sunday brunch instead of … *Sunday Dinner*.

Crabmeat Newberg

- **1 pound of crabmeat**
- **2 tablespoons butter**
- **Salt, cayenne pepper to taste**
- **2 or 3 tablespoons cooking sherry**

1 cup light or heavy cream
2 egg yolks, slightly beaten

Pick over the crabmeat to remove any bits of shell. Melt the butter and cook in it the crabmeat for several minutes, being careful not to allow the butter to brown. Season with salt and cayenne, then add the cooking sherry.

Cook over medium heat for a minute, then add the cream. When the cream comes to a boil, add the beaten egg yolks. Stir the egg yolks gently into the crabmeat to thicken the sauce. Don't allow this to boil after the eggs have been added. Serve on triangles of hot, crisp toast. Serves about 4.

Quiche

(Published February 12, 2004)

I knew about quiche before I ate it.

Quiche, in any of its forms, is a delicious, nutritious dish and easy to make. It is described in one cookbook as a "savory baked custard tart" — and that's a good description, but don't be tempted to call it a cheese pie.

Two areas of France claim they originated the tasty dish. Lorraine is in the northeast corner of France and claims the distinction — but Alsace, the province east of it, also makes a claim. These were "provinces," but after the 1789 revolution, the provinces were changed to "departments," so you won't find either Lorraine or Alsace on a modern map of France.

To make quiche, you start with a pie crust — either one you make or a purchased one, but it should be big (a deep-dish, 9-inch crust would be all right). If you are making your own, there are "quiche plates" that are slightly larger than the plates used for fruit pies.

The basic quiche includes eggs, heavy cream and bacon. The variations include adding Swiss cheese — the most usual — or cream cheese. These are put into the crust and baked. Chopped, cooked ham is often added, and other recipes ask for certain vegetables — especially asparagus — but the first recipe I offer is pretty much the basic one.

Let the quiche sit for three minutes or so until it cuts easily, but it should be served hot — about as hot as you can eat it. It is best served at lunch or supper. Add a green salad, a good bread, and — *voila!* — you have a meal.

Several years ago at a pretty restaurant that specialized in "ladies lunches," I ordered quiche and something else, maybe iced tea. When my food came, that was what I got. On the plate was a lonely little triangle of quiche — no salad, no bread, not even a decorative sprig of parsley.

Today, I offer three quiche recipes, plus an "almost" quiche recipe from our daughter Lee. Because these have to cook 45 minutes to an hour, and you don't want to wait that long after church, you may want to have quiche for Sunday supper instead of … *Sunday Dinner.*

Quiche Lorraine
    1 unbaked 9-inch pie crust
    8 slices bacon (fried until crisp, drained and crumbled)
    1½ cups (6 ounces) grated or finely cut Swiss cheese
    3 eggs, beaten
    1 cup heavy cream
    ½ cup milk
    ½ teaspoon salt
    ¼ teaspoon pepper

Dash of cayenne

½ teaspoon dry mustard

Preheat oven to 375 degrees. Put the bacon crumbles in the pie crust, top with cheese. Combine the remaining ingredients and pour over cheese. Bake 45 minutes, until lightly browned and firm. Cut into wedges and serve hot. Makes 6 servings.

Quiche Lorraine with Cream Cheese

1 unbaked 8-inch pie crust

6 slices bacon, cooked and crumbled

8 ounces cream cheese, softened

3 egg yolks

1 egg

¼ teaspoon pepper

¼ teaspoon salt

Preheat oven to 400 degrees. Sprinkle the bacon on the pie crust. Beat together the remaining ingredients and pour over the bacon. Bake at 400 degrees for 20 minutes. Reduce heat to 350 degrees and bake for 10 minutes, until golden brown and slightly puffed. Makes 4-6 servings.

Mushroom Quiche

1 9-inch pie crust

2 cups heavy cream

4 eggs

½ pound mushrooms, sliced

¼ cup green onions, minced
¼ cup melted butter
¼ teaspoon salt
⅛ teaspoon pepper

Preheat oven to 400 degrees. Prick sides and bottom of pastry with a fork and bake 3 minutes. Remove from oven, prick again and bake 5 minutes longer. Combine heavy cream and eggs in bowl; whisk and set aside.

Sauté the mushrooms and onions in butter about 5 minutes. Add salt and pepper, and then add the mushroom mixture to the cream-egg mixture. Pour into the prepared crust. Bake at 400 degrees for 15 minutes; reduce heat to 325 degrees and bake 35 minutes until set.

Broccoli or Spinach Quiche

1 cup steamed broccoli, cut into pieces
    (or 1 cup spinach leaves, cut)
1 cup shredded cheddar cheese
    (or ½ cup cheddar and ½ cup Swiss)
½ cup diced onion
6 slices bacon, cooked and crumbled
    (or ½ cup cooked, cut-up ham)
¾ cup biscuit mix
1½ cups milk
3 eggs
Salt and pepper to taste
¼ teaspoon nutmeg

Preheat oven to 400 degrees. Spray 9- or 10-inch pie dish with cooking spray. Combine broccoli (or spinach), mushrooms, cheese, onion and bacon, and put in dish. Combine the biscuit mix, milk, eggs, salt, pepper and nutmeg, and pour over vegetables. Bake for 30 minutes.

Shrimp and Grits
Carolyn Watts
(Published December 22, 2011)

Every year I wish for the same thing, and every year it doesn't happen. My wish is that we could separate the celebration of Christ's birth from the madness known as the "Christmas season."

We enjoy the trappings of Christmas, the decorating, the gifts, and especially the eating part. Our hope is that one day all the celebrants of the commercial Christmas will know and honor the day for what it is. Perhaps … one day.

In the meantime, we enjoy the season with relatives, friends, and church friends, and most of the time that includes food. Living in South Carolina with its 150 miles of coastline, you have to like shrimp — and living south of the Mason-Dixon line, you have to like grits. Together, you have a regional food that is great for the holidays.

This shrimp-and-grits recipe comes from Carolyn Watts of Good Hope Baptist Church in Conway. The church is pastored by Rev. John Sullivan, who has been there eight years. Good Hope, which has 322 members, offers a full range of Baptist worship programs: Sunday school, WMU, etc. The Christmas observance held Dec. 11 was a special time for the church, with a live nativity and special music.

Living close to the ocean as she does, you just know Carolyn can make good shrimp and grits. The dish can be served for a heavy late breakfast or brunch. It is a natural for lunch, paired with a crisp, green salad and a calorie-laden dessert during your hurried days. If you have guests and serve that menu, they will like it. Carolyn and her husband, Beaman, like it for a light supper.

Carolyn, an Horry County native, has been a member of Good Hope for six years or so, moving there from Langston Baptist Church, also in Conway. Someday Beaman is still a member there, although he usually attends Good Hope with Carolyn. They have a son and daughter-in-law, Jeff and Mandy Watts — who have a son, Hunter, 4, and a daughter, Maci, 1. Jeff and his family live next door to Carolyn, so there is a lot of visiting with grandchildren.

"We love it," Carolyn says of the dish, adding that it is as good as it is simple to make. Someday soon, buy fresh shrimp even if you don't live on the coast, and make this dish for everyone to enjoy as a light meal for … *Sunday Dinner.*

Shrimp and Grits
    1 cup yellow grits
    1 small onion, chopped
    1 tablespoon Worcestershire sauce
    ½ cup water
    5 slices bacon
    2 pounds peeled raw shrimp
    2 tablespoons flour

Cook grits as directed on package. Cook bacon and drain. Sauté the chopped onion in the bacon grease. Add shrimp and cook until pink. Add the Worcestershire sauce and flour. Cook until flour is browned, then add the ½ cup water and simmer for 30 minutes. When ready to serve, put shrimp and gravy over a serving of grits. Crumble bacon on top of the shrimp and grits. Serves 4-6.

Soups and Salads

Acorn/Butternut Squash Soup

(Published May 5, 2005)

A few days ago, I cleaned the telephone desk. There was rejoicing on seven continents.

In addition to information about many passed events, I found a note from Rev. Craig Neil Jr. asking for a recipe for acorn squash soup. He had eaten this in a restaurant, thought it was excellent, and wanted a recipe for his wife, Frances, to make.

Wanting to be a little helper, I began looking. Yea, diligently did I search but, alas, never found the desired recipe. However, I did find instructions for making butternut squash soup; I tried it. It made a good soup — smooth, slightly sweet, and dark golden.

The cilantro sauce adds to both the flavor and the appearance, but you can omit it if you wish. I didn't use the jalapeños suggested, fearing the soup would be too spicy.

Craig says the two greatest things in his life were being saved and being allowed to serve in the ministry. A native of Gastonia, N.C., where his father was a policeman, Craig lived there until he went into the Army during World War II. His first assignment was training troops in chemical warfare. One day he stopped by the office supply unit, and when it was learned that he knew about such things, he soon found himself in that department and out of the chemical warfare section.

After his military service, Craig began work with Harper Brothers Office Supply in Greenville, but soon went into the ministry. A *magna cum laude* graduate of Anderson College, he also attended Erskine College. His first pastorate was at Martha Drive Baptist Church (now Pleasant View Baptist Church) when it was organized as a mission of First Baptist in Anderson. From there he went to Southside in Abbeville, then to Homeland

Park Baptist in Anderson for 16 years.

For four years, he was director of the Haven of Rest Ministries in Anderson while also serving at Shiloh Baptist. Since his retirement, Craig has been interim pastor for several churches.

He and his first wife, Grace Grizzle Neil, had three daughters — Patricia Hawkins and Joy Brickman of Anderson, and Madonna Ferguson of Abbeville — as well as six grandchildren and eight great-grandchildren. He and his second wife, Frances Melton Neil, have been married six years. He has always enjoyed photography and woodcarving, and he and Frances share the cooking. Maybe they'll make this soup for ... *Sunday Dinner*.

Acorn/Butternut Squash Soup with Cilantro

- 1 medium (2 pounds) butternut or acorn squash (peeled, seeded and cut into 1-to-2-inch chunks)
- 3 teaspoons olive oil, divided
- 1 tablespoon butter
- ½ cup finely chopped onion
- 3 tablespoons finely chopped shallot
- 1 tablespoon finely chopped jalapeño pepper with seeds
- 2 teaspoons grated fresh ginger
- 2 cans (14½-ounce) chicken broth
- ½ cup chopped fresh cilantro
- ⅔ cup unsweetened coconut milk

Heat oven to 400 degrees. Toss squash with 2 teaspoons of olive oil in a large shallow pan. Bake about 30 minutes, until tender. In a large saucepan, melt butter; then add onion and shallot, cooking 2-3 minutes until they begin to brown. Add jalapeño and ginger. Cook 1 minute, then add broth. To make cilantro puree, place in a blender 3 tablespoons of broth, cilantro, and remaining 1 teaspoon of olive oil. Puree until smooth. Put in a cup and set aside. Wash blender.

Add roasted squash to broth mixture and bring to a boil, cooking for 5 minutes and then cooling for 5. In two batches, puree mix. Return all to saucepan, add coconut milk and heat through. Pour into serving bowls and top each with 1 teaspoon of cilantro puree. Makes 8 servings.

Catfish Stew

Charles Jackson
(Published November 17, 2005)

"That's my husband," the very pleasant voice from the Farm Bureau Office in Dorchester County said.

Mystery solved!

I had searched many cookbooks for a catfish stew recipe and found one in "The Golden Taste of South Carolina" published by the South Carolina Farm Bureau in 1994, and now I was trying to find the Charles Jackson who submitted it.

"Is he a Baptist?" was my next question (what with this being a Baptist newspaper and all). "No, but I used to be before I became a Methodist," answered Pat Jackson.

Close enough.

She also said it was her recipe originally but that when Charles retired from Holcim Cement in Harleyville, he began cooking the stew and made some changes.

Pat was formerly a member of Canaan Baptist Church, Cope, in Orangeburg-Calhoun Association. She and Charles have been married about 35 years and have one son, Lee, who lives in Eutawville.

Charles makes this stew maybe a dozen times a year, she said. If he is going to serve it on Friday, he will make it a couple of days ahead, allow it to cool, refrigerate it, then reheat it before serving. She emphasizes that this making ahead and reheating is necessary for the flavors to blend for the best tasting stew. It also freezes well.

I am giving you Charles Jackson's recipe, and I'm also including my adaptation (forgive me, Charles), which makes a much smaller amount. This stew is great for a casual gathering of friends or a large family on a cold day for ... *Sunday Dinner*.

Catfish Stew

10 pounds catfish fillets

1½ packages (16-ounce package) frozen hash brown potatoes

2 quarts fresh tomatoes, stemmed and mashed

1 32-ounce bottle ketchup

2 10½-ounce cans cream of tomato soup, undiluted

½ cup Worcestershire sauce

1 gallon water

1 pound slab bacon, cut into ½-inch pieces

1 pound onions, chopped

¼ cup sugar

2 tablespoons hot pepper sauce, or to taste

Salt and black pepper to taste

½ cup butter

Cook fish until flaky. Drain, remove any bones, and set aside. Combine potatoes, tomatoes, ketchup, soup, Worcestershire sauce and water in a stock pot and cook over medium heat. Meanwhile, sauté bacon until golden brown and add to vegetables. Sauté onion in bacon drippings until golden brown and add to vegetables. Stir in sugar, pepper sauce, salt and black pepper. Simmer for an hour.

Transfer to a double boiler, add fish and simmer for 1 to 2 hours or until thickened, stirring occasionally. Add butter just before serving. Yields 11 quarts.

Catfish Stew (easier version/smaller amount)
- 2½-3 pounds whole catfish or fillets
- 4 cups cooking liquid from catfish
- 8 ounces frozen hash brown potatoes
- 1 28-ounce can diced tomatoes (basil, garlic or other flavors)
- 1 cup ketchup
- ¼ cup Worcestershire sauce
- 4 slices thick-cut bacon, cut into ½-inch pieces
- 1 large onion, chopped
- 1 tablespoon sugar
- 1 teaspoon hot sauce
- ½ teaspoon each salt and pepper, or to taste

Cover fish with water, cook, debone, and set aside. Save cooking liquid. In a large pot, combine the 4 cups cooking liquid from the fish with the vegetables, etc., adding the cooked bacon and onion. Follow cooking instructions above. Makes 4 or 5 quarts.

Hearty Potato Soup
Mrs. Gladys DeBoer
(Published January 22, 2009)

The conversation at the dinner table on New Year's Day was beginning to take an unpleasant turn.

Son Tom had said the only thing he wanted for Christmas was for me to clean the office, and there followed some unflattering comments by almost everyone in the group about the office's untidy condition.

About 10 steps from the carport is the office. It contains a large room where I have my little clutter corner and an office corner for Tom, which he protects from clutter as a tigress does her cub; my Ed's office, which he has been in twice in the last 10 years; a small dark room where I, in times past, enjoyed photo processing; an even smaller restroom; and a storage room. All the rooms are full.

"I don't understand," our son-in-law Ron Smith said, "how a 16-by-20 building can hold 19 tons of recyclable and landfill material."

"It's neither recyclable nor landfill material," I answered with only a touch of huffiness, making a mental note to call our lawyer and change the will.

So the next day Tom thought I was starting on the office. I wasn't. I was making potato soup.

The recipe is from the Taste of Home magazine collector's edition published in 1994. Diligently I have tried to get in touch with the magazine's editors for permission to reprint. I couldn't, but my heart is in the right place, and I hope I don't get sued.

There will be times this month and next when soup is just what you need for a cold, rainy, windy day, and this one will be a good choice. The recipe was submitted by Mrs. Gladys DeBoer of Castleford, Idaho. If you give me a minute, I perhaps can connect Mrs. DeBoer to South Carolina Baptists.

Okay. Wait. Here it is: We are celebrating 400 years of Baptist history. The first baptismal service of adult believers was performed in Amsterdam, Holland, in 1606 by John Smyth, one of the group of English Christians (a.k.a. Dissenters), worshiping there. They called themselves Baptists. Mrs. DeBoer was born in Holland of Dutch ancestry. Her husband, Harold, was born on a Dutch farm.

In commenting on the soup, Mrs. DeBoer, according to Taste of Home, said the original recipe called for bacon fat and heavy cream, but she trimmed it down. When I made the soup, I added small pieces of Christmas ham with the potatoes, carrots and celery. That was good. I also found I needed to add liquid for a good consistency. Using cream for part of the milk ingredients would be good. I cut the ingredients in half for my Ed and me, and that worked well.

Please don't sue, Taste of Home and Mrs. DeBoer. All over South Carolina, people will thank you for your delicious recipe, especially on a blustery day, for ... *Sunday Dinner.*

Hearty Potato Soup

    6 medium potatoes, peeled and sliced or cubed

    2 carrots, diced

    6 celery stalks, diced

    2 quarts water

    1 onion, chopped

    6 tablespoons butter or margarine (or bacon drippings)

    6 tablespoons all-purpose flour

    1 teaspoon salt

½ **teaspoon pepper**
1½ **cups milk**

In a large kettle, cook potatoes, carrots and celery in water until tender, about 20 minutes. Drain, reserving liquid and setting vegetables aside. In same kettle, sauté onion in butter until soft. Stir in flour, salt and pepper and gradually add milk, stirring constantly until thickened.

Gently stir in cooked vegetables. Add 1 cup or more of the reserved cooking liquid until soup is desired consistency. Yields 8-10 servings (about 2½ quarts).

Broccoli-Cheese Soup
Lucy Garner
(Published March 15, 2010)

The worst of winter is probably over, but March will bring wind and some cold, wet days. On one of those days, you will be glad to have Lucy Garner's broccoli cheese soup. This is a good soup, easy to make, and keeps well in the fridge for a couple of days.

I was happy to receive the recipe because I had made a similar soup some time ago but had used too much salt. I usually go easy on the salt, but that time I didn't and then lost the recipe so I couldn't correct my mistake in a second cooking.

Lucy has been a member of First Baptist Church of Rock Hill, in York Baptist Association, for around 60 of her 91 years. The pastor there is Steven Hogg. Now, because of health reasons, she is unable to attend worship service often and had to stop Sunday school several years ago, but she has many warm and loving memories.

She lives alone, but two of her children — Phil Garner and his wife, Cheryl, and Anita and her husband, Kirk Leslie — live nearby. Another son, Foster Garner, and his wife, Sib, live in Myrtle Beach. Lucy has five grandchildren.

She still enjoys cooking and makes "real meals," especially on weekends (although most days she like sandwiches or frozen dinners). She makes this good broccoli cheese soup often.

Lucy enjoyed gardening before she became somewhat limited in what she can do. She says that she cut her grass until she was 87 and had flowers, which she loved. She also had a small vegetable garden, started by her late husband, Leon Garner. She planted six vegetables each time, and when one was harvested she planted another.

Her outdoor work has been replaced by reading. She reads the newspaper each day (and The Courier), gets her books from her local library, and is on her second reading of the Bible.

In making this soup, chop the broccoli, and you can substitute whole milk for the half and half.

The soup recipe was given to Lucy about five years ago, and is one I want you to keep. Have the ingredients on hand, so on that cold, windy day you can make this soup in the morning and have it waiting for you after church for a hot and delicious … *Sunday Dinner*.

Broccoli Cheese Soup

5 cups water

1 medium onion, chopped

6 tablespoons butter

1 pound Velveeta cheese, cubed

6 chicken bouillon cubes

- 2 bunches (about 1 pound) broccoli florets
- 6 tablespoons plain flour
- 2 cups half and half

Bring water and bouillon cubes to boil. Add the onion and the broccoli florets and cook until tender, about 1 hour on low heat. In a separate pan, make a roux by melting the butter and stirring in the flour. Cook and stir one minute. Add to the broccoli and stir until smooth. Stir in the cubed cheese until melted. Add the half and half or the milk and stir. Heat until hot. Makes about 3 quarts.

Gumbo Creole

(Published February 14, 2013)

Imagine the setting. It's winter. It's cold. You have had to be outside for church, for work, doing yard maintenance, have-to-have shopping, or doing good deeds. You and your family are hungry. This recipe can be prepared in about an hour, and it is worth the time.

Although the list of ingredients is long, most of them are seasonings. The main things are the shrimp, okra, bacon, and the ham you still have in your freezer from Christmas.

This is a good dish to make ahead of time and then freeze. Thaw, add the shrimp, cook the rice, and enjoy for a winter's ... *Sunday Dinner.*

Gumbo Creole

- 2 pounds okra, fresh or frozen
- 3 slices lean bacon, cubed

½ pound cubed ham or small hambone without fat
2 large or 3 small onions, finely minced
3 minced garlic cloves
½ large green pepper, minced
¼ teaspoon dried thyme
1 teaspoon salt or to taste
1 tablespoon sugar
1 tablespoon minced celery
2 tablespoons dried parsley
2 bay leaves
1 16-ounce can whole tomatoes
1½ tablespoons flour
½ teaspoon black pepper
2 dashes hot sauce
1 tablespoon Worcestershire sauce
3 or 4 whole allspice
2 pounds peeled and deveined shrimp
   (or 1 pound shrimp/1 pound crabmeat)

In a large heavy pot, fry the bacon until crisp and remove from pan. Break bacon into pieces. In bacon drippings, sauté the onions until limp and golden, gradually adding the garlic and green pepper. Stir in the flour, then add the thyme, bay leaves, salt, pepper, sugar and hot sauce. Add the okra, cooked bacon, ham, Worcestershire sauce, parsley, allspice and tomatoes.

While the mixture cooks, cut the tomatoes into pieces with a spoon and continue cooking until the okra loses its gumminess. If the mixture gets too thick, add one or two cups of water.* Add the shrimp or the shrimp/crabmeat mix. Cover and cook 30-40 minutes until mixture *thickens. Serve over rice. Serves 4-6.*

*Mixture may be frozen at this point. When ready to use, thaw and add the shrimp, which have been cooked with butter in a skillet until pink.

Yum-Yum Chicken Soup with Cornbread
Annie Ruth Yelton
(Published February 2014)

An old children's nursery rhyme says, "The north wind doth blow and we shall have snow." That must have been written for another area of our country, because we shall all be surprised if these winds bring snow. We would be pleased, however, if they did blow and we had a pot of Annie Ruth Yelton's Yum-Yum Chicken Soup, especially if it were accompanied by her Yum-Yum Cornbread.

Annie Ruth is a member of First Baptist Church in Simpsonville, where Rev. Randy Harling has served as pastor for 16 years. The church is part of the Greenville Baptist Association. Simpsonville First Baptist was organized in 1888 and celebrated its 125th anniversary last year. The large, 4,300-member church has campuses at the Connector Church in Laurens, the Delta Church (primarily for young adults), and the Happy Trails Cowboy Church in Pelzer (which meets on Tuesday nights). At the main church, Simpsonville First Baptist has Sunday school, WMU and a men's group. The youth groups meet on Sunday evening.

If there were any church secrets, Annie Ruth would know them. She served as minister of children for 10 years at Simpsonville First Baptist. At the other end of the age group, she currently leads the monthly worship service at Bel-Aire Assisted Living. She wrote two books for Bible skills — one for children and one for youth — and both have been translated into

Spanish. The children's book has been translated into Romanian as well. She has been on several mission trips.

A multi-talented person, in her spare time Annie Ruth enjoys doing watercolor painting, knitting and reading. A seasonal pleasure for her is "eggery," which means she decorates egg shells.

She and her husband, Harold — retired from the South Carolina Department of Transportation and now Annie Ruth's go-to guy who helps her with props, displays, etc., when she gives programs — have three children. David, a pharmacist, lives in Texas. John and his wife, Adina, and their three children — Caleb, Luke and Lidia — live in Greer. Elizabeth, the Yeltons' youngest, lives in Oregon, where she is a linguist teaching English as a second language.

Annie Ruth gives her husband credit for the chicken soup recipe, especially the combination of spices he uses. She also suggests that the soup is a good keeper in the fridge and will be good two or three days after it is made. She tweaked the cornbread to make it the recipe it is, and I like the cornbread as much as the soup. Because it makes a skillet full, you will have leftovers from it also.

If you want a recipe for good chicken soup, and one that is easy to make, do try Annie Ruth's. It is good anytime, but especially on a cold church day for ... *Sunday Dinner*.

Yum-Yum Chicken Soup

 3 small potatoes, peeled and diced

 1 medium carrot, sliced

 1 medium onion, chopped

 1 stalk of celery, diced

 1 14-ounce can chicken broth

1 10¾-ounce can cream of chicken soup
½ soup can of water
1 12½-ounce can cooked chicken breast with liquid

Seasoning:
¼ teaspoon black pepper
¼ teaspoon sage
1 teaspoon minced garlic

In a medium saucepan, combine the potatoes, carrot, onion, celery and chicken broth. Cook until vegetables are tender. Add chicken soup and water. Add seasonings. Stir well to mix ingredients. Heat until bubbling, stirring frequently.

Add chicken breast with liquid from the can. Use stirring spoon to break chicken into small pieces. Stir soup well to thoroughly mix all ingredients. Heat to bubbling. Serve with Yum Yum Cornbread and enjoy!

Yum-Yum Cornbread

2 cups yellow self-rising corn meal
¼ cup canola oil, plus 2 tablespoons, divided
1¼-cups milk (2 percent or fat free)
1 large egg, beaten slightly
1 jalapeño pepper, seeded and finely diced
1 cup medium cheddar cheese, grated
½ cup chopped onion
¼ teaspoon salt

Preheat oven to 400 degrees. Oil a 10½-inch iron skillet with the 2 tablespoons of canola oil and preheat in oven. Mix together all other ingredients until thoroughly moistened. Pour into the hot skillet and put into oven.

Cook approximately 25 minutes, or until edges are brown and have separated from sides of pan. Top should look crusty and golden. A toothpick inserted into the center of the cornbread should come out dry. Slice immediately and serve with butter. Enjoy!

Salads and Dressings

(Published January 31, 2013)

When you say "salad," you can mean a couple of things. Some older persons use the word "salat" to mean turnips or other green leafies that must be cooked.

A "salad" can be a lot of things. It can be a mixture of fruit, hence fruit salad; a mixture of some kind of meat, hence chicken salad or tuna salad; or a dish made with gelatin (a.k.a. Jell-O, which appeared first around the mid 1920s), and commonly called a congealed salad.

All these have the dressing incorporated within them and are good choices for light lunches, club meetings, etc. Where would missionary circles and garden clubs be without chicken salad?

The salads I like best are those some people called "tossed salad," but which I prefer to call a "green salad" made with fresh vegetables. These appear on many restaurant menus, and if you order one it will be served while your main dish is being prepared.

The "good-manners gurus" don't like this. A salad, if served as a separate course, should be served properly following the main course and before dessert. However, I think the restaurant people are going to win this one.

A fresh green salad is an asset to almost any meal. You can serve it on a separate plate following the main course and before the dessert or you can put it on the table or buffet and serve it along with the meat, vegetables, etc. In these days when not many people have a household staff who can properly serve a dining table, the "serve yourself" buffet table is popular.

It is equally correct to put the serving dishes on the table and pass them to the right until everyone is served. A fresh green salad in a pretty glass bowl is both a healthy and an attractive addition to the buffet table, but the traditional wooden bowl is better because it holds the flavor of the dressing.

The basis for most of these green salads is lettuce. Tear it with your hands into one-inch pieces. It isn't very graceful to spear a piece of lettuce as large as an oak leaf and try to eat it without opening your mouth to the size of Mammoth Cave.

Although lettuce is usually the basic for this green salad, fresh baby spinach is often mixed with the lettuce or used alone. Most supermarkets now offer bags of mesclun — a fancy word meaning several young, tender mixed greens, including arugula, radicchio, etc. Other additions to your green salad may include chopped tomatoes, carrots, green peppers, onions, cucumbers, cooked beets, etc.

Plan soon to have a fresh, crisp salad and dress it with one of these dressings for a pretty and healthy dish for … *Sunday Dinner*.

French Dressing

1 cup olive oil
1 tablespoon tarragon vinegar
¼ teaspoon salt
Juice of 1 lemon

1 tablespoon cider vinegar
¼ teaspoon pepper

Shake together in a covered jar. Store in refrigerator.

Variation 1: Add to the above 1 teaspoon each of dry mustard, paprika, sugar, onion salt, celery salt, and 1 clove garlic.

Variation 2: To make creamy French dressing, increase oil to 2 cups and vinegar to ½ cup. Add 2 tablespoons brown sugar, 4 tablespoons catsup, 2 tablespoons grated onion or onion juice, 1 unbeaten egg white, and 2 cloves garlic. Shake vigorously.

Thousand Island Dressing

1 cup mayonnaise
¼ cup chili sauce
2 tablespoons chopped pimiento
1 teaspoon grated onion
¼ teaspoon Worcestershire sauce
2 hard-cooked eggs, chopped
1 tablespoon stuffed olives, chopped

Combine all ingredients.

Variation: Add 1 tablespoon finely chopped sweet pickle.

Roquefort Cheese Dressing

1 tablespoon salt
1 teaspoon paprika
2 cups olive oil

1 teaspoon sugar
1 cup lemon juice
½ pound Roquefort cheese, crumbled

Combine all ingredients and beat together until smooth.

Frozen Fruit Salad
Miriam Bobo Templeton
(Published July 21, 2006)

If you want a pretty salad for a special occasion, a family reunion, to take to a bereaved family, or to carry to a church supper, Miriam Bobo Templeton of First Baptist Church in Laurens has the dish for you.

We thank Miriam for sharing her frozen fruit salad with us. She says it is one of her prized recipes because everyone likes it, and a couple of people have told her it is the best salad they ever ate. That's pretty good. Men like it, too, Miriam says.

Miriam grew up in Gray Court, went to Limestone College, taught home economics three years, and, on June 19, 1942, married Jack Templeton. The next week, they both joined Laurens First Baptist and were immediately put to work. She has had many responsibilities at the church, including serving as WMU director for many years and on the Laurens Baptist Association Leadership Committee for WMU, as an officer in the senior adult organization, etc. Bev Kennedy is the current pastor.

Miriam and her late husband, Jack, former manager of the Laurens Electric Co-op, were blessed with two daughters. Nancy and her husband, Keith Stroble, have one daughter, Kent Stroble Brannon. Nancy and Keith have recently moved to Simpsonville, after living in Florida for a couple of years and in Indiana before that. Miriam and Jack's daughter Anne and her husband, Richard Poole, have two daughters, Temple Poole Holland and Amanda Poole.

In addition to 32 years of teaching home economics, for about 20 years Miriam has been part of the Martha Franks Singers, a community choral group sponsored by Laurens First Baptist and the Martha Franks Baptist Retirement Center. Several years ago, after performing at Boiling Springs Baptist Church in Spartanburg, the group was served a meal, and one of the many delicious dishes was this frozen fruit salad. Miriam thought it was so good that she kept hanging around the buffet table, waiting to talk to the person who came to pick up the serving dish. Miriam has served this dish many times since, and it's always a favorite.

The recipe can be used as a salad on lettuce or as a dessert. For a salad, she says you could put a little dollop on mayonnaise on top. As a dessert, it would be pretty served on a glass plate with a couple of fresh, fan-sliced strawberries. If frozen in the paper cupcake liners, which she suggests in her notes, it is very pretty with the ruffled edges when turned upside down and the paper removed.

It will keep a long time in the freezer, she says, or as long as "you can keep your hands off it!" Make this salad some time this week, freeze it, then take it from the freezer about 10 minutes before serving it for … *Sunday Dinner.*

Frozen Fruit Salad

    1 8-ounce package cream cheese

    ¾ cup sugar

    1 10-ounce package frozen sliced strawberries and juice

    1 8-ounce can crushed pineapple, drained

½ cup chopped pecans
2 bananas, sliced
1 16-ounce carton dessert topping, thawed

Mix remaining ingredients and fold into cream cheese mixture. Pour into desired container (such as a glass dish) and freeze, covering with waxed paper topped with aluminum foil. To serve, cut into squares and serve on lettuce.

Cook's Note — I made the following adjustments:
- *I used 2 of the 10-ounce packages of strawberries.*
- *I used 3 bananas, cutting the bananas in half lengthwise, then crosswise into little half slices.*
- *I put the bananas into the drained pineapple juice to keep them from turning dark while working with the other ingredients. Drain the juice before mixing them with the cream cheese mix.*
- *I increased nuts to 1½ cups.*
- *I froze the mix in paper cupcake liners set in muffin tins to make individual servings. When frozen, remove from the tins and store in plastic freezer bags. These ingredients fill 36 cupcake liners.*

Cabbage Slaw
Belinda Todd
(Published July 17, 2008)

"I want you to give Angie this recipe," our son Tom said on July 4 while eating the cabbage slaw featured today. His wife, Angie, is a good cook, and good cooks always like to use new recipes. This is a good one.

It is from the cookbook "Recipes and Remembrances" sent to me by Jenell Burke of Good Hope Baptist Church in Conway, and I thank her for doing so. Good Hope's pastor is John Sullivan, and the church is part of Waccamaw Baptist Association. The recipe for cabbage slaw was submitted by Belinda Todd, a 25-year member who moved there when she married George Todd.

For 20 years, Belinda taught fifth grade at Homewood Elementary School but retired when her husband, George, became ill. Since his death in 1993, she has worked part-time. She currently has responsibilities with her mother, Mrs. Doris Chandler of Hemingway, who has been ill but is doing better.

Belinda and George had two sons. Marshall, an accounting major, is a rising senior at Coastal Carolina and works part-time at Horry Electric. Von, the older son, graduated from Coastal Carolina and works with Horry Telephone, but is back in school part-time working on his MBA. Both young men are involved in Good Hope's activities.

Over the years, Belinda has taught the college and career class, done children's church, helped with VBS, etc., and currently is substitute young adult Sunday school teacher at Good Hope. She is also the co-leader for discipleship training. Belinda has several other interests as well, including flower gardening, cooking and reading.

Today's recipe is one you will want to keep and use often. Belinda says it is always a "big hit" when she carries it to gatherings, and that people often ask for the recipe. I can understand why. It is fresh and crisp and different from many cole slaw recipes. Our son Tom says it needs a bit more celery seed, but you can adjust that to your taste.

It will keep for a few days in the fridge. Belinda suggests stirring or turning the container upside down (with proper precautions against spilling, of course) to get the dressing well distributed. With our sweltering summer weather, a crisp green, tangy salad dish is just the thing we need for any day, and especially for … *Sunday Dinner.*

Cabbage Slaw

- ½ cup oil
- ¾ cup vinegar
- 1 cup sugar
- 1 teaspoon celery seed
- 1 teaspoon mustard seed
- 1 medium cabbage, shredded
- 1 medium onion, finely chopped
- 1 bell pepper, finely chopped
- 1 teaspoon salt

In a small saucepan, boil the oil, vinegar, celery seed, mustard seed and ¾ cup sugar for one minute. Let the mixture cool while you prepare the cabbage. In a large bowl, combine the shredded cabbage, chopped onion, and chopped pepper. Sprinkle with the remaining ¼ cup sugar and the salt. Stir. Pour the cooled oil mixture over the cabbage. Stir, cover, and refrigerate overnight.

Chinese Slaw
Betty Rice
(Published August 13, 2013)

We have a lot for which to thank the Chinese: checkers, porcelain, lanterns, the chinaberry tree, and others. We can thank them also for this dish shared with us by Betty Rice of Holly Springs Baptist Church in Inman.

We have written about this church previously. It is one of our state's oldest, organized in 1804 with 56 members, on land with "a spring surrounded by holly trees" and donated by Joseph Smith.

Brother Smith wouldn't recognize the church today. It has an active membership of around 350. They are busy Baptists with Sunday worship, Sunday school, discipleship training, WMU and VBS, and are supporters of the mission programs. Their pastor is Rev. Tim Clark, who has served there for many years.

Involved in some of these programs over the years is Betty Rice. She grew up in Duncan but moved to Inman, where she has been a member of Holly Springs for 35-40 years. She hasn't been active in the last couple of years because of illness, and especially misses her Sunday school class.

Betty, whose husband, Melvin, is deceased, has two children — her son, Conrad Wilson, his wife, Lindsey, and their two daughters live in Florida; and her daughter, Denise Brunson, and her husband, Jack, live in Taylors.

A lot of people will know Betty because she is retired from Mountain View Family Practice in Inman, where she worked for 23 years.

I always like hearing where the recipe-of-the-day person got the recipe, and Betty says it was given to her by her late husband's brother-in-law at a wedding 17 years ago. She doesn't make the recipe often now because of the quantity, and although it keeps well in the fridge, that's still a lot of Chinese Slaw for one person. Maybe you should serve this on the day you are having a missionary luncheon honoring Lottie Moon.

This is also a good dish to make in advance of a day you know you'll be busy.

It is a pretty salad to serve in a glass bowl for your family, and it carries well if you are going to a picnic or to Aunt Susie's house for … *Sunday Dinner*.

Chinese Slaw

> 1 16-oz. can French-style green beans
> 1 16-oz. can fancy Chinese vegetables
> 1 6-oz. can water chestnuts, sliced
> 1 medium onion, thinly sliced
> ¾ cup vinegar
> 1 5-oz. can mushrooms, sliced
> 1 16-oz. can English peas
> 1½ cups diced celery
> ¾ cup sugar
> Salt, pepper, garlic salt to taste

Heat sugar and vinegar to dissolve sugar. Cool. Rinse and drain the Chinese vegetables and drain the remaining vegetables. Combine all the vegetables in a large bowl. Pour over them the cooled sugar-vinegar mix. Add seasonings and stir. Cover, refrigerate and allow to marinate at least 24 hours. Yields 8-10 servings.

(Note: You will find LaChoy mixed vegetables in the Chinese section of your supermarket.)

Marinated Cukes and Onions
Jean Rushing
(Published June 10, 2010)

Soon home gardens and farmers' markets will be providing South Carolinians with fresh, locally grown vegetables. Almost always, we (or they) don't see among the leaves all the cucumbers when picking and consequently have several that grow too large for slicing.

Ta-dah! Today's recipe, although a secondhand one, comes to the rescue.

The recipe itself is from Clara Hendricks, a Methodist currently living in Florence, and comes to us by way of Jean Rushing of Providence Baptist Church in Pageland. Part of the Chesterfield Association, Providence is pastored by the Rev. Jonathan Cox and has an active congregation of 275-300 with an even larger membership.

Jean was on the committee that created the "Tasteful Treasures" cookbook the church did a few years ago and asked her friend Clara, who lived in Pageland at the time, to contribute a recipe.

Jean herself has been a member of Providence Baptist since she was a teenager, except for the time she and her late husband, Billy, lived in Charlotte before returning to Pageland in 1972. For 15 years, Jean worked with BellSouth, making the commute to Charlotte every day.

Now retired, she has time to participate in five activities she likes.

The first is Providence Baptist, where she works with the greeters for all the church services and works in the church library. She, of course, is in Sunday school, etc.

The second is genealogy. She is secretary of the Chesterfield County Genealogy Society.

The third is quilting. A member of the Magic Needles Quilting Guild of Lancaster, Jean is currently working on three queen-sized quilts and has completed others.

She also enjoys working in her yard, but the thing that brings her the most pleasure is her daughter Julie. Jean and her husband had one child, Julie, who works with the Arts Center in Monroe, N.C. Julie bought her grandparents' house in Pageland and now lives about a mile from Jean, so they see each other or talk on the phone each day.

There are several things appealing about this recipe from Clara and

Jean. It is pretty, with its pale green color and flecks of parsley, and is attractively presented in a glass bowl. It is a good way to use these oversized cucumbers. It is tasty, but the flavor is not overwhelming. It has only a few ingredients, most of which are on the average kitchen shelf. It is easy to make, although the peeling and slicing of the cucumbers will take 30 minutes or so.

We thank Jean for sharing her summer-fresh recipe with us. Another thing I like about it is that it makes a large amount. You can make it during the week and still have plenty of marinated cukes and onions for ... *Sunday Dinner*.

Marinated Cukes and Onions
6 large cucumbers, peeled
1 large onion
⅔ cup mayonnaise
½ cup sugar
¼ cup vinegar
1 tablespoon parsley flakes

Cut the cucumbers in half lengthwise. Using a spoon, scrape out and discard all the seeds. Cut the halves crosswise into thin half-moon slices. Peel and cut onion into bite-sized pieces. Soak onions and cucumbers for 20 minutes in ice water. Drain and pat dry.

To make the dressing combine in a small bowl the mayonnaise, sugar, vinegar and parsley flakes. Mix well. Add mixture to the cucumbers and onions. Chill in a covered dish and keep refrigerated. Keeps for several days. This is a good way to use the large cucumbers because the seeds are discarded.

Regal Chicken Salad

(Published May 10, 2012)

"What are you doing here?" I asked our daughter Elizabeth after I gave her a hug and a kiss. I didn't mean to sound inhospitable, but it was a mid-week afternoon when most people were working.

"Because I own my own business and I can do this," she answered.

I need my own business.

She had come to carry her father for an outing to check that the world was running as it should. I was making chicken salad, and I was pretty sure that would help.

This Regal Chicken Salad is an old recipe from a cookbook I have had for years, "Cooking for Company," published in 1968. Many dishes can be prepared in a variety of ways — vegetable soup, potato salad, beef stew, etc., depending on the habits and preferences of the cooks — and chicken salad is one of these. I checked the Internet, which stated there are 23,000 recipes for chicken salad. Either that is excessive, or I misread it.

Cooks in other parts of the country make chicken salad, but it seems to be a typical Southern food — just right for our hot summer days.

Prepared many ways, chicken salad can be made with apples, pineapple and grapes; with green pepper, finely diced sweet pickle, onions, chopped pimiento; with almonds, pecans and peanuts. One can use lemon juice, wine vinegar or curry to add taste. For a binder, one can use salad dressing, mayonnaise or sour cream.

Chicken salad can be patted firmly into a measuring cup to form a shape and then turned onto a plate. It can be prepared with gelatin, chilled and cut into squares. It can be chilled in a ring mold, filling the center with fruit, vegetables or cottage cheese. It can be served in a pretty glass bowl.

It can be made with all white chicken or the whole chicken. The chicken can be boiled, baked or grilled.

Chicken salad is versatile in its use. It can be the main course at a light lunch, one of the items on a mixed buffet, as a spread for crackers or toast points for an appetizer, or for sandwiches — either hearty ones for a take-a-long lunch, or dainty ones. If the salad is to be used for sandwiches (a staple for ladies club meetings), the chicken should be cut into very small pieces for spreading on the sandwiches — which are then cut into halves, fourths or other shapes after the crusts are cut away.

For sandwiches, one can use white, whole wheat or other bread — but most people like the thin, white sandwich bread. Sandwiches can be made a day ahead of serving, covered with plastic wrap and refrigerated. The salad can also be covered and kept two or three days in the refrigerator.

Chicken salad is an institution in the South, so try this or another similar recipe this weekend. Make it on Saturday and put it in the fridge so it will be waiting for you when you return home from church the next day for a warm-day ... *Sunday Dinner.*

Regal Chicken Salad

4 cups cooked chicken

1 1-lb.-4½-oz. can pineapple chunks

1 cup seedless green grapes

1 cup chopped celery

½ cup coarsely chopped dry salted peanuts

Salt

¼ teaspoon dried tarragon

1 cup mayonnaise

2 tablespoons lemon juice

2 tablespoons pineapple juice

Drain the pineapple, saving the juice. If grapes are large, cut into halves or fourths. Combine the chicken, pineapple, grapes, celery and peanuts. Taste for salt and add if needed. Stir in the tarragon.

Combine mayonnaise, lemon juice and 2 tablespoons of the saved pineapple juice. Gently fold into the chicken mixture. Serve on lettuce with parsley or small celery leaves for garnish. Serves 8.

Note: Although the recipe asks for peanuts, I used pecans. If you prefer, you may used drained pineapple tidbits instead of the chunks.

Layered Lettuce Salad
Ruby Baskin
(Published August 4, 2014)

Every household and every restaurant serves them. People living alone or large families serve them.

Some say green "salat" — others say mixed salad, fresh salad, tossed salad, garden salad, etc.

Regardless of the name you use, this dish is part of the menu for every household and restaurant, with the recipe varying based on ingredients you deliberately purchase or those you find in your fridge.

Today's recipe for a layered salad is an old one and a bit dressed up from the basic green salad, and, unlike the basic green salad, can and should be made a day ahead of use. If you don't have this among your recipe collection, consider adding it and making the dish soon.

It is from the late Ruby Baskin of Unity Baptist Church in Simpsonville, and her recipe was among those in the church cookbook published in 2004. Mrs. Baskin died a few years ago. She had been a member of Unity for several years, moving her membership from Standing Springs Baptist

Church (also in Greenville County). She was active at Unity, where she taught Sunday school and was the WMU leader at one time. Her husband is also deceased. They had three sons — John, Jerry and David.

Back to the "tossed salad." There are reasons for the perpetual popularity of the simple "green salad": It is easy to prepare; often the ingredients are on hand; it fits with almost all other foods on the menu; it's pretty on the table; and it's versatile.

This green salad can be made with only lettuce and a dressing and be part of your menu of meat and veggies — or you can add other ingredients to the salad mix, increase the amounts, and — *voila!* — the salad becomes a light lunch.

One writer suggests that fruits and vegetables should not be combined in the same salad. Use all vegetables with their dressing, or all fruits with their dressing.

The simplest salad includes only the greens — whether lettuce, romaine, endive, young tender spinach, etc. — topped with a simple dressing. The greens should be bite-sized. Purists would say the lettuce leaves should be torn apart, never cut. Well, maybe, but who hasn't had to deal with a large piece of lettuce on his or her fork? Cut or tear the lettuce into one-inch (or smaller) pieces.

To this you may add many other raw vegetables: carrots, celery, cucumber, radishes, chopped cauliflower, chopped or finely sliced onion (especially green spring onions), etc.

It can be served dressed simply with an oil and vinegar dressing, or with one of the many commercial salad dressings at your grocery. The dressing should be tossed with the salad greens immediately before serving, or it can be offered on the side.

We are glad that Ruby generously shared her layered lettuce salad recipe with the cookbook committee, and therefore with the rest of us, and we thank her for that. This is a healthy, easy-to-make dish. It has more ingredients than the simple greens/dressing salad, and gives you protein in the eggs, bacon and peas.

Make this pretty and fresh-tasting salad the day before you plan to serve it for a church gathering, family reunion, or to enjoy at your own home for family and guests for … *Sunday Dinner*.

Layered Lettuce Salad

- 1 head crisp lettuce, cleaned
- 1 cup celery, diced
- 4 eggs, hard-cooked, sliced
- 1 10-ounce package frozen English peas, uncooked
- ½ cup diced green pepper
- 1 medium sweet onion, sliced
- 8 slices bacon, fried and diced
- 2 cups mayonnaise
- 2 tablespoons sugar
- 4 ounces cheddar cheese, grated

Tear lettuce into small, bite-sized pieces and place in a 9×12 glass dish. Layer celery, eggs, frozen peas, green pepper, onion and bacon on lettuce. Add the sugar to the mayonnaise and spread over the top as you would frosting. Top with the grated cheese, cover and refrigerate for 8-12 hours. At serving time, garnish with additional bacon and parsley. Serves 10 or more.

Cherry Congealed Salad
Gayle Taylor
(Published June 4, 2015)

They were more popular a few years ago, but one doesn't see them as much now as previously. I like them. They are pretty on the plate or buffet, simple to make, and usually must be made a day or so before serving.

I'm talking about the molded, or "congealed," salads, as they are often called. One of the reasons for their failing popularity is that most recipes (like today's) have as a base one of the sweetened gelatins: Jello or Royal. Because of that, the result may have more calories than one wants.

Today's recipe is from Gayle Taylor, who has served as church secretary for Providence Baptist Church in Pageland for 37 years. The pastor, Dr. Rogers Wall, has been there a couple of years. The church, organized in 1894, has the full range of Baptist programs: Sunday school, Bible study, WMU, GAs, RAs, Mission Friends, etc., and a 30-to-35-member choir.

Gayle and her husband, Steve, who is in transportation, have two sons. Michael and his wife, Sherry, live in Chicago; and the younger son, Berton, is part of the Providence church staff and works with the media.

When not working full-time at Providence, Gayle enjoys reading, cooking (most of the time), and especially the trips she and Steve take to visit their son in Chicago.

Gayle got the recipe many years ago from Steve's aunt, Johnie P. Taylor.

You can enjoy this pretty salad without guilt by using one of the sugar-free gelatins. Besides, you probably aren't going to eat the whole thing by yourself, and this is so good that you should consider making it soon. It will be the prettiest thing on the table or buffet for … *Sunday Dinner.*

Cherry Congealed Salad

   1 6-ounce package cherry gelatin
   1 cup boiling water
   1 20-ounce can cherry pie filling
   1 15-ounce can crushed pineapple, undrained
   1 8-ounce package cream cheese, softened
   1 8-ounce carton sour cream
   ½ cup sugar
   Chopped nuts, if desired

Dissolve gelatin in boiling water in large saucepan. Add pie filling and pineapple. Mix well. Pour into a 9×13-inch dish and refrigerate until congealed. In a small bowl, mix cream cheese, sour cream, sugar and nuts. Spread over top of cherry mixture and refrigerate. Cut into squares. Yield: 12 servings.

Vegetables and Side Dishes

Macaroni and Cheese
Jerry Baskin
(Published March 9, 2015)

Who or when, I don't know — but to someone at some time we owe a great thank you for, first, developing pasta (specifically, macaroni), and, second, for combining it with cheese to make that staple of tables everywhere.

This versatile macaroni and cheese goes to church suppers, picnics, company meals and Sunday dinners, is carried to the sick, is a mainstay for almost any menu, is always good-tasting, and is easy to prepare. It can be part of many menus and is also considered a meat substitute.

Macaroni, made in more than 100 shapes and sizes (although most of us see only a few of them), has been with us for hundreds of years, and no one knows for sure who developed it. According to World Book, it was probably the Chinese, and then the Germans and Italians introduced it to Europe.

And aren't we glad they did! In addition to the mac and cheese that everyone likes, how could you have a vacation Bible school without macaroni to string into a necklace?

Although almost all recipes are similar, today we are using one from Jerry Baskin of Holly Springs Baptist Church in Inman. A large church, Holly Springs averages around 280 in Sunday school. The pastor, Rev. Tim Clark, has served the church for 20 years or so. The church also has an active group of men who annually go on mission trips, and Jerry is part of this. The group — calling itself "Men on A Mission" — has gone to Iowa, Louisiana, Mississippi and other places. Started in 1987 by Holly Springs, now other churches have joined, and a large group goes on the trips each year around Memorial Day. While most of the men are building, Jerry is in charge of the kitchen.

Jerry also teaches a men's Sunday school class named for him, and has served as a deacon and in many other positions.

With his wife, Brenda, he has two stepchildren — Stephen Eubanks and his wife, Melody, who live in Denver, and Allison Eubanks Malach and her husband, Wayne, of Holly Springs — and a daughter, Andrea Baskin Evans and her husband, Brian, who live in Lyman.

Jerry is proud of his macaroni dish. He used a dish his wife, Brenda, made and "tweaked it." He suggests running a knife around the inside edge of the dish once or twice while it is baking. Brenda has learned not to offer her help, because, as Jerry says, "I don't let anybody touch my macaroni and cheese."

If you are lucky enough to be invited to their home, hope that Jerry and Brenda will serve you his Mac and Cheese for ... *Sunday Dinner.*

Macaroni and Cheese

2 cups macaroni

1 small can evaporated milk

24 slices American cheese, cubed*

4 eggs

1 stick (½ cup) butter (or margarine)

Approximately 1 cup milk

1 12-ounce can evaporated milk

Salt and pepper to taste

Cook macaroni until tender and drain. Preheat oven to 375 degrees. Mix evaporated milk, eggs and pepper, and set aside. Drain noodles and place into a 9×13-inch glass baking dish. Add the butter, and stir until the macaroni is coated and the butter is melted. Add milk and egg mixture, stirring well. Stir the cheese into the mixture, then add the milk so that it almost covers the macaroni.

Bake 10 minutes, then reduce heat to 350 degrees and bake for 45 minutes, checking to make sure the macaroni is not cooked dry. Leave it a little runny, as it will continue to cook when removed from the oven. Serves 10-12.

*Amount of cheese can vary.

If you don't want the eggs, try the following recipe:

Eggless Mac and Cheese
1 cup macaroni
3 tablespoons butter
3 tablespoons flour
1 cup milk
1 cup shredded cheese
1 cup cubed cheese
Salt and pepper to taste

Cook macaroni according to package directions. Preheat oven to 350 degrees. Meanwhile, melt butter in saucepan and stir in flour. Gradually add the milk and stir until mixture thickens. Stir in the grated cheese until it melts.

Pour cheese mixture into pot with drained macaroni, stirring to mix well. Empty into a glass baking dish. Scatter the cubed cheese on top; then, using the back of a fork, gently press the cheese cubes down into the mac and cheese mixture, smoothing the top. Bake about 25-30 minutes. Serves 5-8.

Note: The dish may be topped before baking with finely crumbled saltine crackers if desired.

Crock Pot Macaroni
Jane Fussell and Mary Berry
(Published September 16, 2008)

This is the way she describes it: "Simple to make, can be made ahead of time, doesn't tie up oven space, and usually no leftovers."

Those are the words of Jane Fussell of Calvary Baptist Church in Florence. Mike Mills is the new pastor. The church (a large one with 1,065 resident members) is in Florence Baptist Association, and Jane has been a part of the congregation for 35 years.

The dish she is describing is Crock Pot macaroni. "Crock Pot" is a brand name, and the recipe would probably do just as well in another slow cooker.

At one time many years ago, Jane was a member of First Baptist Church, Darlington, but since then she and her family have lived in other places. Jane and her late husband, Bob, who died in 1991, have three children. Their daughter, Susan Williamson, and her husband, Paul, have three children — Drew, Jon, and Elise — and they also attend Calvary. The Fussells' two sons — Berry and John and their families — live in the Raleigh, N.C. area. Jane's biggest pleasure is being with her family. She also enjoys traveling somewhat, but only short trips.

At her church, Calvary, Jane's main work for the past 25 years or so has been with the library, which she says is larger than the usual library for a church its size. In addition to books, it has videos, tapes, etc., and is open during most church activities and on Wednesday mornings.

Another Calvary member, Mary Berry, worked for a long time with the library program there, and it was she who gave Jane this Crock Pot macaroni recipe. Jane describes Mary Berry as "a good friend, longtime member and faithful member at Calvary Baptist." Some time ago, Mary moved to Methodist Manor Retirement Home in Florence.

"She was a good cook," Jane said, and is glad to have Mary's recipe, which she uses several times a year for holiday meals and when her family gathers. One grandchild always asks immediately if she has made the macaroni!

Jane says this is a good dish to take to church suppers, family reunions, and other informal gatherings because it can be served directly from the cooking pot. Jane was not quite sure about the number of servings. If you increase the ingredients by one-half, they almost fill a 3½-quart cooker. To double the recipe, you'll need a larger cooker. Don't remove the cover while cooking.

Now that fall is almost here, we like hearty comfort foods, and none could be better than Crock Pot macaroni. You will thank Jane for sharing this recipe with us when you are enjoying it for … *Sunday Dinner*.

Crock Pot Macaroni

- 8 ounces elbow macaroni, cooked and drained
- 16 ounces (4 cups) shredded sharp cheddar cheese
- 12 ounces (large can) evaporated milk
- 1½ cups milk
- 2 eggs, lightly beaten
- 1 teaspoon salt
- ½ teaspoon pepper

Lightly grease 3½-quart crock pot. Place macaroni in crock pot. Add all other ingredients, except 1 cup cheese. Mix well. Sprinkle remaining cheese on top. Cook on low 5 hours or until firm and golden around the edges. Do not remove cover while cooking. Serves approximately 16.

Macaroni and Cheese My Way

(Published January 13, 2005)

One of our daughters had a friend visiting for the "First Thanksgiving" — the Sunday before Thanksgiving when all the children were home. He probably thinks I have only one menu, and he is right about that, in a way.

For holidays, you don't mess with the menu! You have the turkey, the dressing, the giblet gravy, the sweet potatoes, etc.

And, especially, you have macaroni and cheese.

The dish is sometimes called "comfort food" because everyone likes it, and it is easily made.

Every cook has his or her own way of making this, and I'm going to tell you mine, but first I say these things: I don't like eggs in the mac and cheese. They give it a custard taste that I don't like. This is purely a matter of personal taste; many people use eggs and have gone on to live useful, happy lives.

You have to have sharp cheddar cheese. The macaroni should be cooked well before it is added to the cheese mixture. The cheese mixture will need salt and pepper. You can make the whole dish several hours before baking. Cover and keep in the refrigerator if it is to stand overnight, or on the counter if not.

One other thing: The measurements don't have to be exact. If you get those basic ingredients in a dish and cook them, the result will be good.

I make a cheese sauce, which is basically a medium white sauce with a whole bunch of sharp cheddar in it. Sometimes I use processed cheese — Velveeta. Some purists don't like Velveeta, but it does make a smooth mixture. One of the things I do right before baking is to push half-inch cubes of cheese into the mixture. This means that when one dips out a serving, he occasionally gets a partially melted chunk of cheese. Good!

Grease (or coat with cooking spray) the baking dish on the bottom and sides, up to the top, so the macaroni won't stick to the sides. Don't overcook. Everything in the dish is already cooked, so about 25 to 30 minutes is adequate.

The matter of topping is also optional: Some cooks don't use any topping, some use crushed saltines or buttered bread crumbs, some used grated cheese. I like the cheese, but occasionally use the crushed saltines.

However you make it, macaroni and cheese is a dish that everyone enjoys. If you don't have a favorite recipe, assemble this one before Sunday school this week and bake it when you get home from church so that it will be warm, comforting and tasty for ... *Sunday Dinner.*

Macaroni and Cheese My Way

    16 ounces elbow macaroni

    ½ teaspoon salt

    Water

    6 tablespoons butter

    6 tablespoons flour

    3 cups milk

    1 pound medium or sharp cheddar, grated (sharp is better)

Or you might want to try this combination:

1½ pounds or more processed cheese (Velveeta)
½ pound (or more) sharp cheddar cheese,
   cut into ½- to ¾-inch cubes
Salt and pepper to taste

Topping:
Grated cheese
Crushed saltines (or buttered, fine bread crumbs)

Grease a bake-and-serve dish. Preheat oven to 350 degrees. Bring water (enough to cover macaroni a couple of inches) to a boil, add salt and macaroni. Bring water to a boil again and cook according to package directions, usually 8 to 10 minutes.

Meanwhile, over medium to low heat, melt butter in large skillet. Add the flour, stirring until blended. Then gradually add the milk, stirring, to make a medium white sauce. Add salt (about a half teaspoon or less) and black pepper to taste. Add the grated cheese (or Velveeta cut into chunks). Stir until cheese melts. Now you have a cheese sauce.

Remove from heat. Drain macaroni and add to cheese mix. Pour into prepared baking dish. Evenly sprinkle the cheese cubes on the macaroni, and with the back of a spoon, push them down into the macaroni and cheese. Sprinkle with topping. Bake about 25 minutes (until lightly brown for saltines or bread crumbs, or until the grated cheese is melted). Serve hot. Serves about 15.

Infallible Rice Casserole
The late Wilma Brown
(Published October 3, 2013)

We are all survived by things we have done. Mr. Bell gave us the telephone, someone I don't know gave us the paper clip, and we have the late Wilma Brown of Gaffney to thank for Infallible Rice Casserole.

This simple recipe has a lot in its favor. It has only four ingredients, and you probably have these in your pantry and refrigerator. It is easy to assemble, and it can bake while you are doing something else. It is a dish that will go well with almost any menu and is good for family or guests.

Mrs. Brown and her late husband, Clyde, were members of Goucher (pronounced Go-cher) Baptist Church of Gaffney, originally Goucher Creek Baptist because it was located near Goucher Creek. The creek is still flowing, but the church dropped that part of its name many years ago.

Goucher Baptist Church, one of the state's oldest churches, has been in the church business since 1770 and is currently served by Rev. Norman Gardner, pastor, and Rev. James Sean McElworth, the new student minister. The church offers the programs of most Baptist churches.

The late Mrs. Brown, who died more than a year ago in her mid-90s, and her husband were members of Goucher for decades, serving in many capacities.

Professionally, she was a school teacher in several local schools and on different levels, but liked 7th and 8th grades the best.

She loved her church and taught both adult and youth classes, but preferred the junior and senior high age groups. In her retirement, she liked knitting, and it was her pleasure to knit items and give them to others. She was also known as a good cook, but we don't know where she got this recipe. The Browns had one son, Barry. He and his family live in the area.

Mr. Brown worked in the textile industry and loved children, often spending the Sunday school hours in the children's department. A testimony to their lives was given by Mrs. Dell Byers, church secretary, who said, with affection and respect, "They were well thought of."

And we thought well of Wilma's casserole. You will, also. It is a good recipe to accompany beef, pork or chicken. It is good for a family, and good and pretty enough for company. It is easily put together, so you can make it when you get home from church, or you can make it in the morning and reheat it briefly. Either way, you will thank the late Mrs. Brown for her contribution to your ... *Sunday Dinner.*

Infallible Rice Casserole
- 1 medium onion, minced
- 2 tablespoons butter
- 1 cup regular white rice
- 2 cups chicken broth (hot)

Sauté onions in the butter over medium heat until clear. Combine onions, rice and hot broth. Bring to a boil on top of stove. Put into a casserole baking dish and cover. Bake in a 325-degree oven for 20 minutes. Serve hot and listen for the compliments! Serves 4 hungry or 6 polite people.

One-Pot Potatoes
(Published January 19, 2007)

Emily has been with us this morning. Our 10-year-old granddaughter lives around the corner and drops by. We are always delighted to see her, and this morning she has been using the shredder I gave my husband, Ed, for Christmas. He didn't know he needed a shredder until I gave him one. Emily likes to shred, but she is an indiscriminate shredder, so I was careful that none of the recipes I was studying strayed over to the shredding pile.

I like recipes, and as I was looking at them I became aware of how many of them use prepared foods such as baking mixes, soup, puddings, seasonings, etc.

Let's talk about packaged foods. I'm not a package snob, and I do use them, but not much. There are two reasons. First, I like things in their natural state. Both canned and frozen peaches are good, but a peach from the tree is better. The second is that I like to be able to pronounce the things I eat. For example, I like cooking with butter. When you are at the grocery next, look at the ingredients in butter: "Cream, salt." Then look at the ingredients in margarine. There are a lot of syllables. Of course, all the packaged foods are safe because our Food and Drug Administration takes care of that.

Because of our busy lives, I (and most cooks) frequently use the packaged products — and that's all right, but when time allows, go to your farmers' market or your grocery and buy the fresh vegetables.

Today's recipe jumped out at me as I was looking through a collection. I don't think I clipped it very long ago; there is no date on it. I made it for lunch, and we liked it. It's one I think you will want to keep and use frequently, because it gets several veggies in one pot and is easy to make.

It doesn't have any water because the vegetables — especially the yellow and zucchini squash — will release enough liquid for cooking. As you see, the amounts don't have to be exact.

The cheese is optional. It tastes good and is a bit more nourishing, but the vegetables are good without it. Don't overcook this or it will get mushy. You can cook the bacon before Sunday school then add the vegetables when you get home letting it cook to enjoy for … *Sunday Dinner*.

One-Pot Potatoes

    5 or 6 medium red or white potatoes
    2 carrots, sliced crossways
    2 medium onions, sliced
    ½ green bell pepper, sliced
    1 medium yellow squash
    1 medium zucchini squash
    4 slices bacon
    Salt and pepper to taste
    ½ cup grated white cheese (optional)

Cut bacon into ½-inch sections and cook about 10 minutes in a large heavy pot such as a Dutch oven. Wash potatoes and slice with skin on. Slice all vegetables and put into pot with the bacon. Add salt and pepper. Cover and cook about 30 minutes or so until the vegetables are tender. Stir a couple of times. Don't overcook or stir too often or vegetables will be mushy. A few minutes before serving, sprinkle the cheese over the vegetables and let it melt. Serves 6-8.

Stuffings and Dressings
(Published December 4, 2003)

During the holiday season, there are many meals other than Thanksgiving and Christmas Day when we serve stuffing/dressing. And today I am offering several recipes for these. But first, an old joke:

    The celebrated hostess was having a lavish dinner party. The maid brought into the dining room the perfectly browned and beautifully presented turkey on a large platter. Suddenly, she missed a step and dropped the turkey, which went skidding across the floor. The quick-thinking lady of the house said, "Look what you've done, Essie. Now pick up that turkey, carry it back to the kitchen, and bring the other one you have out there."

I hope Essie didn't drop the dressing as well.

The recipe for both stuffing and dressing is the same. For stuffing, the mixture is put inside the turkey/chicken/goose/duck cavity and cooks when the fowl is cooking. For dressing, the same recipe is used but is baked separately and served usually with gravy as an accompaniment to the turkey, chicken, etc.

Whichever you do is purely a matter of choice. I personally like the "dressing" baked separately with a lightly browned, crusty top, bottom and sides. If you cook the dressing separately, time it so that it comes hot from the oven near the serving time.

There are several do-aheads to cut time and work. You can crumble and measure the bread; cook, cool, crumble and measure the corn bread if you are making that kind of dressing; or mix the two together. You can cook the onions and celery and have them in the fridge. If you are doing the chestnuts, boil and prepare them the day before; brown the sausage and refrigerate it; slice the mushrooms if you are using those, etc. Prepare the baking dish and set it aside until you need it.

The first recipe, corn bread dressing, is the one I have used forever. The measurements don't have to be exact. I like a lot of sage; you may not want as much.

Corn Bread Dressing

    4 cups finely crumbled corn bread

    4 cups finely crumbled bread (leftover biscuits, white bread, etc.)

1 tablespoon poultry seasoning (or to taste)
1 teaspoon sage
1 cup finely chopped celery
1 cup finely chopped onion
4 or 5 eggs, beaten
Broth (from baking turkey or canned)

Preheat oven to 400 degrees. Grease a large baking dish, about 9x15. Combine white bread and corn bread crumbles, poultry seasoning and sage, and stir to evenly distribute the seasonings.

Add celery and onions, and mix. Add the beaten eggs, which serve as a binder, and enough broth to make a moist mixture. Pour into prepared dish and bake until top is browned, about 45 minutes or so. Serves 15-20.

Bread Crumb Dressing

5 cups crumbled or cubed stale white bread crumbs
2 teaspoons poultry seasoning or sage
½ teaspoon salt
½ cup butter
Small onion, chopped (about ½ cup)
1 stalk celery (including leaves), finely chopped
Water, milk, or broth

In a skillet, sauté the onion and celery in the butter until tender. Combine all ingredients, adding as much broth, milk or water needed to make a moist mixture. Bake separately or use for a 5-pound chicken or small turkey.

Mushroom stuffing — Add ½ pound of sliced mushrooms to onions when cooking.

Chestnut — Decrease bread crumbs to 3½ cups and butter to ⅓ cup, and add 1 pound chopped chestnuts. To prepare chestnuts, cut an "X" on flat side of each chestnut. Cover chestnuts with water, bring to a boil, then simmer 20 minutes. Leave chestnuts to cool in the water, then remove the outer shell and brown skin, then chop.

Sausage-Prune Dressing

- **16 ounces packaged corn bread stuffing mix**
- **1 pound pork sausage**
- **12-ounce box chopped prunes**
- **½ cup water**
- **2 tart cooking apples, peeled and chopped**
- **¼ cup finely chopped onion**
- **¼ cup raisins**
- **¼ cup molasses**
- **1 cup water**

Preheat oven to 300 degrees. Grease a 9x13x2 baking dish. In a skillet, cook sausage until lightly browned, stirring frequently. Remove from skillet and drain drippings. In a small saucepan, combine the ½ cup water and prunes. Bring to a boil, reduce heat and simmer the prunes 2 minutes, stirring constantly. Do not drain. Set aside.

In a skillet, melt the butter, add the onions and apples, and cook until just tender. Mix all ingredients in a large mixing bowl. Put into the prepared dish, cover and bake about 40-45 minutes. Serves 12-15.

Oyster Dressing

    4 cups bread stuffing mixture
        (your own mixture or the purchased kind)
    1 cup oysters, drained and chopped

Combine the dressing and oysters, using the oyster liquid to moisten the mixture. Add warm water if more liquid is needed. Use for stuffing, or bake separately in greased baking dish at 400 degrees until lightly browned. Serves 8 or so.

Zesty Vegetable Casserole
Virginia Beck
(Published October 30, 2008)

Today's dish is from a friend of a friend. It is in the cookbook "In Good Taste: Tasty Recipes" printed by the WMU of St. Helena Baptist Church on St. Helena Island. If you don't recognize the name, it is a small town in Beaufort County across from Parris Island and on the way to Hunting Island.

The pastor is Richard Spearman, and the church is part of Savannah River Baptist Association. Gerald Roper, retired associational missionary in Easley, is serving as a supply pastor while Rev. Spearman is on a sabbatical.

The church began in 1965, according to the info in the cookbook, in prayer meetings sponsored by The Baptist Church of Beaufort. After the decision to form a church was made, 38 people adopted a church covenant and articles of faith. For several years, the young church met in a house.

Groundbreaking for the first sanctuary was in 1966, and in 1980 there was another groundbreaking ceremony for a new sanctuary and fellowship hall. The growing church is currently constructing a multi-purpose building for worship, fellowship and ministry. It is almost complete, and a dedication date is set for early November.

The cookbook was published this year, and mystery woman Virginia Beck submitted the Zesty Vegetable Casserole recipe. She isn't a member of the church, but she sure makes a good vegetable dish. The Garrison Detective Agency has tried unsuccessfully to find Mrs. Beck, who is probably a friend of someone on the cookbook committee. We hear she has moved to California. Whatever Mrs. Beck's connection, we thank her for the contribution.

This is an easily prepared dish because you will probably have on hand all the ingredients. You can probably substitute cheddar cheese for the processed cheese and saltine crackers for the butter crackers. When I made it, I followed the recipe exactly, and it got a good report at our church supper.

Another plus for the dish is that you can assemble it the day before or on Sunday morning, put it in your prettiest baking dish, refrigerate, then bake it after church for all to enjoy for … *Sunday Dinner.*

Zesty Vegetable Casserole

½ cup chopped onion

½ cup chopped bell pepper

½ cup chopped celery

One 14½-ounce can sweet corn, drained

One 14½-ounce can green beans, drained

One 10¾-ounce cream of celery soup, undiluted

1 cup sour cream

1 stick (½ cup) butter
1 stack (36) round buttery crackers
8 ounces (½ stick small package) processed cheese,
   cubed small

Preheat oven to 350 degrees. Grease an approximate 7×12 baking dish. Mix the drained corn, green beans, sour cream and soup together in a large bowl. Stir in the additional chopped vegetables. Stir in the cheese cubes. Pour mixture into the prepared baking dish. Melt the butter and add the crushed crackers. Mix well and spread over the vegetable mixture to form a crust. Bake approximately 30 minutes, or until golden brown and bubbly.

Corn Casserole
William Conner
(Published February 8, 2006)

"Can I get you on alternate weeks?" I asked William Conner, a member of First Baptist Church of Georgetown. We were discussing his corn casserole, which he is sharing with us this week, and he said he does almost all the cooking at his house.

This situation began, he explained, when his wife, an elementary school teacher, came home each day with loads of school work. He began helping a bit so she would have some free time in the evening, and after a while it became the norm.

Ted Sherrill is pastor at Georgetown First where William and his wife, Angela, have been members for about 17 years. The Conners have two sons. The younger son Jeffrey has recently returned from service in Iraq and immediately afterward married his new bride, Jennifer. The older son

Christopher works at a surfing resort in Nicaragua.

William and Jennifer are part of the Sunday school and the church's music program. She is part of the Singing Christmas Tree, and William handles the lights.

They also work with the church-sponsored, city-wide program called Upward Basketball that involves more than 350 children. Angela is a referee, and William is the photographer. A similar soccer program has 200-plus young people.

A weekly activity for the Conners is helping with the Wednesday-night church suppers. One group cooks during the day; the Conners and others come in the evening to serve and do the clean-up.

William, a professor with the Clemson University Forestry Department, works at the forestry lab in Georgetown, where he is mainly involved in research and writing. On alternate years, he teaches. Angela is at Waccamaw Elementary.

He likes to cook soups and stews, and, of course, living in the Lowcountry, he likes Frogmore Stew. He doesn't remember when he got this corn casserole recipe, but it slightly resembles the corn pudding his mother made.

When I made the corn casserole for our group, everyone liked it, and it's a good recipe to have when you need "something else" for the menu. William says that it can be assembled, put in the refrigerator, then baked after church to serve hot and delicious for … *Sunday Dinner*.

Corn Casserole

- 1 16-ounce can cream-style corn
- 1 egg
- 1 small onion, chopped

¼ cup grated cheddar cheese

1 tablespoon sugar

¼ cup chopped bell pepper

2 teaspoons pimento, chopped

Dash of hot pepper sauce

1 cup cracker crumbs

1 tablespoon fresh chopped parsley

Mix all ingredients together and pour into baking dish. Bake in a 350-degree oven for about 30 to 35 minutes. Serves 6.

Fresh Corn Pudding
The late Hazel Lusk
(Published September 4, 2013)

"Jake wanted me to call you," daughter Elizabeth said, calling from Greenwood. "He says there is a storm — with the possibility of a tornado — coming to your area."

"Thank him for me," I answered. I had just readied myself for bed, and my pajamas had a small slit in the seam on the left side. I would have to change to another pair.

"Mother," she replied, "no one is going to see your pajamas."

"Well, if I go flying all over the neighborhood like Dorothy in 'The Wizard of Oz,' someone surely will!" I answered.

There was no tornado, and I was glad because it would have interfered with my making Hazel Lusk's fresh corn pudding. Whether the corn is from a local farmers' market, your supermarket, or your own garden, corn is good for taste and health.

I am sorry to tell you that Mrs. Lusk is no longer with us. She died in January 2012, after having spent almost a lifetime as a member of Barker's Creek Baptist Church near Honea Path. Organized in 1821, Barker's Creek is one of the state's oldest churches, with a membership of roughly 400. Rev. Wesley Taylor has served as pastor since 2007. The church has nearly all the Baptist programs in place, and these "are well attended," including worship services, Sunday school, WMU, RAs, GAs, Mission Friends, etc.

Hazel and her late husband, Marvin, had three children, all members of Barker's Creek: Kathy Lusk Fisher, Billy Lusk, and Dennis Lusk.

When Mrs. Lusk died, she had been in poor health for several years. Before the health problems arrived, she was active in her church doing "whatever needed doing," including being in the choir. One thing friends recall about Hazel was that when she was in high school, she was the beauty queen for her class.

She liked to sew, making many of the children's clothes when they were young and sewing for home decorating including making curtains, etc. In her later years, she enjoyed traveling and reading, and always loved her church.

We don't know where she got this recipe for corn pudding; her daughter Kathy doesn't know. Fresh corn prepared almost any way is good, but this is a healthy recipe to serve guests because, as tasty as it is, corn-on-the-cob is not a very dignified way to eat this valuable vegetable. Leave that for family dinners or cookouts; for the dining room, consider Hazel's recipe.

This corn pudding is better if the directions are followed, but if you are in a hurry, simply cut the corn from the cob but don't cut too closely and then scrape the cob with the unsharpened side of the knife blade. Make this in the morning, let it rest in a warm place, and it will be waiting for you and your guests for … *Sunday Dinner.*

Corn Pudding

   3 cups fresh corn kernels, about 5-6 ears
   3 tablespoons flour
   1½ teaspoons sugar
   ¼ teaspoon pepper
   1 cup milk
   3 large eggs
   1½ teaspoons salt
   ¾ teaspoon baking powder
   3 tablespoons melted margarine

Husk and remove silks from the fresh corn. Preheat oven to 350 degrees. Grease a 6-cup casserole dish and set aside. Cut down the center of each row of corn. Stand the ear on its end and scrape down the cob to release pulp and milky juice.

Beat eggs lightly; add corn and remaining ingredients, and mix well. Place corn mixture in the prepared casserole dish. Bake 35-45 minutes in prepared oven or until golden brown and just set in the center. Remove from oven and let stand 15 minutes before serving. Serves 6-8.

Corn Pie
Claudia Meadows Burdette
(Published February 17, 2011)

She has a connection with four South Carolina Baptist churches and feels a close association with all of them. Her name is Claudia Meadows Burdette, and she lives in Hampton County.

Claudia's recipe for corn pie is one you'll want to clip. All the ingredients will be available almost any time in your refrigerator or pantry for you to use on that day when you need another dish for dinner.

Her Aunt Mary gave her the original old family recipe, but Claudia has adjusted it to bring it to the useful dish it is today.

Claudia grew up in Brunson in Hampton County and was a member of Brunson Baptist Church. Her father and a brother were both deacons.

After college, she lived in North Carolina a short time, then moved to Edgefield. She was an involved member at Edgefield Baptist Church for eight years as GA leader and teacher for a young members' Sunday school class.

Claudia now lives with her husband in Blackville, where she is a member of Mt. Calvary Baptist Church in Elko. David O'Donnell has been pastor there almost four years.

Claudia and Stephen frequently attend Barnwell First Baptist Church to visit family members. Keith Richardson is pastor of the large church. They offer three services on Sunday with an attendance of 420-plus.

Stephen is a forester working with American Forest Management. Claudia is program coordinator of the continuing education program at Denmark Technical College.

One thing that has remained a constant — and comforting — dinnertime experience for Claudia's family, no matter where they were attending church, is her corn pie.

This is a good recipe Claudia is sharing with us. Cook it in a bake-and-serve dish, because, although the interior is somewhat soft, it can still be spooned onto a plate. This will be good anytime, but plan to have it this weekend when you prepare it after church and have it for a late … *Sunday Dinner.*

Corn Pie

- 1½ cups milk
- 2 eggs
- 1 tablespoon butter, melted
- Salt and pepper to taste
- ¼ cup flour
- 1 tablespoon sugar
- 1 15-ounce can whole kernel corn

Beat eggs with egg beater. Add milk, sugar, butter, salt and pepper. Beat all together. Mix flour and corn and add the liquid mixture to the corn. Bake in a 9-inch square, greased casserole dish at 450 degrees for 40-45 minutes. Serves 8.

Stuffed Tomatoes with Yellow Rice
Jenny Myers
(Published May 24, 2012)

My children have an obsession with orderly clothes closets.

Daughter Elizabeth was "emptying and organizing" mine. While my Ed and I were errand-running, she had come for a visit and in our absence had organized her father's closet and was starting on mine.

"That is the ugliest sweater I've ever seen," stated Elizabeth as she tossed it onto the "out" pile, adding, "You've had it forever."

"All the more reason to keep it," I countered. "People have been born who have never seen that sweater, and it will be new to them."

Several months ago, her older sister Gaye had made a similar attack.

The residue from that raid is still packed into two large boxes upstairs.

Our children agree that my inability to toss, give away, sell, or in any way dispose of any possession is because I was born in the waning months of the Depression, and one never knows when one may need something one has thrown out.

One thing you probably won't throw out is Jenny Myers' recipe for stuffed tomatoes. The recipe is in the book, "The Pastors' Wives Cookbook," compiled by Sybil Dubose several years ago. Our contributor Jenny is Sybil's sister, who now lives in Pensacola, Fla.

At the time, Jenny was a member of Edisto Baptist Church in Cordova, located in Orangeburg County.

She and her husband have since moved to Charleston. They both are amateur radio enthusiasts and with that do a lot of charitable work.

This recipe will be a good one for you when the local tomatoes from the farmers' market, your supermarket or your own garden are available. It makes a pretty dish for both dining room and picnic table. If you have an abundance of tomatoes, this will be another useful recipe for them.

We thank Jenny for sharing the recipe. You can make it Sunday morning or even Saturday, refrigerate it, and bake it when you get home from church for a pretty and good-tasting addition to your … *Sunday Dinner*.

Stuffed Tomatoes with Yellow Rice
- 1 8-ounce package yellow rice
- 1 small jar chopped pimento
- 1 cup sharp cheddar cheese, grated
- 1 10½-ounce can beef consommé
- 1 tablespoon chopped parsley
- 8 or more medium tomatoes

Cook rice according to package directions, using consommé for the water required. Remove ½ inch from bloom end of tomato. Scoop out pulp; save for another use or discard. Turn tomatoes cut side down to drain. Mix together the cooked rice, ¾ of the cheese, parsley and pimento. Stuff the tomatoes and top with remaining cheese. Place in baking dish with a small amount of water. Bake at 350 degrees for 15-20 minutes or until done.

(Note: Vary the amount of cheese if you like. Also, the rice mixture may fill more or less tomatoes indicated, based on size. If a larger amount is needed, use the 16-ounce package of rice and more tomatoes.)

Bacon and Tomato Pie
Wendy Cruce and Julie Murden
(Published May 19, 2005)

Looking at the recipe the first time, one would think there is no such thing, but there is — and it's good, and it's original.

The recipe is from "Recipes for Delightful Dining," the Charleston First Baptist Church School cookbook that I used previously. For lunch, I baked a tomato pie by Dianne Earp, who for several years was the school's librarian. She has since moved with her husband, Walter, to Boone, N.C. Everyone at our table liked Dianne's recipe.

Today's recipe, bacon and tomato pie, is somewhat similar, yet different, and was the creation of two women associated with the school. They have been friends about 10 years or so since meeting in Sunday school at Charleston First, where they are members.

Their names are Wendy (Mrs. Jeff) Cruce and Julie (Mrs. Herman Jr.) Murden. Wendy's two daughters, Hayward and MacKenzie, attend the church school — and Julie's son Drew did go there but is now attending the

Academic Magnet High School in North Charleston.

Wendy teaches the church's high schoolers in Sunday school. Julie teaches in vacation Bible school and does the VBS clinic for the Charleston area. Julie taught at the Charleston First Baptist Church School for 20 years, but now teaches at the Addlestone Hebrew Academy.

The women went regularly to Leland Farms, where they purchased fresh vegetables, and began to consider ways to use the excellent tomatoes they bought there. They worked on the recipe together, and then they each cooked it. After the first baking, Wendy suggested adding the bacon. They each tried that, and agreed that the bacon made the dish better.

In assembling the pie, place only one layer of tomatoes. If you have more, the cooked pie will have too much liquid. The bottom crust should be brown, and the cheese/mayo topping cooks to a pretty color. Julie says that she has transferred the pie shells to a glass baking dish and made bacon and tomato pie in it, which makes for easier cutting into serving pieces.

In not too many weeks, we will have fresh, local tomatoes from home gardens and farmers' markets all over the state. Use two of them in this dish for … *Sunday Dinner*.

Bacon and Tomato Pie

- 2 ripe tomatoes
- ½ teaspoon salt
- 6 tablespoons chopped basil
- 3 cups grated cheddar cheese
- 2 eggs, beaten
- 2 purchased 9-inch pie crusts, baked
- 1 teaspoon pepper
- 1 cup sliced onion

    1 cup mayonnaise
    6 strips bacon, cooked and crumbled

Preheat oven to 350 degrees, prick bottoms of pie shells, and cook about 10 minutes or according to directions. Allow to cool. Peel tomatoes, cut into slices, and then cut slices into fourths. Divide tomatoes and all the ingredients into two parts. The ingredients will be placed in layers in the pie crusts.

Cover the crusts with the tomato slices/pieces. Sprinkle with the salt, pepper and basil. Layer the onion slices on top of the tomatoes.
Mix together the mayonnaise, eggs and cheese. Cover the onions and tomatoes with this mixture. Top with the crumbled bacon pieces. Bake pies for 30-35 minutes. Allow to rest for 20-30 minutes before serving. Makes 12-16 servings.

Baked Onions
(Published March 14, 2013)

Today's recipe is one you are going to use and one for which you will thank me.

It is baked onions from the cookbook "Garden and Field" I assembled a couple of years ago. The recipe has a lot of qualities we like when selecting a dish for ourselves and our families.

Most of the ingredients you already have. The dish is easy to prepare. It goes into the oven and out of the way while you are doing other things. It has good stuff in it and, most importantly, it tastes good.

Onions and tomatoes are the most consumed vegetables, and the reasons are obvious. They are extremely versatile, being used not only fresh but also in many cooked and frozen dishes.

Young green onions are eaten raw and are eagerly anticipated by all gardeners. When the onions mature, they will keep for weeks or months in a dry setting and are always available at the supermarket. Don't store them in the same bowl or bag with potatoes.

When you have a bit of time, prepare and chop several onions. Measure them into ¼-cup portions and wrap each portion in wax paper or plastic wrap; then put several of these individual packets in a plastic freezer bag. When you need ¼ cup (or whatever) of chopped onions for a recipe, they are waiting for you, already chopped and measured.

Onions are low in calories. They are not especially grown for food value, but are very high in flavor. Sometimes they are eaten fresh just as "onions," but much more often they are part of many stews, soups, casseroles, etc. It would be hard to run a kitchen without onions.

Growing onions is easy. Soon you will see "onion sets" — or scallions, as they are also called — in garden shops. These "sets" are small onion plants which have not yet formed a fat bulb at the base. You put them into your garden and allow them to grow to salad size. Even if you do not normally grow vegetables, a pot of these onion sets and their later size will be welcomed in your kitchen for salads and to be eaten by themselves (probably with salt) as an accent to your luncheon or dinner plate.

Here is the onion recipe. It will be a good choice for this or any … *Sunday Dinner.*

Baked Onions

    4 to 6 large onions, peeled
    ¼ cup butter or margarine
    Brown sugar to taste

½ cup sour cream
1 tablespoon lemon juice
Paprika and parsley (sprinkling of each)

Heat oven to 375 degrees. Rinse onions, cut off the hard root, the dry top and one layer of peel. Place in a bake-and-serve pan, cover loosely with aluminum foil, and bake 1½ hours.

While onions bake, combine the butter, sour cream, lemon juice and brown sugar. Spread mixture over onions, then return onions to oven for a few minutes to heat the sauce. Sprinkle with the paprika and parsley to serve. Allow one onion per serving.

Green Bean Casserole
Donna Hubbard
(Published December 19, 2008)

As a general rule, men don't like several foods mixed in a dish, topped with grated cheese, baked at 350 degrees for 30 minutes, and called a casserole. They like a meat, a vegetable, a starch, a bread, a dessert, etc., separated and each easily recognized.

To be accurate, a casserole is a covered dish in which food can be both cooked and served. In the early 1950s, there was an explosion of "casseroles" — when all manner of meats, pasta, vegetables, soups, juices, etc., were put into these casserole dishes for "one-dish meals," possibly because of the number of wives in the work force.

Anyway, casseroles (the mixture of several foods baked and served, not the container) are here to stay and are a part of many family and church supper/potluck meals. You'll like today's recipe from Donna Hubbard of

Pleasant Grove Baptist Church in Greer. Her green bean casserole has a crisp taste and a lot of good stuff in it.

Donna is from Jacksonville, N.C., but moved to Greer after marrying Eric Hubbard. He works at BMW, and they have a daughter, Cheyenne, 9, and a son, Zachariah, 5. Donna teaches first grade at Buena Vista Elementary, a position she has held for four years.

She has been a member of Pleasant Grove for 10 years. Danny Emory is pastor, and the church is in the Greer Baptist Association.

At Pleasant Grove, Donna teaches the 4- and 5-year-old Sunday school class, is one of the helpers for the nursery, and is one of the teachers at children's church.

As do many teachers, Donna enjoys reading. She also enjoys scrapbooking and family time. She doesn't like cooking, but it's a requirement! This green bean casserole recipe is from her mother-in-law, Sherrill Carithers of Taylors.

The recipe calls for almonds. I think it was developed by someone in the Campbell Soup kitchen who didn't know how good pecans are. Donna and I agree that you could substitute pecans for the almonds. Whether you use the almonds or pecans, try this dish for your next ... *Sunday Dinner*.

Green Bean Casserole

    1 large can white shoepeg corn

    1 14½-ounce can French-style green beans

    ½ cup chopped celery

    ½ cup chopped onions

    ¼ cup chopped green peppers

    ½ cup grated sharp Cheddar cheese

    ½ cup sour cream

1 10¾-ounce can cream of celery soup, undiluted
1 box of crumbled cheese crackers (about ½ cup)
½ stick butter or margarine, softened or melted
1 pack (about ½ cup) slivered almonds

Combine the corn, green beans, celery, onions, green peppers, cheese, sour cream and soup. In a separate bowl, combine the crackers, butter and almonds.

Preheat oven to 350 degrees. Into a 9×13 bake/serve dish, put the vegetable mix, then top with the cracker mix. Cover the dish (casserole, that is) with aluminum foil and bake for 30 minutes. Remove the foil and cook an additional 20 minutes.

Green Beans
Betty Ruth Rentz
(Published November 12, 2013)

Fresh green beans from your supermarket, farmers' market or your own garden are a staple in American cooking. They may also come from a freezer packet or a can, but the green bean is probably the third-most-used vegetable after the onion and potato. Correct me on this if you can.

In these paragraphs, we deal not with exotic foods, but with those that are available, easy to prepare, nourishing — and the kinds you want to make for yourself, your family or guests.

Therefore, today I am going to share with you how Betty Ruth Rentz of The Baptist Church of Beaufort cooks green beans. The Baptist Church of Beaufort is one of our state's oldest, going back to 1804, and still growing with around 1,000 members. This summer, the church conducted four vacation Bible schools: one at the church, one in Hilton Head, one on Daufuskie Island, and another in Washington, D.C. Rev. Jim Wooten serves as pastor, and the church is in the Savannah River Association.

I know you will like these beans. My mother cooked beans with a piece of salt pork for two or three hours, and they were good. As a young bride many years ago, I did things differently, cooking the beans 20 minutes, as the cookbooks said.

I threw out a lot of beans that first summer.

I went back to the three-hour pork-seasoned beans, and have cooked them most often that way, but sometimes with butter, canola oil, or bacon drippings.

Then I read and cooked Betty Ruth's recipe, and all who tasted it said they were the best beans they had ever eaten. She got the recipe from a cookbook years and years ago, and that recipe is the one I am sharing with you — and the one I shall be using.

Betty Ruth and her husband, Ed, are both retired and have been members of The Baptist Church of Beaufort since 1954 — he coming from Hopewell Baptist in Hampton, and she from First Baptist in Hampton. Ed is now deacon emeritus, having served 40 years as a deacon and usher.

Betty Ruth and Ed have two daughters: Betty Jean (and George) Russ, who live in Myrtle Beach; and Judy (and Ron) Hill, who live in Princeton, N.J. Betty Ruth and Ed also have five grandchildren and four great-grandchildren.

In her retirement, Betty Ruth enjoys reading and cooking. This works out well, because Ed enjoys eating.

You will be serving fresh, healthy green beans many times throughout the year for yourself, family, guests and church suppers, so try Betty Ruth's recipe. When you do, you may want them every week for … *Sunday Dinner.*

Green Beans

    1½ pounds fresh green beans
    1 cup water
    Scant stick of butter
    ¾ teaspoon garlic salt
    1 tablespoon sugar
    ½ teaspoon basil
    Salt and pepper to taste

Wash, trim and break or cut beans into 1-inch (or more) lengths. Cook beans in water for 30 minutes. Most of the water will be gone. In a frying pan, melt the butter. Add the garlic salt, sugar, basil, salt and pepper. Add beans and stir well. Cook on medium heat for 15 minutes. Serves 5 or 6.

Broccoli

(Published January 7, 2008)

As of today, three things probably have occurred: (1) You have just about put the house in order after the holidays; (2) you have eaten the collards, black-eyed peas, and jowl or pork roast (to ensure a healthy, prosperous New Year); and (3) you have made the annual weight-loss resolution.

    I can help you with the latter. Broccoli. Three and a half ounces of raw broccoli has only 32 calories. It is a great source of iron, calcium, vitamin A, riboflavin, is one of the best sources for vitamin C among the vegetables, and its bright green color on the plate is pretty. Broccoli also tastes good.

    Broccoli is easy to prepare. Simply take a slice off the larger stem that may be tough and remove the leaves. If the stalks are long, cut them vertically down through the buds, and peel the stems if necessary. You may also cut the florets from the stems, as is usually done when the florets or buds are used raw in salads.

Cook broccoli three ways. The most nutritious is to steam. Do this by standing the stems in a deep pan and add water, about two inches or so. Bring the water to a boil, cover pan and cook about 10-15 minutes until tender. Open the cover occasionally to allow the steam to escape. This lets the broccoli keep its bright green color.

To boil the broccoli stems, lay them flat in a large skillet, cover with water and cook uncovered about five minutes. Add about ½ teaspoon salt, then continue cooking until stems are tender. Total time will be 10-15 minutes.

If you like sautéed dishes, try broccoli. Simply cut the buds/florets into small pieces and slice the stems. Put a small amount of olive oil in a skillet, add the stems and let them cook a bit then add the florets. You may prefer to boil the broccoli first, then cut and sauté it.

An easy and delicious way to serve the steamed or boiled broccoli is to dress it simply by sprinkling it with lemon juice or with three parts lemon juice and one part melted butter. You can also sprinkle it with Parmesan cheese. Broccoli seems to be a good mix with almost all cheeses.

Another popular way to serve broccoli is with hollandaise sauce. Below are a couple of more recipes you may like.

Broccoli is a pretty dish to serve for family or company. Use it as fresh as you can from your own garden, local farmers' market or your supermarket — but do include the pretty and nutritious vegetable for anytime, or maybe this weekend for ... *Sunday Dinner*.

Blender Hollandaise Sauce

    3 egg yolks
    2 tablespoons lemon juice
    ¼ teaspoon baking powder
    ¼ teaspoon cayenne pepper
    ½ cup hot, melted butter
    Salt to taste

Combine egg yolks, lemon juice, salt and cayenne in blender. Cover and switch blender on and off several times. Remove cover, switch blender to high speed and gradually add melted butter in a steady stream until just blended and thickened. Serve immediately. Makes 1 cup of sauce.

Broccoli and Cheese Custard

    1 bunch broccoli (two or three stems, depending on size)
    3 eggs
    ⅔ cup milk
    1½ cups grated sharp cheddar cheese
    Salt and pepper to taste

Remove leaves and cut away bottom of stalks if tough. Split stems from top to bottom so stalks will cook as quickly as florets. Cook uncovered in about an inch of water for about 10-15 minutes until barely tender. Lift broccoli from water and place in a greased shallow casserole.

Beat eggs, then add to them milk, cheese, salt and pepper; pour mixture over broccoli. Set dish, uncovered, in a pan and add water so that it is about an inch deep. Bake at 350 degrees for 30 minutes or until firm. Serves 4.

Okra Casserole
Bobbie Tucker
(Published September 22, 2005)

Some people (and I am in the group) think okra is good almost any way you cook it. Others don't like it at all. I like it soft fried, crispy fried, in soups, gumbos, and boiled using the small pods, but I had never made an okra casserole until a few weeks ago, when Mrs. Bobbie Tucker of Taylors sent me a recipe to share with you.

Bobbie and her husband, Ronnie, are members of Camp Creek Baptist Church in North Greenville Association. Jake Darnell is their pastor. She attends the Ruth Bible Class Sunday school, the monthly WMU meetings, and is chairman of the bereavement committee of Camp Creek. Ronnie also attends Sunday school, and they both serve on the hospitality committee.

Bobbie is retired from Union Carbide and her husband from Mohawk Mills in Landrum. Bobbie used to do a lot of sewing but not so much now, and, yes, she still has stacks of fabric! Bobbie enjoys doing tatting, which she calls almost a lost art, and crocheting. She used to participate regularly in the Greer Community Ministries and still goes sometimes. She also has a vegetable garden, where she grows the okra for this good dish.

They have three children: Alan Tucker, Juanita C. Smith, and Michael Center, seven grandchildren, and one great-grandchild.

Bobbie found this recipe in a cookbook a few years ago. That recipe had only the hush-puppy mix, so she added the cup of onions, and later the peppers — which contribute both flavor and color to the dish. A few cookings after that, she added the cheese. Someone told her that she had added sage, but Bobbie hasn't tried that. Some cooks like to cover the dish with aluminum foil for the first 45 minutes of baking to help with the browning, but Bobbie doesn't.

The cooked dish freezes well, she says. You can also prepare it ahead, refrigerate it, then bake. If yours is a small family, bake the mixture in two dishes; freeze one and serve the other. Whether from the counter, refrigerator, or freezer, do try this okra casserole for a meal soon, maybe ... *Sunday Dinner.*

Okra Casserole

- 6 cups (about 2 pounds or so) very thinly sliced okra (about ⅛-inch thick)
- 1 cup chopped red pepper (hot or sweet, or some green pepper)
- 1 cup chopped onions
- 1 cup grated cheese (any kind)
- 1 8-ounce package hush puppy mix (1½ cups)
- 1½ teaspoons each of pepper, salt, and Accent (adjust to taste)
- 3 eggs, beaten
- ⅔ cup vegetable oil
- 1½ cups whole milk

Preheat oven to 350 degrees. Spray or grease a 9×13 bake-and-serve dish or two 8×8 dishes. Combine all ingredients. Pour into the prepared dish. Bake for 45 minutes. Sprinkle on additional cheese if desired, and bake an additional 15 minutes. Serve warm.

Cabbage Casserole
Anna Forbes
(Published May 12, 2011)

I must drop a few pounds. If I don't, my family will be unable to find pallbearers for my funeral. But eating this good cabbage casserole featured today won't help.

The recipe is from Anna Forbes of Spartanburg. I'm sure you're going to like this recipe — and you should, because Anna, a chef, knows her cooking.

She and her husband, Danny, are members of Fairview Baptist Church in Spartanburg, where the Rev. Ty Childers has been pastor three and a half years. Part of North Spartan Association, Fairview is a growing church, averaging 150 or so in Sunday school and 250 in Sunday morning worship. His wife, Jan, a nurse, is leader of the Acteens and works with the WMU.

Anna and Danny are from North Carolina and have been members of Fairview about four years. Danny is a residential and commercial builder, and Anna is a chef. She received her training in culinary arts at A-B Tech in Asheville. Currently, she is cafeteria coordinator at Mt. View Church Academy, where their two children attend school: Ashlyn in the first grade and Chase in the fifth. Anna has also worked for several restaurants but likes her current position because she can be near the children.

She also serves as Fairview's church hostess, is chairman of the fellowship committee and does Kids Connections, a teaching session held while adults are in discipleship training or choir practice.

Anna, who grew up on a North Carolina farm, works at instilling in her children the values she learned there. The family grows a vegetable garden together, and they have horses. She laughs that their "at home" meals are simple, basic, healthy food — not the elaborate dishes she learned to make in culinary arts!

This recipe was given to her by her mother-in-law, but Anna tweaked it some, and suggests you can use other soups such as cream of celery or cream of onion to vary the flavor slightly. It is a different way to serve cabbage and can be assembled Sunday morning, then baked when you get home from church — or both make it and bake it, then keep it warm, waiting for you and your family to enjoy for ... *Sunday Dinner.*

Cabbage Casserole

1 small cabbage, chopped or shredded
1 medium onion, chopped
½ stick (4 tablespoons) butter, melted
½ teaspoon salt
¼ cup mayonnaise
1 10¾-ounce can cream of mushroom soup

Topping:
1 sleeve buttery crackers, crushed
1 cup grated cheddar cheese
1 stick (8 tablespoons) butter, melted

Place chopped cabbage in a 9×13-inch baking pan. Place onion on top of cabbage and sprinkle with salt. Melt ½ stick (4 tbsp.) butter and pour over cabbage. Mix soup and mayonnaise together and spread over cabbage.

To make the topping, mix 1 stick (8 tbsp.) melted butter with the crushed crackers and cheese and spread over cabbage mixture. Bake at 350 degrees for 45 minutes.

Cabbage, Collards and Kale

(Published January 5, 2015)

Cabbage and collards and kale. Oh my!

I'm not saying that if you regularly eat these you will be able to leap tall buildings in a single bound, but you will be healthy and smile more.

It's fall, so it's time for the fall vegetables, specifically the fall greens. You can often get these, which find their way from around the country to your supermarket, throughout the year. However, it is in fall and winter that local growers start bringing these to your local farm markets, or perhaps you have a few in your own garden.

And how good they are!

And healthy! There are other greens, but cabbage, collards and kale grown in our areas are the ones most anticipated.

All of these are high in potassium and Vitamins A, C, E and K. They are also low in calories. Cooked without any fat, one cup of kale has 36 calories, 3½ ounces of collards has 45 calories, and a cup of cabbage has 15.

It is generally believed that the darker green a vegetable is, the more nutritious it is. This doesn't speak well for cauliflower.

If you buy them at the grocery, all three of these are good keepers in your refrigerator, although, as with any vegetable, the quicker you can use them once they have left the soil the better.

Collards take longer to cook than the other two, perhaps even 1½-2 hours. Cabbage takes the shortest time, and if you overcook it you'll get a pink color. Don't do that. Generally, the kale and cabbage will both cook in about 15 minutes. All three are cooked in a small amount of water and salt. You can add bacon drippings or salt pork, which improves the flavor — especially the collards, and especially if you live in the South.

To do this, simmer the bacon or the salt pork (a.k.a. fatback) in a small amount of water until tender, add the greens, salt and more water, cover and cook until tender. Using two knives and a crisscross motion, cut the greens while still in the pot for easy serving and eating. Cutting the cabbage into small slices before cooking will eliminate this step.

Before cooking collards and kale, strip off the leaf from the center stem. You can cut this center stem into 1-inch lengths and cook separately, or you can put them on your compost pile for your flowers to enjoy.

It's obvious that if you are ever going to amount to anything, you must eat cabbage and collards and kale, and that however you cook them, these three cold-weather vegetables are good for both taste and tummy. Plan to serve one of these this weekend for ... *Sunday Dinner.*

Scalloped Cabbage

    1 medium head cabbage, coarsely chopped

    1 teaspoon salt

    1 cup Parmesan cheese

    1 cup buttered cracker crumbs

    1 cup medium white sauce*

In a saucepan, combine the chopped cabbage and salt. Cover with boiling water and boil gently 7 minutes over medium heat. Set oven at 350 degrees. Drain cabbage and place half of it into a buttered 9×9 baking dish and pour on ½ cup white sauce. Sprinkle with half the cheese and half the cracker crumbs. Repeat. Bake 20 minutes. Cut into squares. Serves 8.

*White sauce: Melt 2 tablespoons butter, add 2 tablespoons flour and cook until it is blended and bubbles; heat 1 cup milk. Remove butter-flour mixture from heat; add the hot milk and stir quickly until well-mixed and thick. If mixture is not thick enough, return to stove and cook until it thickens.

Sweet-Sour Cabbage

- 4 cups shredded cabbage
- 2 sour apples
- 2 tablespoons vinegar
- 2 tablespoons fat
- 4 tablespoons brown sugar
- 2 tablespoons flour
- Salt and pepper to taste

Core and slice apples, combine with shredded cabbage, salt and pepper. Heat fat in large skillet or saucepan and add the cabbage-apple mixture. Cook over low heat until tender. Sprinkle with the flour, then add the salt and vinegar. Cook a few minutes longer.

Boiled Kale

Option 1: Wash and strip leafy part from stem. Steam or cook in small amount of water. Bring water to a boil, then lower heat and simmer until tender. Add salt, pepper and butter, or, if your Southern palate shows, add a couple of spoonfuls of bacon drippings.

Option 2: Prepare as above, but add strips of bacon (cut into 1-inch pieces) to the cooking water.

Creamed Kale with Onions

- 1½ pounds kale
- 10-12 small white onions, peeled
- ¼ cup shortening
- 3 tablespoons flour

1½ cups milk
Salt and pepper to taste (if desired)

Wash kale and remove large stem. Cook leafy part in salted water until tender (about 15 minutes). In another pan, cook the onions until tender (about 15 minutes). Meanwhile, make a white sauce with the shortening, flour and milk. Drain kale and onions, and combine in a serving dish. Pour the hot white sauce over the mixture. Serves 6.

Collards and Potatoes

2 pounds collards
½ pound salt pork, coarsely chopped
2 quarts water
4 medium potatoes
Salt to taste

Coarsely chop the salt pork; combine with the water and cook on a slow boil about 30 minutes. Remove and discard center stems of collard leaves and tear leaves into small pieces. Add collards to pot with the salt pork and water. Cover and cook about 1½ hours. Peel potatoes and add to pot with the collards. Cover and cook about 30 minutes, or until potatoes are tender.

Panned Collards

Amount of collards needed to fit the pan
3-4 tablespoons bacon drippings
Salt to taste
Water only if needed

Prepare collards as above. Use bacon drippings, or cut and cook 2-3 slices of bacon in large skillet. Remove stems and cut or tear leaves into small pieces, then add the cut collards to pan with the salt. Cover. Cook on high until collards begin to steam, then reduce heat to medium or low and cook until tender. Stir frequently and add a bit of water if necessary.

Collards and Cabbages
Annie Cole
(Published February 4, 2008)

You may think I am obsessed with green vegetables. Last year I wrote about collards, and last issue it was broccoli. Well, I've just recently learned something new about cooking collards that I want to share with you. (Actually I had heard of the practice but didn't think it credible.)

The thing is that Annie Cole's recipe, which was given to her by her sister, uses vegetable oil. I always thought it was in the U.S. Constitution — or certainly in the Constitution of the Confederacy — that collards had to be cooked with fatback, salt pork, or, as a poor substitute, bacon. This new information comes from Mrs. Annie Cole of South Main Street Baptist Church in Greenwood.

Mrs. Cole has been a member there since 1945, and pretty much knows most everything about the church. For 28 years, she worked in the Sunday school with young people from nursery to 6th grade "primaries," as they used to be called. She also was part of the choir and worked in the church office for seven years.

Now that she has seen a lot of calendar pages turn, she isn't quite as active as formerly, but goes regularly to the senior members group. She enjoys being with the group, and she says they always have a good lunch!

She attends Sunday school when she can.

Mrs. Cole and her late husband, Eugene, had one daughter, Pat, who is married to Mike Maffett. They live in Greenwood and have two sons, Kin and Tim — who with his wife, Kathy, have a daughter, Miranda Leigh Maffett. The late Eugene Cole liked fishing and metal detecting, Annie said. One of his best finds with the metal detector was a man's belt buckle at Star Fort. The buckle is now in a museum in Canada, where it was made.

Collards and cabbages are both good for you and are excellent sources of vitamin A, iron, calcium and vitamin C — and a fair source of thiamine, riboflavin and niacin, with collards having slightly more of these.

Annie says there is no "collard cooking" odor in the kitchen when this method is used. This method is similar to the panned collards, where the vegetable is parboiled, drained, and then cooked in a skillet.

Cooked collards keep well in the refrigerator so you can (1) prepare the leaves, place them in a plastic bag in the fridge and cook them on Sunday or (2) cook the collards or cabbage on Saturday and reheat them after church for a nutritious ... *Sunday Dinner*.

Collards and Cabbages

    1 bunch of collard greens, or 1 head of cabbage

    1½ cups water

    2 cups water

    6 tablespoons vegetable oil

    1 teaspoon sugar

    Salt to taste (about 1 teaspoon)

To prepare: Remove each leaf from the main stem. Save the small bunch of white tender leaves on the inside. Working with each leaf, remove the green part from the white stem and cut or tear into bite-sized pieces. Cut the stem into 1- to 1½-inch pieces. One bunch of collards or one head of cabbage will produce about 2½ pounds. The weight doesn't have to be exact.

Wash the collard pieces through two or three sinks of water, lifting them from the water each time. Put in large pot, and add the 1½ cups water. Let water come to a boil and boil 1½ minutes. Drain.

Add the 2 cups water, the sugar, vegetable oil and salt and stir well. Bring to a boil then cook, uncovered, over medium heat for 30 minutes. About 15 minutes before the collards are done, add the small, white tender part that was in the center of the collard. If needed, add a small amount of water during cooking to prevent sticking.

Luncheon Vegetable Dish and Squash Casserole
Syble McInvaille and Ann McGuinness
(Published November 6, 2003)

There probably isn't a cook south of Connecticut who doesn't have or hasn't used a recipe for squash casserole. However, it is possible that there are new, young cooks or more experienced ones who have been asleep for 20 years who do not. Today we are offering two vegetable "casserole" dishes. One is for squash and the other is a vegetable medley. Both are good and will be useful in your meal planning.

Casseroles started gaining great popularity in the early 1950s, and after that, everything that was mixed together and cooked in one dish was called a "casserole." Traditionally, a casserole was a baking dish with a cover, but now many foods are cooked in baking dishes that don't have covers, and we still call them casseroles. That's all right. If your dish needs a cover, use aluminum foil.

Both of today's recipes are from the cookbook published by the Ashley River Baptist Church in Charleston. Originally published in 1980, the book has gone through four printings and sells for $15.

Ashley River was organized in 1943 with 165 charter members. Today, the membership is 2,900. The pastor is David Brady. Both of today's recipes are from members of the church's staff.

The Luncheon Vegetable Dish is from Mrs. Syble McInvaille who works with the church's financial records. In the late 1960s, Syble and her late husband, Charles, lived in Greenville and were members of Edwards Road Baptist Church. They relocated to Charleston because of her husband's business and joined Ashley River.

Syble has one daughter, Kathy Kerr, and she and her husband, Bob, live in Manchester, England, where he works with Michelin. There are four grandchildren, and Syble is trying to wait patiently until they will all be back home in a couple of years.

In addition to her staff work, Syble serves as director of the young marrieds Sunday school, and is on the church's hospitality and flower committees.

The Luncheon Vegetable Dish recipe was give to her by her sister-in-law, Peggy Furr of Lancaster, maybe 25 years ago. Syble uses it often, and says it is an excellent side dish for baked chicken or beef.

Staff member Ann McGuinness handles the church's printing needs, including the bulletin, newsletter, etc. She grew up in Lake City, and when she finished high school and moved to Charleston to attend college, she never returned. She and her husband, Jim, have been members of Ashley River about 25 years, and for 20 years or so she taught in the children's Sunday school. Some time ago she left that department so that she and Jim could go together to a couples class. Jim is director of the Sunday school department and has served as a deacon. Ann and Jim have two daughters

— Patricia McGuinness, who lives in Charleston, and Christy Ann Smith, who lives with her husband in Oklahoma.

Ann got the recipe for squash casserole from her sister, Jessie Gaskins, years ago and uses it every summer during the fresh vegetable season.

Both recipes can be made the day before, refrigerated, then baked when you get home from church, as an important part of your ... *Sunday Dinner.*

Luncheon Vegetable Dish

½ stick butter or margarine
2 tablespoons flour
1 15-ounce can green peas
1 8-ounce can mushrooms
1 small 4-ounce jar chopped pimentos
1 15-ounce can sliced white potatoes
1½ cups sharp cheese, grated

Melt butter, add flour and stir until smooth. Add juices from the cans of peas, pimentos and mushrooms. Stir until thickened. Add 1 cup of the cheese and stir until melted. Add potatoes and vegetables.

Transfer to a casserole dish and sprinkle with the remaining ½ cup of cheese. Bake 30 minutes at 350 degrees. Serves 6 generously. May be prepared the day before and baked at the last minute.

Squash Casserole

2 pounds yellow summer squash
1 teaspoon salt

½ cup chopped onion
1 small bell pepper, chopped
1 teaspoon sugar
½ stick margarine
1 cup grated cheese (medium or sharp)
1 egg, beaten

Boil the squash, onion and salt until tender. Drain and mash. Stir in the pepper, sugar, margarine, cheese and egg. Pour into a greased baking dish. Cover with the topping and bake at 350 degrees for 30 minutes.

Topping:
1 cup bread crumbs
½ cup grated cheese
Margarine

Mix bread crumbs and cheese together. Sprinkle on top of casserole. Dot with margarine.

Glorified Squash
Donna and John Ridgle
(Published July 26, 2007)

So give me a quick guess: In your collection of recipes and cookbooks, how many recipes for squash casserole do you have?

There are six in the Bread of Life cookbook by the First Baptist Church of Hardeeville. I selected this one because of the green pepper and the red pimento, which give added flavor to the dish and make it pretty.

If you have a vegetable garden, your garden basket is probably running over with squash, which is one of the easiest vegetables to grow. If you don't garden, the farmers' markets and your supermarket shelves have big displays of the pretty yellow vegetable.

Squash is the dieter's friend. One cup has only 20 calories. When you add the cheese, eggs, and bread crumbs, that goes up a bit, but you'll think the dish is worth the calories.

Donna Ridgle of Hardeeville contributed the recipe to the church's cookbook. Jay Coder has been the pastor at First Baptist for almost three years, and the church is in Savannah River Association. John and Donna Ridgle joined the church in 1994 after moving to Hardeeville from Savannah, Ga., where they had lived for 31 years.

When I called, Donna wasn't home and I chatted with John.

Donna, a former floral designer, has not been well for a year and has had to curtail her church attendance. John, who owns and operates a garage in Hardeeville, is a deacon and attends Sunday school. The couple has two daughters. Victoria and her husband, Jon Parker, live in Waycross, Ga.; and Kenna and her husband, Roy Robertson, live in Walterboro with their children Kelly, Ashley, Adam, and Jamie.

The Ridgles enjoy camping, and for 13 years had a permanent camp site at Lake Marion but had to release it because of Donna's health.

This Glorified Squash recipe is from his mother, Jane, says John, and she cooked with a pinch of this and a cup of that. Donna's recipe is really good, but probably you could be a little relaxed in the measuring. When I made it, I think I used a bit more onion and pepper but followed the other instructions.

Everyone at our lunch table liked the dish, and seconds were taken.

Let this be your squash casserole. We thank Donna, John, and John's mother, Jane, for sharing it. This is the kind of recipe we like — it can be prepared early in the day, refrigerated, then baked after church just in time for a healthy ... *Sunday Dinner*.

Jane Ridgle's Glorified Squash

    2 cups cooked yellow summer squash
    ¾ cup bread crumbs
    3 tablespoons butter or bacon drippings
    ½ cup milk (or enough to make a "soupy" mixture;
        it thickens while baking)
    2 tablespoons onion, chopped
    2 tablespoons green bell pepper, chopped
    2 tablespoons pimento, chopped
    1 teaspoon Worcestershire sauce
    2 tablespoons tomato ketchup
    Salt and pepper to taste
    ¾ cup grated cheese
    2 eggs, slightly beaten
    Buttered bread crumbs

Mash the squash well, then add remaining ingredients except the buttered crumbs. Pour into a greased baking dish. Top with the buttered crumbs and bake.

Squash Casserole
Nannie Mae Pratt
(Published November 3, 2014)

Hearty menus increase as the thermometer reading decreases, but one meal a day — whatever time of year — needs its vegetables, so try squash.

There must be a dozen or more recipes called "squash casserole," and you will like this one. One of the good things about this vegetable is that local squash are available for a long period in the summer — but the days of autumn and frost put an end to local squash. Because of our farming friends in warmer winter climates, it is usually in the supermarket throughout the year.

The crook neck yellow summer squash is a prolific producer, and there is the running joke of home gardeners during the summer trying to give squash to their neighbors. After a while — whether they are cooked or canned, frozen or pickled — one can use only so many squash.

Squash is also a dieter's friend; a half cup is only 15 calories.

Whether you get the squash from the supermarket, a local grower, your own garden, your freezer, or your enthusiastic gardening neighbor during the summer, you will like this recipe from Nannie Mae Pratt. It makes a large dish for 10-12 servings — good for a family or church gathering.

Nannie Mae and her husband, Bonner, have been members of Overbrook Baptist Church in Greenville for 18 years or so. Organized in 1950, Overbrook is part of the Greenville Baptist Association and has a current active membership of around 225. It has a Sunday school, worship service, WMU and youth groups, including preschool and children. This year's VBS was quite a successful one. Rev. Dale Sutton has served the church as pastor for 12 years.

Nannie Mae retired from a longtime teaching career at Lake Forest Elementary, mostly with second graders. The school was located about a block from her house in Greenville, and for many years (with agreeable weather) she could walk to school. Later, a new school was built not much farther away.

This summer she and her husband celebrated their 59th wedding anniversary by going out for a quiet dinner. Before and since their retirement, the couple has traveled to 30 countries and has been to Europe three times.

As most teachers, Nannie Mae enjoys reading. Over the years, she has enjoyed gardening but doesn't do that so much now, and Bonner has become the family gardener. Nannie Mae and Bonner attend worship service and Sunday school regularly, where Anna Marie Robertson teaches the class Nannie Mae attends.

When you make this recipe, you may want to decrease the amount of stuffing mix, both in the dish and as the topping. You may also want to decrease the baking time to about 20 minutes. At 30 minutes, my dish was too brown on top — but good!

We thank Nannie Mae for sharing the recipe with us, both because it is a new way to use squash and because it will serve a large number. If the dish is too large, the ingredients can be easily decreased by half, and you and your family/guests will still have plenty to enjoy for … *Sunday Dinner*.

Squash Casserole

    4 cups cooked yellow squash

    2 carrots, finely grated

    1 onion, minced

    1 cup sour cream

    1 stick butter or margarine

- 1 cup cheddar cheese, grated
- 2 eggs, beaten
- 1 10¾-ounce can cream of chicken soup
- 1 small package Pepperidge Farm stuffing mix

Heat oven to 350 degrees. Mix cooked squash, carrots, onion, soup, cheese, eggs and sour cream in a large bowl. Put stuffing mix into a large bowl; melt butter or margarine and stir into the stuffing mix. Put half the stuffing-butter mixture into the squash mixture and mix well.

Put squash mixture into a large baking dish. Spread remaining stuffing-butter mixture evenly on top. Bake for 30 minutes. (Check the dish frequently; it may need less than 30 minutes to brown evenly.)

Note: You may not need all the stuffing mix.

Ever Best Eggplant
Louise Stroud
(Published August 12, 2004)

It's one of the oldest churches in the state, and if its latest cookbook is representative, it has produced some good cooks.

The church is Chestnut Ridge Baptist Church, a few miles from Laurens. It was given the name because the first meeting house in 1821 was on a ridge where many chestnut trees were growing.

That first building has been enlarged and renovated, and other buildings also have been built, enlarged or renovated to accommodate the 800-plus members. Tony Crouch has been pastor of Chestnut Ridge, part of Laurens Baptist Association, since 1984.

The cook is Mrs. Louise Stroud, and the recipe that she shares with us today is Ever Best Eggplant. She has been a member of Chestnut Ridge for 35 years.

Louise says she "made up" the recipe she submitted for Chestnut Ridge's "Cooking with the Fellowship of Amazing Love" cookbook. It is similar to other eggplant casseroles, but the sharp cheese used both in the dish and as a topping gives this recipe extra flavor.

Eggplant, available almost year-round and easily grown in home gardens, is a rather bland vegetable and is at its best when something is added to it: onions, tomatoes, cheese, etc. There are recipes for frying, baking and stuffing eggplant, and for combining it with other foods. One of the best-known recipes, and the one requiring perhaps the most time to prepare, is eggplant Parmigiana, in which sautéed slices of eggplant are layered with a tomato-meat sauce, Parmesan and mozzarella cheeses, and then baked.

Recently, our church celebrated its 110th anniversary with the morning worship service in the one-room, wooden-frame building constructed in 1894. Afterwards, we moved to the current church building, where we had a covered dish dinner, and in the afternoon our special guests were the Martha Franks Singers from Laurens. We loved hearing them, and all in all it was a wonderful day. As my part of the lunch, I carried a double recipe of Ever Best Eggplant and told the Singers and others I was considering using the recipe for this space and that I wanted their opinions. Several people said they liked it, so here it is. It is easily made, is great tasting, and would be just the right thing for you to have this weekend for … *Sunday Dinner*.

Ever Best Eggplant

    1 large eggplant (peeled, cooked and drained)
    2 eggs, beaten

¾ **cup saltine crackers, finely crushed**
½ **cup grated cheese (sharp cheddar)**
¾ **cup milk**
2 tablespoons melted butter or margarine
½ **teaspoon each of salt and pepper, or to taste**
½ **cup grated cheese**

Preheat oven to 325 degrees. Grease a baking dish, about 7x9 or so. Mash the cooked and drained eggplant, then stir in the beaten eggs. Add remaining ingredients except the last ½ cup of cheese. Put into prepared dish and bake about 30-35 minutes. Put the remaining ½ cup of grated cheese on top of the eggplant mixture and bake an additional 5 minutes.

Grated Sweet Potato Bake
Gayle Harley
(Published September 30, 2010)

They arrived in our community many years ago, fresh from seminary and excited about the ministry. Pretty Gayle Harley and her husband, the Rev. Jimmie Harley, had graduated and accepted a pastorate at our church. While in seminary, the Rev. Harley was a full-time pastor at a small church in that area, but this was a new era for him and for Gayle.

I came across Gayle's recipe in "The Pastors' Wives Cookbook," which Tom Brown in West Columbia sent me four years ago.

The Harleys' name will be recognized quickly by many South Carolina Baptists. From Welcome Baptist, he went to Wagener First and then to Eastlan in Greenville, followed by a 22-month period with the Annuity Board at the South Carolina Baptist headquarters. From there he began a

22-year-long pastorate at Florence First.

Then he retired 10 years ago. Well, maybe. Sort of. He served three interims, and is now associate pastor of Taylors First Baptist Church.

All this time, Gayle was active in the churches and reared four children who were born in three different churches. Little Harleys just popped up everywhere.

Their oldest child, Michael, his wife, Elizabeth, and their two children, Will and James, live in Barrington, Ill. Debra and her husband, Tom Carico, and their children, Bill, Sam and David, live in Statesboro, Ga. David has two children, Andrew and Carolina, and lives in Lake Bluff, Ill. Rachel and her husband, Preston Rish, live in Arlington, Ga. She has a stepson, Hayden, and she and Preston will have another little bundle at the end of the year. His name will be Noah.

Gayle grew up in the area where she now lives. Jimmie was from Denmark. It was of great importance to Gayle when they moved back "home," because for several years she could be near her mother who died at age 102. Now Gayle is able to be near and visit regularly her mother's younger sister, age 104, who is in a nursing facility nearby.

When she and Jimmie were at our church, she taught piano lessons, and over the years has been a part of many church choirs and played the piano for services when needed. She also taught kindergarten in several churches. Now she assists her husband in many ways, one being to help with the trips.

Once or twice a year, they lead groups on excursions, and the next one is soon. They will go to Vancouver, then visit the California coast.

Gayle has had this recipe for a long time, has made it many times, and has shared it frequently. She got it during a ministers' wives meeting from Mrs. Jeslyn Wilson, who was the wife of the associate pastor at Eastlan in Greenville.

You may already have a similar recipe that you like, but try this one. It will probably be the one you choose to use from now onward for ... *Sunday Dinner.*

Grated Sweet Potato Bake

    1 cup sugar
    2 teaspoons vanilla
    1 stick (¼ cup) butter, melted
    3 to 3½ cups peeled and grated raw sweet potatoes
    2 eggs, beaten
    ¼ teaspoon salt
    1½ cups milk

Preheat oven to 350 degrees. Mix together the sugar, eggs, vanilla and salt. Combine the grated sweet potatoes and milk, and blend well. Add melted butter to a 9×12 baking dish or put butter in dish and melt in oven. Pour the sugar-egg mixture into pan, then spoon in the sweet potato and milk mixture. Stir to mix.

    Bake 1 to 1½ hours, until potatoes are firm around edges of dish. Serves 10-12.

Sweet Potato Crunch

Jo Ann Comer
(Published October 25, 2012)

"This is really good," said Jay, one of our grandsons, who has a business next door and, to our delight, joins us for lunch most days. He was talking about the sweet potato crunch we were having for lunch as our bow to one of the first cool days of fall.

The recipe is from a cookbook published in 2003 by Overbrook Baptist Church in Greenville. It comes from Jo Ann Comer, who was Overbrook's church secretary for a long time — beginning her tenure when Rev. Cooper Patrick was pastor and ending with Rev. Dale Sutton, the current pastor. Rev. Sutton has served the congregation of 225 or so for about 10 years. Overbrook has the full range of Baptist programs: WMU, Sunday school, etc. The church, a newcomer when judged by some of South Carolina's Baptist churches, was organized in 1950 and is on the northeast side of Greenville.

Although she was associated with Overbrook for 34 years in the church office before her retirement in 2005, Jo Ann was never a member there, as is true of office personnel of many churches. She and her husband, Ralph, who retired from MetLife, are members of Calvary Baptist Church in Simpsonville.

Jo Ann and Ralph have no children, and they travel a lot. On the day I talked with her, they had returned only the previous day from a trip. They frequently go to Virginia, where Ralph owns property.

Jo Ann got this recipe from a cousin, and over the years she made it often. Now she doesn't cook as much as previously. We are glad she got the recipe and shared it with us. It almost screams "Thanksgiving!" It can be served room temperature or made the day before serving and refrigerated. It serves a large number, at least 12.

I used only a half cup sugar in the middle layer and that seemed to be enough. Once you make this, it will be in your "keeping pile," whatever the season, to make and serve to a large group for ... *Sunday Dinner*.

Sweet Potato Crunch

First layer:

1 stick butter, softened

1 cup self-rising flour

1 cup finely chopped nuts

Second layer:

8 ounces cream cheese, softened

1 cup sugar (or ½ cup)

8 ounces whipped topping (Cool Whip)

Third layer:

3 cups cooked sweet potatoes, mashed

1 cup sugar

1 stick butter

1 egg

First layer: Heat oven to 300 degrees. Mix ingredients well and press firmly into a 7×11-inch oven-proof serving dish. Bake until lightly browned and let cool.

Second layer: Beat together the three ingredients and spread evenly on the cooled first layer.

Third layer: Combine ingredients in a saucepan and beat with a mixer until well blended. Cook on medium heat until mixture begins to bubble and thickens. Let cool, then spread onto the second layer.

Dish may be served warm immediately or at room temperature. Serves 10-12.

Main Dishes

Julie's Roast Beef
Julie Tuttle
(Published April 8, 2014)

It can be a balmy spring Sunday, or one where the wind is banging on your house and whipping shrubbery to and fro. If it is the latter, you'll be glad to be indoors. You'll be even more glad if you have Julie's Roast Beef ready to come from the oven. You'll have the people at New Salem Baptist Church near Sumter to thank for it, and you will need a pencil and paper to chart how I got the recipe.

New Salem Church is a new version of the original church, which was organized in 1913 as Salem Avenue Baptist Church. In 1978, the church (at the time, located in Sumter) closed, moved to a new building outside of town, and changed its name to New Salem. The current membership, which includes both resident and non-resident members, is 284. The pastor, Rev. Kevin Massey, new to the congregation, began his duties in December.

New Salem has most of the Southern Baptist programs, but has a Bible study instead of a worship service on Sunday evenings.

Julie Tuttle, whose recipe is here, is a Baptist, but not the South Carolina version. She and her husband, Rev. Terry Tuttle, live in Georgetown, Ky., and he was conducting a revival at New Salem in Sumter when the committee there was working on a cookbook. Her brother-in-law, Johnny Tuttle, and his wife, Sharon, were members of New Salem.

I don't usually state whether the recipes for *Sunday Dinner* are taken from cookbooks or submitted, but this one was straight from the cookbook. While Julie and her husband were there for the revival, the cookbook committee asked her to give them a recipe, and she did. Julie has had the recipe for years, and, like many cooks, doesn't recall where she got it.

Some time after that, the other Tuttles — Johnny and Sharon — moved their membership from New Salem to Dalzell Baptist Church in Sumter, where they are active members.

Julie's Roast Beef is a substantial recipe — rich, filling and satisfying. It is not much different, perhaps, than one you have used, but the dry soup mix and the mushroom soup may give a new and different flavor for you. Try serving it with a green salad that has lots of crisp, fresh vegetables in it and hot rolls.

The day before I did my testing of this recipe, I made a quiche for lunch. This is a fact: Quiche will never replace roast beef!

After getting the two groups of Tuttles, two ministers, and three churches in the right order, I can say this is a good recipe for a roast that can serve a few or many. Put it in the oven early in the morning before church, and you'll have a great meal waiting for ... *Sunday Dinner*.

Julie's Roast Beef

    3- to 5-pound chuck roast
    Potatoes (as needed)
    Carrots (as needed)
    2 10½-ounce cans golden mushroom soup
    1 envelope dry onion soup mix
    1 large onion
    ½ can water

Peel potatoes and cut into halves or thirds. Scrape carrots and cut into thirds crosswise, or purchase the ready-to-use baby carrots. Set oven to 325 degrees. Put roast in center of roasting pan.

Arrange potatoes and carrots around sides. Spread the 2 cans of soup over the meat and vegetables. Evenly sprinkle the dry soup over that. Peel and slice the onion, and lay the slices on top of the roast. Add the half can of water to the sides. Cover and cook for 4 hours or until tender.

Basic Chicken Pie
Polly Atkin
(Published November 6, 2009)

They're called comfort foods, these simple viands prepared in home kitchens for those days when life gets a little heavy. They are satisfying, simple, easily prepared, and taste good. The list varies with individuals, but macaroni and cheese, apple pie, vegetable soup, and certainly chicken pie would be on it.

We have one for you. It is the simplest recipe for chicken pie involving chicken, broth and crust. We can thank Mrs. Polly Atkin for sharing the simple recipe with us. She is a member of Mt. Bethel Baptist Church in the Saluda Baptist Association, where Ronald Culbertson is pastor. Polly has gone to Mt. Bethel all her life and joined when she was 10 years old.

As have so many members, Polly has been involved in several areas of church life. At one time, she was in the choir and served on the church's social committee. Polly currently works with the food committee, serving the bereaved.

Polly and her husband, Joe, had two children. Their late son Joey and his wife had three children — Joie Lynn, Joseph and Justin. Polly and Joe's daughter Jan is married to Rayford Howell.

This recipe is from Polly's aunt, Lena Fisher, her mother's sister. Because the pie serves so many, Polly doesn't make it often with only her and Joe at home. But because the grandchildren often visit, there are many occasions to make chicken pie. Another thing she makes when the grandchildren are there is chicken salad — using chopped chicken, apples, celery, nuts, mayonnaise and salt. Everybody likes that.

There are as many ways to make chicken pie as there are to make potato salad or fruitcake, but this recipe is basic. Some cooks use canned cream of chicken or mushroom soup, adding peas, carrots, sliced hard-cooked eggs, wide noodles, sour cream, potatoes, etc. They are all good.

I am going to offer these distinctions, and if they are not correct you can tell me. Chicken pot pie is cooked in a deep container with a crust only on top and baked in the oven. Chicken casserole is baked in a more shallow dish, about 2 inches deep, with a crust or topped with bread crumbs, crushed cereal, stuffing mix, etc. Chicken pie has pastry on the bottom, sides and top of the dish, and is often layered with the chicken, as in Polly's recipe.

It takes awhile to make a chicken pie, so use Polly's recipe. Cook the chicken and make the crust on Saturday, then assemble and bake it the next day as a comfort food for … *Sunday Dinner.*

Lena Fisher's Chicken Pie
- **1 small hen or large fryer**
- **3 cups all-purpose flour**
- **½ stick (4 tablespoons) butter**
- **2 teaspoons salt**
- **1 cup vegetable shortening**
- **Pepper to taste**

Cook chicken in water with a small amount of salt until tender. Take chicken off bones and leave in broth. Mix flour, salt, shortening and enough ice water to make a stiff dough. Cover and refrigerate overnight.

Preheat oven to 350 degrees. Roll dough thinly. Cut into strips and line sides and bottom of baking dish with the strips of dough. Put in half the chicken and broth. Cover with another layer of the pastry strips. Pour on the remaining half of the chicken and broth. Dot with the butter and sprinkle with pepper. Top with remaining pastry strips. The broth should be level with the pastry strips so that the pie won't be dry.

Bake until pastry strips are a golden brown. Serves 10 or more.

Baked Chicken that Makes Its Own Gravy
Sylvia Freeman
(Published November 11, 2010)

As soon as I saw this recipe, I knew I would like it.

It is in the recently published cookbook, "Kitchen Windows," by Varnville First Baptist Church. There must be many good cooks in Varnville, and this recipe was only one of many that I am preparing and may share with you.

It was contributed by Mrs. Sylvia M. Freeman. She and her husband, Wade, have been members of Varnville First Baptist in Allendale-Hampton Baptist Association for six years. Before that, they were at First Baptist in Hampton for 24 years and at Sandy River Baptist for 40 years.

Sylvia speaks enthusiastically about the church's minister, Dr. Tommy Kelly, who has been at Varnville First Baptist for 16 years. She calls him the "community pastor" because everyone knows him and he is always available. The church was organized in 1877, and, with 350-400 members, has gone to two Sunday morning services. At 9 a.m. there is a contemporary service, followed by Sunday school at 10 and a traditional worship service at 11.

The Freemans were both reared in Hampton County. Sylvia's mother, at age 92, lives nearby in her own house. Although her mother has a caregiver because of poor health, Sylvia is involved in her care. Sylvia and Wade have a daughter, Kaye Eubanks, who lives in Atlanta. One grandson, Scott, has just graduated from the University of Georgia, and their granddaughter, Rachael, is a sophomore at West Georgia University. A tragic accident many years ago, in which all the Freeman family were seriously injured, took the life of their 12-year-old son.

Sylvia and Wade have an insurance business, the Freeman Agency, and Sylvia works there with her husband.

She is also active at Varnville First Baptist. She serves as co-chairman of the church's Christmas bazaar, which will offer crafts and goodies, and the cookbook publication coincides with that. The profits go to the Lottie Moon foreign missions offering. Sylvia has most recently served as WMU director and is currently on the bereavement committee. She taught preschool Sunday school, served as a substitute teacher for the adult ladies class, and is on the committee for the Joy Club, the organization for senior adults.

Wade is a deacon at Varnville First Baptist, a Sunday school teacher, and director of the men's ministries, in addition to other church activities. A busy family!

Sylvia says she has made this recipe (a creation of the Carnation evaporated milk people, and copied from a can label) many times, and that every time she makes the dish she receives compliments.

This is a good dish that will please both the "white meat" and "dark meat" eaters, and if your guest list is small at Thanksgiving, you can use this dish instead of turkey; make some dressing, etc., and you're set to go. We thank Sylvia for sharing it with us.

You can't bake this while you are at church because of the cooking times, but you may do so in the morning, keep it warm, and it will be waiting for you for … *Sunday Dinner.*

Baked Chicken that Makes Its Own Gravy
    3 to 3½ pounds chicken pieces
    ½ cup flour
    1 10¾-ounce can mushroom soup
    1 cup grated American cheese
    1 4½-ounce jar sliced mushrooms
    Salt and pepper to taste
    5-6 tablespoons butter or margarine
    ⅔ cup evaporated milk
    1 small jar onions, drained
    Paprika

In an ovenproof dish, melt butter or margarine. Salt, pepper and flour the chicken and lay in dish skin side down in the melted butter. Bake at 425 degrees for 30 minutes. Turn chicken over and bake until brown, 15-20 minutes.

Remove dish from oven and reduce oven heat to 325 degrees. Remove part of the butter or margarine, leaving the chicken in the pan. Meanwhile, heat the soup, cheese and evaporated milk, stirring until smooth. Cover chicken with onions, mushrooms and soup mixture. Sprinkle with paprika and cover with aluminum foil. Return to oven for 15-20 minutes. Serves 6-8.

Sunday Glazed Ham
Angie Garrison
(Published April 24, 2003)

My apologies, little buddies. I meant for this to appear before Easter Sunday, but I got the dates mixed up. Anyway, this ham is good anytime.

As does Christmas, Easter has two celebrations. There is the one all Christians observe that celebrates the resurrection of our Lord, and we celebrate this with prayer, fasting, sunrise services, choir specials, often the Lord's Supper, lilies placed in the church and cemetery, etc. — and most of all, with great gratitude and praise.

There is another Easter celebration — the secular one — when we celebrate the arrival of spring and all its newness. We have egg hunts, decorate with colorful bunnies, buy new lightweight, light-colored clothing, and perhaps even an Easter hat. Some people celebrate both; others celebrate one but not the other; and some celebrate neither.

And there are family gatherings. For family gatherings, there must be food.

Today's recipe is for Sunday Glazed Ham and is submitted by my dear daughter-in-law, Angie Garrison. Angie, a former member of another Protestant denomination, joined Welcome Baptist Church near Anderson after she and our son Tom married. Tom grew up in Welcome. Angie and Tom are members of the YAMS (Young Adults Married and Single) Sunday school class; Tom has served on the board of deacons and is in the choir.

Angie has served as Mission Friends leader and is on the church directory committee. She is always available for any activity with the youth and children, and also takes her turn providing food for the church's weekly Sunny Side Up breakfast each Sunday morning. Tom and Angie have two daughters, 8th-grader Abbie and 4th-grader Lillie. Their pastor is Mark Wise.

Angie has been baking this ham for 10 or 12 years since the recipe was given to her by Sandra Rankin, her dear friend since junior high school who, Angie says, is a fabulous cook.

"This ham is always a hit at our home for family gatherings such as Easter and Mother's Day," she says. Because this is such a large ham, there are always leftovers for other meals or sandwiches. Try the open-face Hawaiian ham sandwich.

Angie cooks the ham overnight, adds the glaze the next morning, then lets it rest while everyone is at church — and the ham, beautiful and delicious, is ready for … *Sunday Dinner*.

Sunday Glazed Ham
1 16-20 pound fully cooked smoked ham with bone
1 14-to-16-ounce jar honey
1 16-ounce can of pineapple rings
1 tablespoon (approx.) soy sauce
1 tablespoon (approx.) white vinegar
2 1-pound boxes light brown sugar
Whole cloves
1 tablespoon prepared mustard

Preheat oven to 325 degrees. Place ham on rack in roaster. Pour in about 2 inches of water. Cover ham and bake for 8 hours. (To make the glaze, drain pineapple and save juice. In a saucepan, combine pineapple juice and 1 box of the brown sugar. Add a heaping tablespoon of mustard, then the soy sauce and vinegar to taste. Add the jar of honey and cook over low heat until the sugar melts.)

Remove roaster from oven and pour off the juices. Place pineapple slices over the ham and secure them in place with the cloves. (You may have to use a few toothpicks as well.) Pour the glaze over the ham. Crumble the remaining box of brown sugar over the glaze.

Increase the oven temperature to 450 degrees and bake the ham, uncovered, about 45 minutes until brown and crispy. Remove from oven and let rest 1-2 hours. Slice and serve.

Boiled Ham

(*Published November 27, 2006*)

Ham. Pictures of ham and instructions for cooking are in almost every home-centered magazine you find this time of year.

Ham is good. It can be used many ways in your culinary plans, including baking, braising, broiling, and barbecuing. You can find fully cooked ham, slices for sandwiches, center cuts for broiling, etc., but the best ham is a boiled fresh ham.

Almost all hams in the meat counter are cured. Sometimes the word "cured" is used and sometimes the label will read "smoked," but both mean the ham has gone through a process that will lengthen both its shelf life and flavor.

In the "old days" before supermarkets, the grocery store or meat market owners would buy the fresh hams, sometimes called "green" hams, from the abattoir. Our state was more agrarian then, and most farm families would slaughter their own animals and the meat was used immediately or cured, the only way to keep the meat over a period of time in the age before refrigeration and freezers.

Both the meat processing companies and home owners would smoke the sausage, bacon, and hams. Often the hams were rubbed with a mixture of sugar and spices, salt, etc., wrapped in a cloth and hung in a curing room or smokehouse to age. The salt, spices, etc., penetrated the meat, thereby preserving it.

So today, we have similar products at every supermarket meat counter. Once in your kitchen, these cured hams, often with the labels "Smithfield" or "Virginia," are most often baked and sometimes boiled. There are many glazes used: brown sugar and mustard, pineapple and honey, orange juice and brown sugar, etc. They are good, but the best ham is still the boiled fresh ham. It is also the simplest way to cook a ham.

I am already making my arrangements for my ham.

This week, I talked with the meat counter man, asking if he would have the fresh, green, uncooked hams and saying that I will want one about 12 pounds. He then told me that he would have such a ham, or order/save one for me, but that I would want to buy a half ham because the whole hams would be about 20-24 pounds.

Hmmm. That's a lot of ham.

So I will get my 12-pound half-ham and boil it. A boiled fresh ham has a different flavor than the cured one. You can serve it sliced immediately, but the far better way is to cook it, then let it cool in the cooking water, remove and wipe it dry, wrap it in waxed paper and a dish towel, and refrigerate it until cold. Then you slice it for the best sandwiches you ever ate. Combine equal amounts of mayonnaise and mustard, and use this mixture for the bread when making sandwiches.

If you've never boiled a fresh ham, do so this month, but remember that a 12-pound ham won't last long, especially during the busy Christmas season when you serve boiled ham sandwiches for … *Sunday Dinner*.

Boiled Ham
    1 fresh whole ham or 10- to 12-pound half ham
    2 teaspoons of salt, or to taste (optional)
    Water to cover

You'll need a large pot, because the ham should be covered with water at all times. Place the ham on a rack in the pot, cover with water, cover pot and place on high heat. Bring water to a full boil. Let boil rapidly about 10 minutes, then reduce heat to a simmer and cook about 25 minutes a pound for a 12-pound ham, or about 4 or 5 hours until the internal temperature is about 160 degrees F.

Remove pot from heat and leave the ham to cool in the cooking water. Lift ham from cooking water, wipe dry, wrap, and refrigerate. Serve sliced for a meal or for sandwiches.

Pork Chop Casserole
Nookie Harling
(Published April 25, 2013)

"Aren't you going to pick up that paper?" a visiting child asked as I stepped over a newspaper that had slipped off the table onto the floor.

"No," I answered. "I'm waiting until I drop something else. Then I can make one bend-over do two pickups." She rolled her eyes, picked up the paper and went home.

Besides, I was thinking not about a paper on the floor, but about our lady today. She's ill now and has been in a nursing facility for more than a year, with only minimum response to communication — but when she was still up and about, she made a really good pork chop casserole.

Nookie Harling has been a member of First Baptist Church in Edgefield for 66 years. The church, founded in 1823, is a member of Edgefield Baptist Association and has WMU and all the youth mission programs. Rev. Stacy Williams has served as pastor since 2005.

Nookie's late husband, Jimmie, will be remembered as clerk of court for Edgefield County, a position he held for many years. Nookie and her husband had two children. Their daughter, Teresa Harling Harvey, lives in Edgefield. Their son, Jimmy Harling, and his wife, Connie, who is administrative assistant at Edgefield First Baptist, have a son and a daughter. Their son, Johnson, and his wife, Mandy, have two children, Jackson and Molly; their daughter, Fran, and her husband, Brandon Clary, have two children, Huiet Ann and Ella Grace Clary — all members of Edgefield First.

Nookie, who lives at Trinity Mission Health Care in Edgefield, served for many years as the church Sunday school secretary. She was also an active member of the WMU. Known for being a great cook, according to her daughter-in-law Connie, Nookie had three special dishes, and the family always hoped that at least one would be on the menu when they visited: chicken salad, chicken and dressing, and ambrosia.

There are a couple of phrases that Nookie's family associates with her. The first is one that she would tell her children and grandchildren often: "Waste not, want not." This is still good advice, as is the second: "Let the past be a springboard, not a sofa."

Her recipe is good also. You can add another chop or so if you wish. We wish for Mrs. Harling good days ahead and are happy to have her recipe to serve to family or guests for ... *Sunday Dinner.*

Pork Chop Casserole

    4 pork chops
    2 tablespoons uncooked rice for each pork chop
    ¾ cup water
    Bell pepper
    1 can beef or bouillon soup
    Salt and pepper to taste
    1 tablespoon bacon grease
    Tomatoes
    Onions

Grease casserole dish, add rice and set aside. Preheat oven to 350 degrees. Salt and pepper pork chops, and brown on both sides in the bacon drippings. Place pork chops on top of the uncooked rice. Add the water to the drippings left in pan, stir and pour over pork chops.

Place sliced tomatoes on pork chops. Seed and slice the bell pepper and place on the tomatoes. Peel and slice the onions and place on top of the peppers. Add more salt and pepper if desired. Pour the bouillon over this, cover tightly and bake 1 hour or longer, until rice is done. Serves 4.

Baked Savory Pork Chops
The late Linda Culberson
(Published September 2, 2010)

You could have called it a mill church, this once large, now small, church in Upstate South Carolina.

That is no longer a good description, because it has been almost three decades since the members were primarily workers in Riverside Mill. The mill, constructed in the early 1900s, produced "greige" material, a cotton fabric of many uses, and employed 400-600 people. It ceased textile operations in the mid-1980s. For a time after Riverside's closing and sale, it housed a silk-screening concern, retail services, and a warehouse. Some years ago it burned.

This 109-year-old Riverside Baptist Church in Anderson is served by a bivocational minister, Wayne Adams. Although small in number, averaging around 40 for Sunday services, the church has a full range of Southern Baptist programs: two services on Sunday, Sunday school, a Wednesday night prayer meeting, WMU, and a children's ministry. It is in Saluda Association.

The church was organized in 1901. The members met in Riverside Hall, a building used for a church on Sundays and as a school during the week. The first Riverside Baptist Church building was built in 1909 on a lot donated by Riverside Mill Company, which also contributed one-third of the construction cost. In January 1939, the church building was destroyed by fire, rebuilt and completed in August 1939. In January 1975, a fellowship hall and gymnasium were built.

The recipe for Baked Savory Pork Chops was printed in one of the first cookbooks published by the church and was submitted by Mrs. Linda Culberson. Mrs. Culberson died in December 2002. She was active in the church for 20 years or more as a member of the Sunshine Mothers Sunday School Class and a frequent helper with VBS, among other things.

Linda's children are Lee Brock and Aaron Culberson. She has four grandchildren: Rebecca Culberson, Cameron Brock, Autumn Culberson and Emma Culberson. Her husband, Vernon, now lives in Asheville.

This is a good recipe for several reasons. It has only five ingredients. It is relatively low fat (if you trim all the fat from the chops) because the sauce is fat-free. The taste is good. It is easy to prepare by putting it unattended in the oven for an hour, unlike food you may be steaming, sautéing, etc. You can select chops with or without the bone.

You will notice the recipe doesn't ask for salt. The ketchup provides all you need, but you may add more if you wish. I did not. Other seasonings that go well with pork are paprika, sage, rosemary, savory, etc.

The printing of this recipe is in honor of Mrs. Culberson and all those who worshiped and worked with her at Riverside Baptist for many years. Try this easy recipe this weekend. If you get up early, you can bake it before you go to Sunday school and it will be there for you to enjoy for … *Sunday Dinner*.

Baked Savory Pork Chops
- 1 cup ketchup
- 6 teaspoons brown sugar
- 6 lemon slices
- 1 cup water
- 6 lean pork chops, ½-inch thick

Preheat oven to 350 degrees. In a medium-sized bowl, combine ketchup, water and brown sugar. Blend well. Arrange the pork chops in a single layer in a baking dish. Place a lemon slice on top of each chop. Pour the tomato-water-brown sugar sauce over all the chops. Bake in prepared oven for 1 hour. Yields 6 servings.

Cranberry Pork Chops
Jimmie McCullough Keller
(Published May 26, 2006)

Jimmie makes this dish often because she can make it ahead and then reheat it. Also, she says, she has cooked this many times over the years and everybody likes it.

We are talking about Jimmie McCullough Keller, a member of First Baptist Church of North Augusta, and her recipe for cranberry pork chops.

Jimmie and her husband, Fred, have been members of North Augusta First Baptist, where Gary Redding is pastor, since Fred retired from North American missions. The church is a member of Aiken Association.

Both Jimmie and Fred are from Birmingham, and his first South Carolina church was at Heights Baptist, a small congregation on Beech Island. From there, he went on to what a lot of us long-timers call "home missions." He served in South Dakota and in California before retiring several years ago due to declining health.

Jimmie teaches a Sunday school class, a job she has held in churches ever since Fred had his first pastorate. Fred served as a student preacher every two weeks at a small rural church in Alabama while he was in school. Jimmie was asked to teach the ladies class. She was quite apprehensive, and even more so when she discovered the first lesson was on adultery! She must have survived all right, though, because she has been teaching Sunday school ever since.

The Kellers have two daughters. Julie and her husband, Tim Cox, and their children Mark and Rachel, live in Greenwood, Ind. Mark, who will be married soon, is a youth minister. The Kellers' daughter Marsha is married to Bobby Huguley, who is the minister of music at Ocean View Baptist in Myrtle Beach. They have two children, Andrea and Paul.

Jimmie found the cranberry pork chops recipe many years ago in a little booklet published by (you guessed it) the Ocean Spray cranberry people. The recipe requires eight chops to make eight servings, but when I made it I discovered one could easily add a couple of more chops for 10 servings and still have adequate sauce. You may use bone-in or boneless chops — whatever is on sale, Jimmie says.

With the chops, she has served various things over the years, but mostly green beans and red potatoes.

This is the way she does the potatoes: In a bake-and-serve dish, melt butter (maybe a couple of tablespoons) and sprinkle over this garlic salt to your taste. Cut medium-sized red potatoes into halves and lay these on top of the salt. Cover with foil and bake at 350 degrees for 30-45 minutes or until tender.

When she is serving the chops to dinner guests, she likes to make the dish early, refrigerate it, then reheat it for 15 minutes or so until warm. We thank Jimmie for sharing her recipe with us, and I know you'll enjoy it for ... *Sunday Dinner*.

Cranberry Pork Chops

8 bone-in pork chops (½- to ¾-inch thick)

Salt and pepper to taste

2 tablespoons vegetable oil

1 16-ounce can whole berry cranberry sauce

½ cup barbecue sauce

2 tablespoons cornstarch

¼ cup cold water

Season pork chops on each side with salt and pepper. In the oil in a large skillet, brown chops on both sides. Drain oil. Return all the chops to the skillet and pour the cranberry sauce and barbecue sauce over them. Cover and simmer 35-40 minutes until the juices run clear.

Remove the chops and keep warm, leaving the cranberry-barbecue sauce in pan. Combine cornstarch and cold water until smooth, then add to the skillet. Bring to a boil, cooking and stirring for 2 minutes until sauce thickens. Spoon over the chops. Serves 8.

Cheeseburger Pie
Tammy Black
(Published April 4, 2007)

A couple of weeks ago, I had my annual cold, which involved losing my voice for three or four days. No one seemed to care. For about a week, my chest ached, I sneezed and coughed and spit, and then it was over. I stepped on the scales and saw that I had lost about five pounds. It was the best cold I ever had.

A few days later, I made today's recipe, which is one of many variations of this dish. I think you will like it. It comes from "Heavenly Delights," the collection of recipes from Pleasant Grove Baptist Church in Greer, where Danny Emory is pastor. Pleasant Grove is a member of the Greer Association.

This recipe was submitted by Tammy Black. When the request went out for recipes, Tammy says she looked through hers and selected a few. She doesn't remember where she got this one but has had it a long time and uses it often.

Tammy and her husband, Dewayne, formerly with General Electric in

Greenville, have one child, Ashley. She and her husband, Justin Ingram, and their daughter Dawn live in Simpsonville. Tammy has been an insurance agent with Lanford and Gibson Insurance in Greer about one and a half years. In her free time, Tammy reads and enjoys their granddaughter, and she and Dewayne walk their dogs.

The Blacks were members of Pleasant Grove for about eight years, but now attend His Vineyard Church, where Keith Kelly is pastor. Tammy and Dewayne are part of one of the "growth groups" that meet weekly in homes for Bible study and fellowship.

This is a good family recipe, easily put together. It has only six ingredients. Tammy says that you can use grated cheddar cheese and adjust the seasonings if you wish. I think it's one you'll want to use for your family. You can assemble it in the morning, cover it with plastic wrap, put it in the fridge, then bake it when you get home from work during the week or after church for … *Sunday Dinner*.

Cheeseburger Pie
- **1 pound ground beef**
- **¼ cup onion**
- **1 6-ounce can tomato paste**
- **½ teaspoon (or more) Italian seasoning**
- **1 8-count package crescent rolls**
- **6 slices American cheese**

Preheat oven to 350 degrees. Brown and drain the ground beef. In a bowl, mix the cooked beef, onion, tomato paste, and Italian seasoning.

Separate the rolls and press the pieces into an 8-inch round pan. Pour the meat mixture in the pan and spread evenly over the rolls. Top with the sliced cheese. Bake for 25 minutes, or until the crust is brown and the cheese is melted. Serves 6.

Meatloaf and Veggies
Tom Brown
(*Published February 22, 2006*)

You will need to call in the neighbors when you cook today's dish.

The recipe is from a man who likes to cook and collects cookbooks.

Tom Brown is a member of First Baptist Church, West Columbia, where Lonnie Shull is pastor. Tom was formerly a member of Lake Wateree Baptist Church.

Cooking is not Tom's only interest. He hunts and fishes and has four dogs and two cats who share his home. Tom, a former president of a hunting club, enjoys going to gun shows and has recently started a gun collection.

Retired as yard conductor for the Seaboard Railroad in Columbia, where he worked for 35 years, Tom has two daughters. Deborah and her husband, Michael Drake, live in the Sandy Run community and have three children: David, Josh and Sheri. His other daughter, Lisa Brown Thomas, has two children, Kyle and Kaleb.

There is another spinoff from Tom's interest in cooking. He is a certified judge with the South Carolina Barbecue Association and travels the state judging barbecue competitions.

Tom, a former Marine, has collected cookbooks for 40 years or more and has "three hundred or so." He likes reading cookbooks, as do many of us, and says he can "mentally taste while he reads" to know if the ingredients will combine to make a good dish.

Although there is a meatloaf recipe in almost every cookbook ever published, Tom says he got this one from a friend and made two or three changes in it to his taste. He also worked out the vegetable additions and says they can be cooked in a separate container on the oven's bottom shelf.

When I tried this recipe, I put them in the same dish and it was full. The recipe says that it serves 8-10, but it will serve more than that. After the dish rests and before you serve it, use a knife and make cuts about halfway through the meatloaf to indicate the serving slices.

You can bake this in the morning before church, keep it warm in the oven or reheat it for a healthy, satisfying, and bountiful dish for … *Sunday Dinner.*

Meatloaf and Veggies

Step 1: Meatloaf

2½ pounds ground beef

1 cup quick or old-fashioned oatmeal, uncooked

1 cup finely chopped onions

¾ cup chili sauce

2 eggs

2 tablespoons Worcestershire sauce

3 or 4 cloves garlic, minced (or to taste)

1½-2 teaspoons dried thyme

1 teaspoon pepper

¾ teaspoon salt (or to taste)

Step 2: Vegetables

2 pounds medium potatoes, thickly sliced or quartered

2 pounds carrots, cut in 1-inch lengths

1 large onion, sliced or quartered

2 tablespoons extra virgin olive oil
3 cloves garlic, finely chopped
1 teaspoon dried thyme

Heat oven to 350 degrees. Combine the first 10 ingredients in large bowl and mix well. Shape into a loaf and place lengthwise in the center of a 10x12x3-inch bake-and-serve dish. Put prepared vegetables in a large bowl. Combine the olive oil, garlic and thyme and pour over the vegetables, mixing to coat them well. Place vegetables around the meatloaf in the baking dish and pour over them any of the olive oil mix left in the bowl.

Bake on middle rack of the oven 55-60 minutes, or until juices of the meat are no longer pink and the vegetables are tender. Remove dish from oven and let the food rest about 10 minutes before serving. Serves 8-10.

Neapolitan Casserole
The late Gail Gunter
(Published October 28, 2010)

The conversation was with Debbie Yon, secretary at Bel-Ridge Baptist Church in Belvedere. The Rev. Earl Welch is the pastor of this Aiken Association church. We thank Debbie for her help.

We all know that some things survive us: children, furniture, our mothers' pearls, etc. But in this case a recipe has survived the late Mrs. Gail Gunter, whose passing was in November 2005. When her husband, Jimmy Gunter, was pastor of Little Horse Creek Baptist Church near Aiken, she contributed this recipe to a collection. It is a good recipe, one that has everyday ingredients and is easy to make.

Her husband served in several churches, the last full-time pastorate being in Sylvania, Ga. Now retired, he does frequent pulpit supply and works with the children's development center at Millbrook Baptist Church in Aiken.

The Gunters had four children: Debra and her husband, Mark Yon, and their children, Shelly and Joshua; Russell Gunter and his wife, Leslie, and their sons, Andrew and Zachary, all of Graniteville; Darlene and her husband, Randy Lindsay, in New Ellenton; and Doris Gunter in Aiken.

Mrs. Gail Gunter was a native of Gulf, N.C., but she and her husband spent most of their years in South Carolina. She was a good cook, her daughter Debra says, and sometimes shared her skill and interest by baking cakes for sale. She was always active in WMU in the churches where she and her husband served.

The ingredients for Mrs. Gunter's dish are easily kept on hand for that day when the "What to cook?" question pops up. I made the dish by the instructions, but our son-in-law Joel, who was having lunch with us, said — and I agreed — that it needed perhaps cheddar cheese instead of the Parmesan for more flavor. You may want to add a bit more salt also. Bake it in a deep dish so that the noodles are completely covered by the top layer of ground beef mix. This is an especially useful recipe for preparation in the morning, refrigerate, and then to bake after church for … *Sunday Dinner*.

Neapolitan Casserole

- 1 pound ground beef
- ½ green pepper, chopped
- ½ teaspoon salt
- ¼ teaspoon pepper
- 1 teaspoon Worcestershire sauce
- ¼ cup Parmesan cheese

8 ounces wide (broad) noodles
1 medium onion, chopped
1 10-ounce can tomato soup
½ teaspoon paprika
1 cup water
3 tablespoons butter

Heat oven to 375 degrees. Sauté the green pepper and onion in butter over medium heat. Add the beef, breaking it into small pieces. Brown the beef. Cook the noodles in boiling water with salt, according to package directions. Drain.

Combine soup, water, salt, pepper, paprika and Worcestershire sauce. Add the drained beef mixture. Pour half the beef mix into a 2-quart baking dish. Cover with layer of noodles. Spread remaining meat mixture on noodles and sprinkle with the cheese. Bake 30 minutes. Serves 8.

Mama's Scalloped Oysters
Mrs. H.L. Coe
(Published July 1, 2014)

We are continuing our bow to South Carolina's long coastline and fishing/seafood industry. Years ago, you couldn't have had today's dish during the summer because oysters were usually not available in months that didn't contain the letter "r." Now, because of the commercial freezing industry, we can have oysters the year round.

The next time you buy oysters, do make this month's recipe. It is from a cookbook published by the Tamassee DAR school about 1974. The recipe is from Mrs. H.L. Coe of Walhalla, but I have been unable to locate Mrs.

Coe to thank her for her recipe.

Unless you are from the Upstate or are a member of the DAR (Daughters of the American Revolution), you may not know about Tamassee. If you travel west from the coast, Tamassee is about as far from our ocean fishing waters as you can get.

The town is in Oconee County, the corner of upstate South Carolina — about five miles from Georgia on the west, and about 10 from North Carolina on the north — and you have to go through Sumter National Forest.

In 1914, the state DAR conference members (I'm sure a lot of them were Baptists) voted to create a school for mountain children in this northwestern corner of our state. Three generous donors gave a total of 50 acres of land, and in 1918 the first building was erected. The next year, in 1919, the first students were accepted.

The school grew. In 1920, after hearing the glowing accounts of the school, the New York state chapter agreed to contribute to the project — and in 1923 the New York State Cottage was built. Many girls were waiting to attend, but classes and space were limited. An administration building was dedicated in November 1924. Both the campus and student number grew, boys being admitted in the 1930s.

In 1965, the major part of the school became part of the Oconee County school system. A school with smaller enrollment of around 20 became the Tamassee Academy for grades 6-8 for students with learning disabilities. These students would then transfer to the Tamassee-Salem public school.

The Tamassee DAR school creators did a good thing, and for 50 years provided an education to an unserved area. We thank the DAR members in our state and those throughout the country for what they did.

There are Baptists in the area, and we don't know if Mrs. Coe was among them, but we thank her for her contribution to the cookbook because this recipe is a good one. As with most dishes, there are variations to the recipe. Drain the oysters, and if they are large, cut them into halves for easier serving. Some recipes call for no eggs and more butter; others use evaporated milk. Instead of the bread crumbs, I used crumbled saltine crackers. Another way to make this "our-state-is-bordered-by-the-ocean" recipe is to layer the crumbs, oysters, salt and pepper, more crumbs, butter cut into pieces, and add milk to be level with the top of the ingredients. Then bake.

This is a good recipe that you can enjoy the year round, even in those months without the "r." Assemble this dish in the morning, refrigerate it, and it will be ready for you to bake and enjoy after church for … *Sunday Dinner*.

Mama's Scalloped Oysters

1 pint fresh oysters

2 beaten eggs

1 cup milk

1 pint bread crumbs

2 stalks celery, finely chopped

1 tablespoon melted butter

Salt and pepper to taste

Preheat oven to 375 degrees. Combine all ingredients well. Place in a greased casserole dish. Bake 1 hour.

Salmon Loaf
(Published May 2006)

Everybody has them. No one knows quite what to do with them, the little plastic boxes and plastic-wrapped bowls in the refrigerator with a bit of this and a bit of that. These are leftovers — too much to throw away and too little to keep. My Ed doesn't like leftovers, but that's because he doesn't do the cooking. Frankly, sometimes I think he was brought up wrong.

Well, after a while, when the contents of the little boxes have served their period of incarceration in their cold prison, they are sent to the compost pile. I say "compost pile" because the gardener in me hopes that you use this form of last residence of your leftovers instead of the trash can or disposal.

There are a lot of uses for leftovers, especially if they are changed or incorporated into another dish, but that is a column for another day.

It really is hard to cook for only one person, but two … well, that's a little easier.

Today's recipe fits two people quite well, and there should be no leftovers. The salmon loaf and egg sauce are made from things you probably have on hand, and can be prepared, cooked and served in less than an hour. To complete the menu, add minted carrots (3 or 4 carrots, cut lengthwise, cooked in boiling salted water, drained, and mixed with mint jelly or fresh mint), and a green salad from the mix in the package in the refrigerator. So, if you are cooking for one or for two, try this recipe any time or for … *Sunday Dinner*.

Salmon Loaf

    1 8-ounce can salmon, drained (reserving liquid)
    ⅓ cup of reserved liquid
        (adding milk if necessary to make ⅓ cup)
    1 egg, slightly beaten
    ¾ cup fine cracker crumbs
    1 tablespoon lemon juice
    1 tablespoon finely chopped or coarsely grated onion
    Dash of pepper

Heat oven to 350 degrees. Spray with oil or grease the slotted top sheet of a broiler pan. Remove the skin and bone from the drained salmon, and flake the salmon. Mix with remaining ingredients. Shape mixture into two loaves and place both, barely touching, on the slotted top part of the broiler pan. Bake uncovered about 30 minutes until center is firm. Serve with egg sauce.

    (Note: To serve three, use same amount of ingredients, but use a 14-ounce can of salmon.)

Egg Sauce

    1 tablespoon butter
    1 tablespoon flour
    ¼ teaspoon salt
    ⅛ teaspoon pepper
    ¾ cup milk
    1 hard-cooked egg, peeled and diced

In a small saucepan over low heat, melt the butter; then stir in the flour, salt and pepper until mixture bubbles. Gradually add the milk and cook until sauce thickens. Remove from heat; add egg. Stir gently.

Catfish

(Published August 28, 2003)

Our daughter Lee Smith, husband, Ron, and children — Emily, 7 and little Garrison, 5 — have moved from Charlotte to live with us for several months while their house is being built.

Lee doesn't like clutter, and that is creating a mystery. I seem to be having more and more space on my kitchen counters, but I don't know what's missing. I haven't actually seen her tossing anything, but I know she is responsible for this new space and order. On my decluttered counters this week, I cooked catfish two days.

In Washington, it's salmon; and in Maine, it's cod. But here in our beautiful South Carolina, it's catfish.

There are people who become almost violent if you suggest cooking catfish in any way but fried, with the possible exception of catfish stew. However, at the risk of their ire, I am offering two catfish recipes. (There is another way, though, I sometimes prepare catfish that is so simple it doesn't need a recipe: Place the fillets on a baking sheet, sprinkle with grated Parmesan cheese and bake at 350 degrees until brown.)

The first recipe I offer is a simple one. Because the fish are baked, the calories are fewer than in fried fish. The recipe calls for brushing the fillets with oil. I omitted that and the fish was good, but the oil would have caused the crushed chips to adhere to the fish more closely. This dish can be prepared and cooked in a short time, maybe 30 minutes.

The second is for a company catfish meal. When cooking the fish, be sure to keep the oil at 375 degrees and the fish will cook to a golden brown. If the oil is hotter, the fish will brown too darkly and the presented dish won't be as attractive. For this dish, you may want to use more crabmeat than the recipe suggests.

To make part of this ahead, cook the fillets and keep them warm in the oven. Then, when you get home from church, heat the asparagus and crabmeat, make the hollandaise, and you will be ready to serve Andrew Jackson Catfish for … *Sunday Dinner*.

Oven Fried Catfish

    4 catfish fillets
    1 6-ounce bag thin potato chips, finely crushed
    2 tablespoons cooking oil
    Poultry seasoning or garlic powder (optional)

Season fillets with garlic or poultry seasoning. Dip each fillet into the oil, then coat each heavily with the finely crushed potato chips. Arrange in a single layer on a slotted broiler pan and bake at 425 degrees about 15 minutes or until done. If fish is not evenly browned after 10 minutes, raise the oven temperature to 450 degrees for the last 5 minutes. Don't overcook. Yields 4 servings.

Catfish Andrew Jackson

    4½ pounds catfish fillets
    Salt and pepper to taste
    1 egg, beaten

1 cup milk
1 cup corn meal
1 10½-ounce can asparagus spears
6 ounces (or more) crabmeat

Combine the milk and egg. Salt and pepper the fillets, dip in the milk-egg mixture, then dredge in the corn meal. Fry in 375-degree oil about 5 or 6 minutes on each side. While fillets are cooking, heat the asparagus and crabmeat in separate pans.

When fish are cooked, place 3 or 4 spears of asparagus on top of each fillet, then top with ¼ of the drained crabmeat. Slowly pour the Hollandaise Sauce over the fillets and serve at once.

Hollandaise Sauce

3 egg yolks
1 tablespoon lemon juice
½ cup melted butter
⅛ teaspoon cayenne pepper

Put egg yolks, lemon juice and cayenne pepper in blender, and blend briefly until well mixed. Slowly pour melted butter into yolk mixture and beat vigorously.

American Chop Suey
Karen Wham and Myra Young
(Published October 14, 2008)

"We are always looking for great recipes to serve a crowd economically," wrote Karen Wham of Mountville Baptist Church. Located in a small rural community between Greenwood and Clinton, Mountville Baptist Church is in Laurens Baptist Association, and David Shiflet is the pastor.

Every Wednesday night, the church — which averages around 40 or so in Sunday school — serves dinner to an equal or larger number, usually about 50. The cost is $4, which Karen correctly says is a bargain. This is also youth night, and following the supper the young people go to Mission Friends, GAs, RAs and Acteens. The adults stay in the dining hall for prayer meeting.

Karen and Myra Young regularly (with three or four other rotating helpers) prepare the meal, which they use as an outreach arm of the church. Many attend Mountville Baptist or even another church. They have been doing this four or five years, and the attendance (and the food!) is always good.

This is not Karen's only job. As with most small churches, the members wear several hats, and Karen is also the Mission Friends leader, church clerk and pianist.

Karen was a teacher and worked with the Council on Aging, but resigned from these after her second child was born.

Karen's husband, Joe, is on the board of deacons. He coached and taught school for eight years, then returned to farming — specifically egg and poultry production involving 85,000 chickens.

There's never a question about his Wednesday night dinner!

Their sons, Jay and Allen, are both Clemson graduates. Jay and his wife, Becca, have a daughter, Livie, and are members at Mountville. He has a contract environmental management business. Allen and his wife, Karen, are in the process of moving to Laurens, where he is an attorney. Their youngest child, Sallie, is at Presbyterian College where she is majoring in early childhood education for a teaching career. She is also a cheerleader.

At each Wednesday night dinner, Karen says, they serve a meat or meat casserole, two vegetables, salad or slaw, bread, dessert and drink. She is asking for recipes to serve about 50. The word here is "economically."

Let us help Karen, Myra and the others. If you have a recipe that serves a large number, please send it and we'll use it here. I am sharing with you, and them, a recipe for 25. I haven't used this, but maybe soon I shall invite a group and have this for … *Sunday Dinner*.

American Chop Suey
- 2 pounds fresh pork shoulder
- 8 cups celery, shredded
- 8 cups onion, sliced
- 4 cups water and stock
- 4 tablespoons brown sauce
- 12 tablespoons soy sauce
- 4 cans bean sprouts (the recipe didn't say what size can)
- **Fluffy boiled rice**

Slice the lean meat (veal or beef may also be used) into thin, small pieces and fry in a little fat until nearly done. Add the celery, onions and water, using the stock from the bean sprouts for part of this. Add brown sauce and soy sauce, and cook about 15 minutes. Add bean sprouts and heat through, seasoning with a little salt. Serve with rice on the side and additional soy sauce. Serves 25.

(Note: If chop suey seems too juicy, thicken with cornstarch.)

Toaster Oven Recipes
Requested by Doris Henderson
(Published August 3, 2007)

"I can't cook anymore," wrote Doris Henderson of Glendale, asking for "recipes that can be put together with a toaster oven, crockpot, or microwave." Now, I think I can help with that.

Doris joined Glendale Baptist Church around 1996. Johnny Bridges is pastor, and the church is in the Spartanburg County Baptist Network.

Doris grew up in Inman and had to leave school to help at home. She worked her way through beauty school in Charlotte to get her beauty operator's license. Subsequently, she worked for 22 years at the Ideal Beauty Shop in Spartanburg. In 1986, she retired from the hair-styling business, and a short time later started another career. She took a training program to do home health care and retired from that in 1994. She attended Sunday school and worship at Glendale, but her attendance has decreased because of health.

Doris now rents an apartment from son Wayne Morris and his wife, Debbie, in their home. She does her own cooking, but her health has meant a decrease in that. She has a microwave, toaster oven, and slow cooker for safer cooking, and we hope she will enjoy these two recipes.

We thank Doris for her request, and if you cook for a family or only for yourself, I think you will like both of these recipes. They can be assembled quickly, and either would be suitable for … *Sunday Dinner.*

Fruit-Topped Ham Slice

¾ pound fully cooked ham slice, cut 1 inch thick
½ of an 8-ounce can pineapple slices
2 tablespoons orange marmalade
Dash of ground cloves

Slash fat edge of ham slice and place on rack of unheated broiler pan in toaster oven. Broil 7 to 8 minutes. Turn; broil 5 to 6 minutes more.

Meanwhile, drain pineapple slices, reserving 2 tablespoons of liquid. Combine pineapple liquid, orange marmalade and cloves. Place pineapple slices atop ham slice and spoon marmalade mixture on it. Broil for 2 to 3 minutes, or until marmalade and pineapple are heated through. Serves 2 or 3.

Barbecue Chicken

4 chicken drumsticks
2 tablespoons ketchup
2 tablespoons water
1 teaspoon vinegar
1 teaspoon Worcestershire sauce
½ cup shredded Monterey Jack cheese (2 ounces)
¼ cup finely crushed corn chips

Place chicken drumsticks in shallow baking pan and bake, uncovered, in 400-degree oven for 15 minutes. Combine ketchup, water, vinegar and Worcestershire sauce, and spoon over chicken. Bake 20-25 minutes longer, or until chicken is tender. Sprinkle with cheese and corn chips; return to oven, baking 3 to 5 minutes longer. Serves 2.

Hay and Straw with Pear Pie
(Published October 13, 2011)

Today's two recipes are the result of trying to bring order to my "office." I have always liked playing office. Once, as a child, I somehow acquired a large refrigerator-sized wooden box, turned it on its side to make a desk, and played office all summer.

My telephone was a stick, and the "desk" appointments were a collection of crayons, coloring books, almanacs, old calendars, etc. I conducted all manner of important business at that back porch "office."

As an only child in that pre-TV era, I don't ever remember being lonely or bored. There were trees to climb, paper dolls to make, play houses to design, "cooking" to be done, pictures to be drawn, and of course, the "office work."

In the years since, I have had six or seven "offices" in nooks and crannies around the house, and then many years ago my Ed constructed an office building which held a room for him, one for me, a darkroom for my camera habit, a restroom, and a storage room. That served for many years.

My Ed has been retired for some time and doesn't do much office stuff, so to be inside with him, I established another "office" in a corner in our laundry area. Most of the children have said unkind things about the site which is visible immediately upon entering the back door. I may leave them out of the will. Anyway, I have now moved out to our sun porch to what will probably be my last "office/clutter" location.

In the moving and arranging, including boxes of recipes, I found and cooked these two. The first can be the main dish for your meal — and the second, a new use for pears. We liked them both. Both the "Hay and Straw" and the pear pie are easily made and should be served warm when you prepare and enjoy them for ... *Sunday Dinner.*

Hay and Straw

    1 16-ounce package linguine
    2 cups finely cut, fully cooked ham
    1 tablespoon butter
    3 cups frozen peas
    1½ cups grated or shredded Parmesan cheese
    ⅓ cup heavy whipping cream

Cook the linguine according to package directions. Cut ham in narrow strips. Melt butter in large skillet, add the ham and cook about 3 minutes. Add the frozen peas. Cook over medium heat several minutes, until peas are heated through.

*   Drain the linguine and combine with the ham and peas, tossing to mix thoroughly. Stir in the Parmesan cheese, then stir in the whipping cream. Add a bit more cream if mixture seems dry. Serve immediately. Makes 8 servings.*

Pear Pie

    Double crust for 9-inch pie
    5 medium pears
    ¼ cup firmly packed brown sugar
    1 teaspoon grated orange rind
    3 tablespoons sugar
    ¼ cup flour
    ⅛ teaspoon nutmeg
    Orange Butter Sauce (optional)*

Arrange one crust in the pie plate. Preheat oven to 400 degrees. Peel pears, cut into fourths, remove cores and slice pears. Combine pears with the two sugars, flour, nutmeg and orange rind in a large bowl. Toss to mix evenly. Place pears in crust, top with remaining crust and press edges together. Make a few slits in top crust. Bake for 45 minutes. Serve warm with orange butter sauce.

*Orange Butter Sauce: In small saucepan, combine 2 tablespoons cornstarch, 1/3 cup brown sugar and 1¾ cups orange juice. Cook until mixture thickens, stirring constantly, then cook an additional 3 minutes. Remove from heat and stir in 4 tablespoons butter until melted and 2 tablespoons vanilla. Makes 2 cups. Serve warm over pie.

Breads and Rolls

Biscuits

(Published February 20, 2008)

Everybody likes biscuits, including our English friends who call them scones. If you ask for biscuits in England, you'll get cookies. I think it was Churchill who said the Americans and English are separated by a common language (or something like that).

Anyway, everybody likes biscuits, and every cook ought to know how to make them. They are tasty enough to be good alone, but bland enough to adapt to many accompaniments: butter, jellies and jams, gravy, sauces, creamed dishes, etc.

They should be light brown on top and bottom, and the crusts should separate easily. The inside should be light and fluffy.

Although there are many variations, the basic recipe for biscuits includes flour, milk and fat. You will want to add a leavening agent, such as baking powder or soda, and salt. Southern cooks most often use self-rising flour to eliminate the adding of the leavening.

The best biscuits are made with lard. Yes, lard and eating one or two biscuits won't kill you. The biscuit interior is flaky, and the crusts bake to a light brown. You may also use a vegetable shortening, and some recipes ask for butter. You can use half butter and half shortening, and some recipes suggest using cream instead of milk. Occasionally a recipe will say vegetable oil, but the usual fat is lard or shortening.

Most recipes use whole milk, but you may choose to use the 1 percent or 2 percent. Other recipes ask for buttermilk, but basically it's flour, milk and fat, plus the leavening and salt.

Most biscuit dough is rolled about ½ to ¾ inch, then cut, and when baked will probably double to 1 inch in height. Most biscuit cutters are 2 inches, but you can make big ol' biscuits using a larger one or make little tea biscuits using a 1-inch cutter.

After the biscuits are cut, you can freeze them by placing them on a cookie sheet in the freezer, and when they are frozen put them in plastic bags. It is best to wrap them individually or to pack with waxed paper or plastic wrap so that the biscuits don't touch. To bake, place the biscuits on a baking sheet and cook at 425 degrees for 15-20 minutes until brown. To thaw and then bake, cook at 425 degrees 10 to 12 minutes.

Here are some recipes you may like for Sunday breakfast or … *Sunday Dinner*.

Basic Biscuits
2 cups self-rising flour
½ cup lard, or lard and shortening mix, or shortening and butter
1 cup milk

Preheat oven to 450 degrees. Sift the flour before measuring. Then sift again. With fingers or a pastry blender, blend in the shortening or lard. Add the milk all at once, stir with a fork until mixture stays together.

Turn dough onto a floured board, dust with flour, and turn and knead about 10-12 times, patting it into a circle. Dough will be sticky. Use a rolling pin lightly, if desired, to make the top smooth. Cut with a 1½- to 2-inch cookie cutter and place on an ungreased cookie sheet. Bake about 12-15 minutes until tops are lightly browned. Yields about 12 biscuits.

(Try adding ¼ cup grated cheese or ½ cup cooked and crumbled bacon to the dry mix.)

Buttermilk Biscuits

    2 cups all-purpose flour
    ½ teaspoon baking soda
    ¼ cup shortening
    2 teaspoons baking powder
    ½ teaspoon salt
    ¾ cup buttermilk

Sift together in a bowl the flour, baking powder, baking soda, and salt, then cut in the shortening. Stir in buttermilk. Turn dough onto a floured surface and turn and knead gently. Roll to ½ inch; cut with a 1½-inch biscuit cutter. Bake on a lightly greased baking sheet for 10-12 minutes at 450 degrees. Yields 10.

Herbed Biscuits

    ¼ cup chopped onion
    1½ cups all-purpose flour
    ½ teaspoon salt
    1 egg
    2 tablespoons grated Parmesan cheese
    2 tablespoons butter, divided
    2 teaspoons baking powder
    ¼ cup shortening
    ⅓ cup milk

Seasoning: 2 tablespoons each of dried oregano, marjoram, and basil; 4 teaspoons dried savory; 2 teaspoons dried rosemary, crushed; 2 teaspoons rubbed sage. Combine these. You'll have some left for another use.

Sauté 1 tablespoon of the seasoning with onion in 1 tablespoon butter. Combine flour, baking powder, salt and cut in the shortening. Mix the egg, milk and onion seasoning and add to the flour mix. Turn out, knead and roll to ¼ inch. Cut and put on ungreased baking sheet. Melt the remaining tablespoon of butter and brush over the biscuits, then sprinkle with the cheese. Bake at 450 degrees for 12-14 minutes. Yields 6 biscuits.

Spoon Bread
(Published March 18, 2009)

I want you to cook a pan of spoon bread.

All my life I have heard of spoon bread but had, until recently, neither cooked nor eaten any.

It has been a wasted life.

Spoon bread is good. It is an old recipe. I have looked in several cookbooks and find it in the "Rumsford Complete Cookbook," published first in 1908, the "Modern Priscilla Cookbook," copyrighted in 1929, and several others. There are two versions in the "Williamsburg Art of Cookery" (1938), one attributed to an "Old Recipe, Petersburg, Virginia, From a Williamsburg Family Cookbook." A spoon bread recipe almost always shows up in cookbooks printed by churches and other organizations.

Spoon bread is just what it says it is. It is served in the pan in which it is baked, so use an attractive baking dish. It would cook great in your cast iron skillet, but that would look rather crude sitting on the table. It is called spoon bread because it does not become as firm as cornbread does. It must be served with a spoon, and it is eaten with a fork. Most of the recipes say to serve topped with butter. That's optional, but good.

I can't document this, but I think spoon bread is mostly a Southern dish. The recipes are all similar, but none of the several I found were identical — somewhat like making potato salad. Some use only water, some only milk, and some require both. Some recipes say to boil the milk/water/milk-water and add the cornmeal. Others say to mix it all together and then bring to a boil. One suggested adding ½ cup grated Parmesan cheese.

The one common instruction is that spoon bread must be served hot, probably to melt that pat of butter. So here are three recipes from different cookbooks. Select one, mix and bake it when you get home from church, and I just know everyone at your table will enjoy spoon bread for … *Sunday Dinner*.

Spoon Bread (1)
- 2 cups milk
- 1 teaspoon salt
- 2 eggs
- ⅓ cup cornmeal
- ½ teaspoon baking powder
- 2 teaspoons melted shortening

Scald the milk, stir in the cornmeal gradually and cook in a double boiler until thickened like mush. Meanwhile, separate the eggs. Beat the whites until stiff and beat the yolks.

Remove meal mix from heat. Add salt, baking powder, beaten egg yolks and shortening to the meal mixture; then fold in the egg whites. Turn into a greased baking dish and bake at 375 degrees for 30 minutes. Serves 6.

Spoon Bread (2)

 1 cup milk
 1 cup cornmeal
 2 eggs, separated
 1 tablespoon butter
 1 cup water
 1 teaspoon salt
 2 tablespoons baking powder

Place milk and water in saucepan. Add cornmeal and salt and cook 5 minutes, stirring as needed. Add beaten egg yolks, baking powder and butter. Beat egg whites until stiff and fold into mix. Pour into greased casserole dish and bake at 425 degrees for 40 minutes. Serves 6.

Spoon Bread (3)

 1 teaspoon salt
 2 eggs, beaten
 2 cups water
 1 tablespoon shortening
 1 cup milk

Place the meal, salt, shortening and water in a saucepan. Cook, stirring until smooth and thick. Allow to cool, then stir in the beaten eggs. Thin the batter with the 1 cup milk and beat well. Pour into a baking dish and bake in hot oven about 30 minutes. Serves 6.

Easy Yeast Rolls
Helen Martin
(Published March 4, 2009)

"They may be better made with butter," Helen Martin said. We were discussing her recipe for Easy Yeast Rolls, which required margarine. I had made them with butter.

We talked about refrigerator rolls in the last issue of the Courier, and here is another recipe, slightly different and good. I'm trying to get you to bake at home with ingredients that you can pronounce. Look at all the stuff on the list of ingredients in things you buy. Exchange those for flour, sugar, butter, etc.

Helen has been making these rolls for a while. She has lived in Beaufort most of her life, having been a member of The Baptist Church of Beaufort since 1945, and has seen a lot of changes in those 64 years.

The Baptist Church of Beaufort has a new pastor, Jim Wooten, who came Dec. 1. The church, which has around 500 in its two Sunday morning worship services and Sunday school, is in a growing mode. There is no evening service.

During her years at The Baptist Church of Beaufort, Helen has held several offices. She was treasurer of her Sunday school class for a while and since 1990 has been on the Sunshine Committee, which sends cards, flowers, etc., to members. For several years, she was on the homebound committee, visiting members who could not attend worship services. She also meets monthly with the church's craft group. Each year they make items that are given to the homebound members at Christmas time. I can't tell you what they are working on this year; it's a secret!

She goes to the monthly first Thursday meetings of OASIS (Older Adults Still in Service) when the 50 or more ("a bunch," she says) adults gather for a covered dish meal and a program.

Helen's late husband, Charlie, died 16 years ago, and she lives alone. She and Charlie have three sons: Chuck and his wife, Donna, who live in North Carolina; Robert, who lives in Maryland; and Henry and his wife, Sandi, of Beaufort; nine grandchildren; and 10 great-grandchildren.

She doesn't bake as much as she did formerly and doesn't remember when she got this recipe, but it's a good one. If these rolls are served at lunch or dinner, then she usually serves butter with them. If they are served at breakfast, she agrees that butter, jelly or jam would be great. She says the recipe could be used to make cinnamon rolls, etc.

Make these rolls and refrigerate them, then as soon as you get home from church on Sunday, roll and shape them. Let them rise, then bake while you are preparing the rest of the meal. Add butter, and you will all enjoy these for … *Sunday Dinner*.

Easy Yeast Rolls
- 1 cup boiling water
- ¼ cup shortening
- ¼ cup butter or margarine
- ⅓ cup sugar
- 1¼-ounce package yeast
- 1 egg, well beaten
- 1 teaspoon salt
- 2 to 3 cups sifted all-purpose flour

In a large mixing bowl, pour the boiling water over the butter (or margarine) and shortening. When the shortening and butter have melted, add the sugar. When the liquid has cooled to lukewarm, add the yeast and stir until dissolved. Add the egg and salt to the liquid. Sift the flour into the liquid about ¾ cup at a time. Add enough flour to make a soft dough. Let rise, or cover and put into refrigerator until ready to use.

When ready to use, take the amount you need, roll, cut into shapes, and let rise about 30 minutes. Preheat oven to 350 degrees and bake about 10-15 minutes. Batter will keep a week or so in the refrigerator.

Refrigerator Rolls
Kathleen Burkett
(Published February 13, 2009)

Her name is Kathleen Burkett. She is 89 years young, has been a member of Lexington Baptist Church in Lexington for 63 years, has seven children and numerous grandchildren and great-grandchildren. And she is a delightful person.

She and her late husband, Max Ezelle Burkett, were from Leesville and moved to Lexington in 1942. Max died 27 years ago, and one of Kathleen's granddaughters, Rhonda Datman, lives with her. Kathleen does most of her housework and is in good health.

During the years she has been at Lexington Baptist, there have been changes. On the first Sunday of January 2009, the church started a contemporary service at 11:30 a.m. to complement the traditional services at 9 and 10:15 a.m. Mike Turner is senior pastor. For the three services, attendance has been 1,500-1,600 each week.

Kathleen has done her part. For 17 years, she and Evelyn Alewine taught in the junior Sunday school department and she also had a children's training union group. Over the years, she has gone on several church-sponsored trips.

There was a period many years ago when her husband was ill that she didn't attend regularly, but now she is in a Sunday school class and serves as the outreach leader. Along with Vienna Teal and others, she goes to an assisted living facility to lead devotionals, and with Jennie Thompson and others she also helps lead the residents with craft projects.

On the second Sunday of each month, her family (or as many who can come) gather for the noon meal. The hostess cooks the meat and other family members fill out the menu.

Kathleen doesn't remember where she got this recipe for refrigerator rolls, but she says it was probably from her mother. She doesn't make these often now, but cooked them frequently in the past. In times past, every homemaker knew how to make yeast-risen rolls, and the instruction for doing so was basic to home economics classes.

There are many recipes, but they are all similar. Some use lard, some potato water, some use only water, others milk, etc. Most require a rising before the dough is punched down, shaped, then allowed to rise again before baking. The refrigerator roll recipe will keep two weeks or so. When I made the recipe, I covered the dough with plastic wrap touching it, then covered the bowl with another piece of plastic wrap.

The people sitting at your table will thank you, just as we thank Kathleen, if you mix and refrigerate these rolls during the week, then take them from the fridge, shape and bake for ... *Sunday Dinner*.

Refrigerator Rolls
- 6 cups plain flour
- 1 teaspoon salt
- ½ cup sugar
- 1¼-ounce package yeast

- 2 cups warm water
- ½ cup vegetable shortening
- 1 egg, slightly beaten

In a large bowl, sift together the flour, salt, and sugar. Dissolve yeast in the warm water. Add the shortening, egg, and yeast mixture to the dry ingredients. Mix gently as you would biscuit dough. Place dough in a large greased bowl, cover with plastic wrap, and store in refrigerator until ready to use. Will keep two weeks or so in the fridge.

When ready to use, remove from refrigerator all or only the portion you need. Roll, shape*, and bake at 375 degrees about 10-15 minutes.

*Plain rolls: Shape as biscuits, cut a slit down center top about ¼ the depth of the roll.

Cloverleaf: Shape dough into 1-inch balls. Place 3 balls in each greased muffin tin cup.

Crescent: Roll dough, cut into triangles, then roll beginning at wide end opposite the point.

Parker House: Cut rolled dough into 2-inch circles. Make a slight cut on top about ⅓ from the edge. Fold the ⅔ part over the ⅓ part.

Strawberry Bread
Peggy Lollis
(Published April 11, 2013)

"And don't forget the sugar!" Peggy laughed.

I had made her recipe, and, amid all the interruptions here, I had omitted the sugar. The next day at lunch, our grandson Jay said it was good without the sugar and I agreed with him. Both of us would be the better if we dropped a few pounds.

Do you need a little something for a snack? Or perhaps to add to a light luncheon? Or even for a breakfast?

Then Peggy Lollis of Crescent Hill Baptist Church in Columbia has just the recipe for you, and we thank her for sharing it with us. The recipe, easily put together and very good, is for strawberry bread.

Crescent Hill has a new pastor, Rev. Lee Butler, who came last August. The church has around 125 members, and offers both Sunday morning and evening and Wednesday night worship services. It has an active WMU and conducts VBS in the summer. Located on Two Notch Road, Crescent is part of Columbia Metro Association.

Peggy, who has been a member since the 1980s, has worn (and does wear) a lot of hats for church responsibilities. She is on the benevolence committee, the church's social committee, and chairs the Lord's Supper committee. She has also served as treasurer of her Sunday school class for 29 years.

Peggy, whose late husband, Carl, died several years ago, retired from the dental lab at Fort Jackson after working there for 31 years. Following that, she worked at the Hallmark shop for three years. Peggy and Carl had three children. Their son, Michael, and his son, Marshall, live in Columbia. Their daughter, Susan, and her son, Daniel, also live in Columbia — as do her daughter, Brittany, and grandchildren, Savannah and Carey. Peggy and Carl's third child, Carol, died several years ago.

The recipe is from Peggy's daughter, Susan. She got it from a neighbor when she lived in Nashville, Tenn.

When making the strawberry bread, Peggy sometimes allows it to cool, but prefers it warm and served with butter. I tried it with the butter and with softened cream cheese, and both were good. It is a good keeper, lasting three days or more at room temperature, and Peggy says she also wraps the loaves in aluminum foil and freezes them. They keep well.

Most store-bought frozen strawberries come in slices or halves. When assembling the ingredients, cut the strawberries into smaller pieces. In determining how much of the juice to use, make the batter about the consistency of that for a pound cake or layer cake.

Someday soon, make Peggy's strawberry bread and enjoy it warm or cold for your next ... *Sunday Dinner*.

Strawberry Bread

- 3 cups all-purpose flour
- 1 tablespoon cinnamon
- 1 teaspoon salt
- 1 ¼ cups cooking oil
- 2 cups sugar
- 1 teaspoon baking soda
- 3 eggs, well beaten
- 2 10-ounce packs of frozen strawberries

Using kitchen shears, cut the thawed strawberries into small pieces. Set aside. Preheat oven to 350 degrees. Lightly grease 2 loaf pans; line each with aluminum foil. Mix flour, sugar, cinnamon, baking soda and salt in a mixing bowl. Make a well in center of mixture,

Pour eggs and oil into the well. Pour strawberries into a bowl. With a slotted spoon, dip out strawberries and add to the oil/egg/flour mixture, stirring gently. Add strawberry juice gradually and stir. Do not make the batter thin. Divide batter between the two pans. Bake for 1 hour.

Popovers
The late Frances Chapman
(Published November 24, 2009)

My first popover experience came in a high school home economics class. Over the years I have made this funny little bread a few times, and did so again this week using a recipe from the late Frances Chapman of First Baptist Church in Edgefield.

Before her death in December 2006, Frances had served as the church's administrative assistant for 27 years. She and her husband had four daughters — Dorothy, Nancy, Eleanor, and Sara — who grew up in the church but now live in other places.

Edgefield First Baptist is a growing church, averaging around 235 for Sunday morning worship. Stacy Williams has been pastor there about four years, replacing the former pastor, Tony Hopkins. The associate pastor is Gregory Pittman.

Edgefield First Baptist is a church with a strong mission feeling. This fall one of their members, Lynn Rearden, a nurse, is in American Samoa working with medical missions.

Frances contributed several recipes to the church's cookbook compiled by the youth missions organizations, but it was the one for popovers that caught my eye.

Popovers are usually served at breakfast but can be served at brunch or lunch. You have to have a good jam or jelly to poke in the little hole.

When you look at the recipe, you will think the baking powder and shortening have been omitted by mistake. Not so. The popovers rise because of the steam they create, so don't open the oven door while they are cooking.

As they rise, they form a hollow in the center. When served, sometimes the little hole forms in the base of the popover and sometimes the base is a solid crust. Then you have to open the little hole with a knife in the bottom crust to get into the hollow center. Into the little hole, put a dab of jam, eat, and enjoy away!

Popovers can be baked in muffin tins. They take on a better shape if you use a popover tin, which is much like a muffin tin but deeper and more narrow.

If you are having house guests over the Thanksgiving weekend, consider serving this bread. You may have to get up a bit earlier to have these ready for breakfast, but the resulting popovers will be worth the effort. Try these this Sunday morning. The recipe makes about 10, so if you have some left it will be all right to reheat them for ... *Sunday Dinner*.

Popovers
- **2 eggs**
- **1 cup sifted flour**
- **½ teaspoon salt**
- **1 cup milk**

Preheat oven to 450 degrees. Grease muffin or popover tins with shortening or lard, no oil. In a small bowl, beat eggs slightly. Add flour, salt and milk, and beat just until blended. (Do not overbeat.) Fill cups half full. Bake at 450 degrees for 15 minutes. Reduce oven temperature to 325 degrees and bake 25 to 30 minutes or until a deep golden brown. Makes 8-10.

Note: To serve, make small hole in bottom of popover to the hollow center. Insert small amount of butter and jelly in hole. Replace hole cover. Serve hot.

Sandwiches

(Published April 15, 2008)

We owe him a lot, this John Montagu (1718-1792), because without him there would be no picnics, no lunch at one's desk, no ladies' afternoon teas, etc. Not even hamburgers. The story is that Mr. Montagu — also known as the Earl of Sandwich — was a dedicated gambler, and, on one occasion, not wanting to leave the gambling table, ordered his servant to plop cold beef between two slices of bread so the Earl could continue to eat while gambling.

We still do that today, and the sandwich (as in "Earl of") is a kitchen basic.

Not all sandwiches are peanut butter and jelly (also known as the world-famous PB&J), or even the Southern standard of the garden-ripe tomato, salt, pepper, mayonnaise and bread. There are many kinds of sandwiches. The heaviest are those made with layers of sliced meat and cheese between oversized slices of bread. The hearty meats include ham, beef, corned beef, chicken, salami, sliced pork, etc.

Sandwiches can be made into roll or pinwheel shapes and the little pocket sandwich, but the most normal is two slices of bread with a filling.

The open-face sandwich is one slice of bread, toasted or not, topped with any number of things (including meat, tomatoes, lettuce, eggs) and is eaten with a knife and fork. The hot open-face sandwich can be meat or chicken with gravy over the top. Some open-face sandwiches are broiled.

A club sandwich is one with three slices of bread. The fillings, usually something hearty, are different between slices one and two, and two and three.

Bread choices include sandwich rolls, the round ones called kaiser rolls (although I doubt if anyone uses the word) for hamburgers, or the long roll used for hero sandwiches — as well as the many kinds of sliced bread, such as white, rye, pumpernickel, Italian, etc. Spread with butter (about 1 teaspoon per slice) to the edge, then fill with any choice of fillings. Sometimes we use mayonnaise instead of butter, but the slices should be spread with something so the filling won't make the bread slices soggy.

If you trim the crusts, do so before spreading the butter and adding the filling. Save the crusts for bread crumbs or croutons, or put them beside (not in) your compost pile, if you have one, for any night critters that may stroll by.

Here are some sandwich fillings you can try:

- Chopped corned beef or tongue, sour-pickle relish, mayonnaise
- Liverwurst, sliced tomato, lettuce, mayonnaise
- Sliced meatloaf, pickle relish, sliced hard-cooked egg, salad dressing
- Finely chop 1 cup deviled ham, ½ cup stuffed olives, 1 hard-cooked egg, 1 small onion, moisten with mayonnaise; serve on white or other bread
- Chopped hard-cooked egg, sardines, mayonnaise, bit of prepared mustard
- Cream cheese and pickled beets
- Drained crushed pineapple, peanut butter, mayonnaise
- Mayonnaise mixed with whipped cream and horseradish, diced cucumbers, thin slices of roast beef
- Toasted cheese: Butter both sides of two slices of bread; put thin slices of soft American cheese between bread; toast slowly on each side so cheese will melt
- Raspberry jam and finely chopped pecans
- ½ cup orange marmalade, ¼ cup moist shredded coconut
- 2 hard-cooked eggs finely chopped, 2 tablespoons pickle relish, ¼ cup finely diced celery, 2 tablespoons finely diced green pepper, 1

tablespoon chopped parsley, salt and pepper to taste, mayonnaise to bind; makes 3 or 4 sandwiches

- Vegetable: Finely chop 1 large ripe tomato, 1 cucumber, 1 green pepper, 1 carrot, ½ small onion; add 1 teaspoon Worcestershire sauce, 1½ teaspoons salt, ½ teaspoon prepared mustard, 1 cup mayonnaise, 1 package plain gelatin dissolved in ½ cup cold water; refrigerate
- Combine one 7½-ounce can salmon, ¼ cup chopped black olives, 2 tablespoons chili sauce and 1 tablespoon fresh lemon juice to make 4 sandwiches
- Split and toast 6 English muffins; combine 1½ cups finely diced cooked chicken, 1 8-ounce pack frozen cooked small shrimp (thawed and drained), ½ cup finely chopped celery, ½ cup mayonnaise, ¼ teaspoon salt, ⅛ teaspoon pepper; and spread on muffins; top each with 1 cheese slice; toast until cheese melts; makes 12

Desserts

Baptist Pound Cake
Connie Whitten
(Published November 18, 2004)

"This is the best and easiest cake I've ever made," wrote Connie Whitten of Dorchester Baptist Church near Belton in the Saluda Baptist Association.

I agree with her, and this will probably be the pound cake recipe I will always use.

"I don't know why it is called 'Baptist Pound Cake,'" she said, "unless it is because I pray each time I make it that it will turn out all right!" It always has, she said.

Connie has had the recipe for 20 years or more, but has started using it frequently within the last two. She remembers that it came from an old cookbook and had the same name then. She never frosts the cake, but says one can do so. She suggested the lemon glaze often used on hot pound cakes immediately after they come from the oven. She says that almost any frosting — chocolate, caramel, etc. — would be good, but she always leaves her cakes unfrosted. When I made it, I didn't use a frosting, and in no time the cake was gone.

Connie grew up in Princeton and attended Columbia Baptist Church in Honea Path until she married. Her parents, Barney and Frances Medlock, still go to Columbia Baptist. Connie has two sisters but no children and lives alone. She doesn't do a lot of cooking because it's hard to cook for one, she says. But when she bakes this cake, everybody loves it.

Retired with a disability from BASF in Anderson, Connie no longer works away from home, but she has served as volunteer organist and pianist at Dorchester Baptist since 1988.

She began taking piano lessons in the second grade. She has loved both the piano and the organ ever since, and is glad she can use her talents in the church. Dorchester has a membership of about 400, with about 100 in attendance each week. The congregation also has a new pastor, Stephen Payne.

If you like pound cakes — and like to bake them, too — you will find yourself using this recipe. You should probably make it this weekend so it will be ready for ... *Sunday Dinner.*

Baptist Pound Cake

- 1 stick (½ cup) butter at room temperature
- ½ cup vegetable shortening (Connie uses Crisco)
- 3 cups sugar
- 5 eggs
- 3 cups plain flour
- ½ teaspoon baking powder
- 1 cup milk
- 1 teaspoon vanilla

Prepare a tube baking pan by greasing and dusting with flour, or use the new spray-on coating for baking. Set aside. Sift the plain flour, measure, and sift again with baking powder. Set aside. Cream butter, sugar and shortening until fluffy. Add eggs one at a time, beating after each. Add the flour mixture and milk alternately a little at a time. Add vanilla and mix well.

Pour batter into prepared pan and put into a COLD oven. Bake at 325 degrees for 1 hour and 15 minutes. DO NOT OPEN OVEN during baking time. Remove from oven and let pan rest about 5-10 minutes, then invert cake onto a wire rack to cool.

Pound Cake
Edna Robinson
(Published May 8, 2003)

There are a few dishes that everyone who cooks should be able to prepare. Most of these are simple, commonplace foods such as fried chicken, apple pie, scrambled eggs, rolls, etc.

And pound cake.

Pound cake has its name because in old recipes it contained a pound each of butter, flour, sugar and eggs, with a touch of vanilla extract. No milk was used because the eggs provided the necessary liquid.

Before the electric mixer was a basic appliance (although many may not remember that time) the beating of the pound cake almost exhausted the cook and anyone else who could be talked into helping.

The first recipe is a pound cake with a variation and is named Kentucky Pound Cake with a Southern Touch. We thank Mrs. Edna Robinson of Greenwood for sharing her recipe. She got the recipe from a friend and has been baking it for years, using it especially for birthdays. Sometimes she serves it plain; at other times, she covers it with a caramel frosting.

Mrs. Robinson has been a member of Harris Baptist Church near Greenwood for 50 years or more, joining the church after coming to the area as a bride from Rosman, N.C. She and her husband, Harold, who goes to another church, have three children — Stan, Hal and Linda — who live in the Greenwood area. One grandson, Jason Burch, also attends Harris Church.

Mrs. Robinson is a member of the TEL Sunday school class and is less active now than she was at one time. The TEL stands for something else, but the members laughingly say it stands for Tired Elderly Ladies! She still helps with the church's mission work, and makes the dessert to carry to bereaved church members when needed, etc.

One activity she did for many years was to dress in a clown costume and assume the persona of "Buttons the Clown," presenting a little act at nursing homes and handing out little treats. Her audience always enjoyed it, she says.

For her recipe, Mrs. Robinson suggests toasting the nuts in the microwave for about 30 seconds or so. You can use all shortening, or part shortening and part cooking oil, but a total of 1½ cups are needed. She has not tried the cake with butter. She says that one can also add about a half-cup of flaked coconut and a half-cup of raisins to the batter. Another possible change is to use two cups sugar and one cup honey.

When I made the cake, it was a bit overcooked at an hour and 20 minutes. Don't open the oven door until the cake has baked at least an hour. Then, because ovens can vary, you can test for doneness.

Because it has the ¼-cup brown sugar and the spices, it is a darker color than the pale yellow of most pound cakes.

I offer you the basic, traditional pound cake after Mrs. Robinson's. Make one, or both, so you will have a large, delicious cake and everyone will ask for seconds at … *Sunday Dinner*.

Kentucky Pound Cake with a Southern Touch

    3 cups self-rising flour

    ½ teaspoon nutmeg

    ½ teaspoon cinnamon

    5 eggs, separated

    3¾ cups sugar

    ¼ cup light brown sugar

    1 tablespoon vanilla extract

1 cup vegetable shortening or oil
½ cup vegetable shortening
1 cup chopped and toasted pecans
1 small can (8¼-oz.) crushed pineapple and juice
   (raisins, coconut optional)

Combine flour, cinnamon and nutmeg; sift and set aside. Beat egg yolks, sugars, and shortening and oil until well mixed. Add flour mixture. Beat at low speed until blended. Add nuts, pineapple and vanilla. Beat egg whites and fold into batter. Pour into prepared tube plan and bake for 1 hour, 15 minutes at 350 degrees. Because ovens can vary, test for doneness after 1 hour. Cool in pan.

Old-Fashioned Pound Cake

1 pound butter (2 cups)
1 pound sifted cake flour (4 cups)
10 eggs, separated
1 pound sugar (2 cups)
1 teaspoon vanilla

Grease two 8x4 loaf pans and line with waxed paper. Preheat oven to 325 degrees. Cream butter, work in flour until mixture is mealy. Beat egg yolks, sugar and vanilla until thick and fluffy. Add the flour mixture to it gradually, beating thoroughly. Fold in stiffly-beaten egg whites. Beat vigorously 5 minutes.

Bake in the two prepared loaf pans in a moderately slow oven (325 degrees) for 1 hour, 15 minutes.

Pineapple Pound Cake
Sisters Alice Plyler Glass, Theresa Plyler Glass, Betty Plyler Ashe
(Published March 8, 2006)

Three sisters worked together to get this cake. The three — plus a whole family.

About 15 years ago, Mary Mackintosh Plyler began a family cookbook. As with many such projects, the response was gradual at first; then, because of certain conditions and her living in Washington State, she couldn't complete the project.

That's when her three sisters-in-law — twins Theresa and Alice Plyler, who married brothers Jim Glass and John Glass, and Betty Plyler Ashe — began work on the collection and printed it in January 2004. The "Plyler Family Favorites" is in its third printing.

All three sisters are active in Baptist churches. For about 30 years, Theresa and Jim Glass have been members of Southside Baptist in Sumter, where Tommy Atkinson is pastor. She is in her 15th year as WMU director and is also on the homebound committee, and her husband, Jim, is a former deacon. They have three children: Jimmie Glass, Patti G. Rogers, and Anna G. Odon.

Alice and her husband, John Glass, are members of Crooked Run Baptist near Winnsboro. She is in charge of meals for the faith ministry team and helps in the church library. Alice and John have two sons, Johnnie and George. Tommy Hutto is the pastor of Crooked Run.

Betty Plyler Ashe, a member of Lowry's Baptist in Chester Association, has taught the ladies Sunday school class for nearly 40 years. She and her late first husband, Albert McKeown, had three sons (Mac, Simmy, and Jimmy) and one daughter, Dorothy — who, with her husband, Everett Burnette, served for a period as missionaries in the Ivory Coast and Senegal in west

Africa. Betty's second husband, Boyd Ashe, is also deceased.

Betty's pastor at Lowry's Baptist is Denver Parker.

Theresa is retired from her position with the Sumter County Department of Social Services, and it was there that she got the pineapple pound cake recipe. Someone brought it to one of their nibbling sessions, she liked it, and asked for the recipe.

We thank Theresa, Alice, Betty and all the Plyler family for sharing, through their cookbook, this recipe with us. It's one you will enjoy. Because of the moistness of the pineapple, this cake is good immediately and, as with other pound cakes, is also good the second and third days. You can decorate it with pineapple slices or leave it plain. Either way, make this good cake Friday or Saturday and have it waiting for ... *Sunday Dinner*.

Pineapple Pound Cake

- 2 sticks (1 cup) butter or margarine
- ½ cup vegetable shortening
- 6 eggs
- 2¾ cups sugar
- 3 cups sifted plain flour
- 1 teaspoon baking powder
- 1 teaspoon vanilla
- 1 cup crushed pineapple (in its own juice, undrained)
- 1¾ cups powdered sugar
- ¼ cup butter or margarine
- ¼ cup crushed pineapple with juice

Have all ingredients at room temperature. Grease and flour tube pan. Preheat oven to 300 degrees. Sift flour, measure, add baking powder, and sift again. Set aside. Mix the 1 cup of butter, vegetable shortening, and sugar to a creamy texture. Add eggs one at a time, mixing after each. Add flour and baking powder. Mix gently with a spoon, then use mixer. Add vanilla, and, last, add pineapple.

Pour batter into prepared pan and bake for 1½ hours. Do not open oven because cake is easy to fall. After 1 hour and 20 minutes, check to see if it is done. When cake is done, cool for a short time — just enough to get cake out of pan. Combine the powdered sugar, ¼ cup butter, and ¼ cup pineapple. Frost the warm cake, covering top and sides.

Note: I buy the 15½-ounce size can of crushed pineapple. Use 1 cup in the cake and the rest in the glaze. You may use an oblong pan, but the 13×9-inch pan is not big enough. I have a 10½x16-inch pan, and I bake the cake in it at 300 degrees for only 50 minutes because it makes a thinner cake. If you use the oblong pan, just leave cake in pan and glaze.

Strawberry Pound Cake

Hazel Merrill

(Published July 2, 2008)

"I have to be there at 8:00 on Saturday," our daughter Gaye explained as she and her sister Elizabeth were trying to work out a running schedule. Gaye wanted to be at her town's farmers' market when the fresh strawberries arrived. She didn't say what her use for the berries would be, but she didn't want to miss them.

Anyway, she thought that fresh strawberries would be good whether in last issue's strawberry pie or today's pound cake. The store-bought berries imported from around the world extend the supply, but the season for fresh, local strawberries is short. Today's recipe can be used with the fresh or frozen berries. As our contributor suggests, the fresh ones can be sliced and sugared and allowed to rest a bit before you make the cake.

It's a good cake. It is also a pretty pink cake, and the recipe is from Mrs. Hazel Merrill, a member of Brandon Baptist Church in West Greenville since 1944. She is currently an assistant teacher for an adult class. Her pastor there is Wilton Maxwell, and the church is in the Greenville Baptist Association.

Mrs. Merrill has had this recipe a long time — so long, she says, that it is yellowed with age but still readable. She clipped it from the old Greenville Piedmont newspaper back in the days when several South Carolina dailies also had afternoon editions. Her recipe from Jan. 17, 1966, had been sent by Mrs. J.G. Mayfield of Lyman. Mrs. Merrill's cousin, Mrs. R.T. Cantrell in Sans Souci, had sent a similar recipe but without the flour and water and increasing the berries to one cup.

Mrs. Merrill and her late husband, John Sr., who died in 1986, had five children. One of them, John Jr., lives in Colorado Springs, and the other four — Jim, Steve, Anne and Phillip and their families — live in the Upstate area.

Hazel has two interests in addition to her church and family. The first is pen pals. Over the years, she has had about 30 or so in a lot of states, including Colorado, Mississippi, New York and Arizona, as well as in England.

Her other interest is calligraphy. She uses this beautifully styled penmanship to write birthday and other greeting cards to friends. Sometimes she uses the special blue ink, which turns a gold color when it is heated and dried. How lovely it must be to get one of Hazel's personally penned cards!

It will also be lovely for you to make Hazel's strawberry pound cake this Saturday, then serve it as a delicious end to ... *Sunday Dinner*.

Strawberry Pound Cake

- 1 18½-ounce package white cake mix
- 1 small package strawberry gelatin
- 4 eggs
- ½ cup water
- ½ cup vegetable oil
- 3 tablespoons flour
- ½ cup sliced strawberries, drained

Grease a tube pan. Preheat oven to 325 degrees. Mix together all the cake ingredients. Pour into prepared pan and bake for 1 hour.

Icing:
- 1 1-lb. box powdered sugar (you may not need the whole box)
- 1 stick (½ cup) butter or margarine, softened to room temperature
- **Juice from berries**

Combine the sugar, butter and juice. Frost cake when cool. (Note: To use fresh strawberries, wash and slice them and add sugar to taste. Allow to sit at least an hour to extract the juice.)

$100 Coconut Cake
The late Dixie Rucker
(Published October 7, 2004)

"Oh, I'm sorry. Mrs. Rucker died about two years ago," said Connie Harling, the administrative assistant at Edgefield First Baptist Church.

Connie had graciously sent me a copy of the church's cookbook, "Sharing Our Best," and in looking through it I had selected and baked Mrs. Dixie Rucker's $100 Coconut Cake. I was calling to get Mrs. Rucker's telephone number and wanted to talk with her. Instead, after hearing the sad news about Mrs. Rucker, I talked with her daughter, Betsy Rucker Martin, who divides her time between Edgefield and Edisto Beach.

I decided that it is such a good recipe that I should use it anyway as a memorial to Mrs. Rucker, and after hearing about her, I think she deserves a lot of memorials for the person she was.

Mrs. Rucker was born in North Carolina and lived her early years there before marrying George Rucker and moving to Edgefield in 1933. She joined the Presbyterian denomination because her husband was that, but later returned to the Baptists and was a member of the Edgefield First Baptist choir.

She and Mr. Rucker had three children: Betsy; George Jr., who lives with his family in Raleigh; and Carolyn, who, with her family, lives in Asheville.

Mrs. Rucker (née Dixie Carriker) worked as a bookkeeper until she was 76, and then her employer had to "buy a computer to replace her." She drove her car until a few months before her death in September 2002 at age 94.

She was active in a lot of things, including being a hospital volunteer, and was involved with a political party that she helped organize in

Edgefield. She received the Order of the Palmetto, the highest honor the state can bestow on a citizen.

Connie, at the church, says Mrs. Rucker was known for her good cooking. After her retirement, she enjoyed making jams, jellies, pickles, chowchow, etc. — which she often gave to friends. She had a recipe for a poison ivy cure that really works, her daughter Betsy said, but Betsy remembers only that it involved St. John's Wort. Betsy says that in her late mother's things there were many recipes she had clipped from newspapers and other places, but she doesn't know where her mother got the recipe for the $100 Coconut Cake.

I don't usually use brand names in the recipes for *Sunday Dinner*. A specific brand would usually be listed "yellow cake mix," for example, and Cool Whip would be called "frozen dessert topping." Ritz crackers would become "butter crackers," etc. — but I am using the brand names in her recipe. In making the cake, I used the white butter recipe cake mix instead of the yellow, and it made a beautiful cake.

I'm sorry I didn't know Mrs. Rucker, but I am happy I can share her cake with you as a memorial. Bake it Saturday, put it in the fridge, and have it ready for ... *Sunday Dinner*.

$100 Coconut Cake

- 1 box Duncan Hines yellow cake mix (butter recipe)
- 2 tablespoons plain flour
- 1½ cups sugar
- 1 8-ounce carton sour cream
- 1 teaspoon almond flavoring
- 2 6-ounce packages frozen coconut
- 1½ cups Cool Whip

Grease and line with waxed paper two 9-inch cake layer pans. Preheat oven to 350 degrees. Mix the cake batter, adding the 2 tablespoons of flour, and bake for 28-33 minutes. Cool, then slice each layer in half horizontally, making four layers.

Mix well the sugar, sour cream and flavoring, then add 1½ packs of the coconut to the sugar mixture. Mix well and put this filling between the layers only. Combine remaining ½ package of coconut with the Cool Whip, and frost sides and top of cake. Put in refrigerator overnight to chill.

Pineapple Cake
Annie Frances Blackman
(Published November 13, 2007)

Today's recipe is from a dear friend of a half-century. Annie Frances Blackman was one of the first persons I met when my Ed and I married and I moved to our community.

Annie Frances and I have been friends, neighbors, and fellow church members all these years in Anderson at Welcome Baptist Church, where William West is pastor. The church is in Saluda Baptist Association.

Annie Frances is an absolute pillar at Welcome — as was her late mother, Fannie Sue Blackman, who was WMU leader for many years; her late sister, Ethel Fred Bishop, who also filled that role; and her brother-in-law, Willard Bishop. Since joining Welcome in 1944, Annie Frances, a soft-spoken person, has held many positions in the church. For many years, she was in the choir, was YWA leader, helped with GA coronations, taught Sunday school, and was a leader of WMU (a job she still has). During these years, she has served on a lot of committees.

Annie Frances attended Anderson and Winthrop colleges. Her

master's degree in library science is from Florida State University. For many years, she did library work in the public schools, then at Anderson's public library — until she accepted a position as librarian at Anderson College. She was there 19 years until her retirement.

She spends a lot of time reading. When she worked in a library with all those wonderful books, she explains, there was no time to read. Now she is catching up. She also enjoys knitting. She likes growing flowers, and she and her late sister always had beautiful plants at the family home. She still does much of that, frequently contributing flowers for the church.

Annie Frances has a reputation as a good cook. She doesn't recall where she got the pineapple cake recipe, but has had it a long time, coming across it again recently. She now makes it often because it's simple and easily put together; one doesn't have to get out the mixer. She says the nuts can be omitted if anyone in your family is allergic to them. We thank her for sharing this good recipe with us. It will be one you'll use.

"The cake is better after it sits in the fridge for a few days," she says, suggesting that you "make it about the middle of the week and it will be just right for … *Sunday Dinner.*"

Pineapple Cake

    2 eggs

    1 20-ounce can crushed pineapple, undrained

    2 cups all purpose flour

    1 cup white sugar

    1 cup brown sugar

    2 teaspoons baking soda

    1 cup chopped nuts

By hand, beat the two eggs till light and fluffy. Add the crushed pineapple, 2 cups of flour, the sugars, and soda. Mix well by hand, then stir in the 1 cup of nuts. Spread in an ungreased 13x9x2 baking pan and bake at 350 degrees for about 30-35 minutes, or until done. Remove from oven and let cake cool completely.

Cream Cheese-Ginger Frosting

1 3-ounce package cream cheese, room temperature
¼ cup butter or margarine, room temperature
1 teaspoon vanilla
2 cups powdered sugar, sifted
½ teaspoon ground ginger
Chopped nuts

To make frosting, beat together the softened cream cheese, butter and vanilla; then gradually add the powdered sugar and ginger. Spread on cake; sprinkle a few chopped nuts on top. Because of the pineapple and cream cheese, the cake is best stored in the refrigerator.

Blackberry Jam Cake with Caramel Icing
Connie Whitten
(Published June 5, 2013)

All the ingredients were on hand, and I was looking forward to baking and eating Connie Whitten's blackberry jam cake when the sock-matching situation came up.

I know there won't be any such thing as this in heaven because we will all be rejoicing to be in God's presence. But, if by chance there is, and I am put in the area dedicated to matching socks for the angels, I am going to be really, really mad about the whole thing.

It all started when our oldest child, Gaye, was an infant wearing the little white socks. Since then it has been baby socks, children's socks, athletic socks, argyle socks, stretch socks, dress socks, and now with the children all gone we are down to my Ed's socks. There is always a pile to be matched, and in this pile there are always socks that have no matches. Many predate home computers, certain countries, several presidents and frozen dinners. The Great Mystery of our time is, "Where do socks go?"

The thriftiness in me won't permit my tossing the unmatched ones because maybe someday, somewhere from under the washer, in a never-opened drawer, or in the dust cloth bag, the mates will appear. But until that happens I'll make Connie's cake.

Connie is a member of Columbia Baptist Church in Princeton, part of the Palmetto Association. The pastor is Rev. Scottie Hendricks, who has been with them about three years. He'll have to stay a while longer to help celebrate the church's 200th anniversary in 2015.

Connie, retired from BASF, grew up in the church and works with both the youth and the senior adults. She enjoys playing the organ and the piano, and serves as the assistant at church when needed. When asked about her interests, her reply was that she enjoys helping people.

The recipe she has shared with us is an old one, says Connie, who got it from her great aunt, Bessie Davis, on her father's side of the family. Connie makes it every Christmas and suggests that this recipe will bring back a lot of memories not only for her family but also for yours. It makes a large cake; I baked it using three cake pans, and they were full. Don't wait until Christmas; carry this cake to family gatherings this summer.

Although her Aunt Bessie's recipe, like many old recipes, doesn't give many instructions, I mixed it as I do most cakes: creaming the sugar and butter, adding the eggs one at a time, adding the jam, sifting together the flour and spices and adding alternately with the buttermilk. I tested it after it baked 30 minutes, then added another five or so until the toothpick came out clean.

Start the caramel icing as soon as you put the layers in the oven. It takes a long time to cook. Using a fork, Connie punches holes in the first layer and spreads on a third of the icing, then repeats with layers two and three. Some of the icing will dribble over the sides.

The cake is best if it sits, covered, a day before serving. We thank Connie and her Aunt Bessie for sharing this good cake with us to enjoy for any occasion, and especially when you have a crowd for ... *Sunday Dinner*.

Blackberry Jam Cake
- 2 cups sugar
- 6 eggs
- 1 cup buttermilk
- 2 teaspoons cinnamon
- 2 teaspoons baking soda in the milk
- 1 cup butter or lard
- 2 cups blackberry jam
- 2 teaspoons cloves
- ½ teaspoon nutmeg
- 4 cups plain flour

Grease and flour pans. Bake at 300 degrees until done. Makes 2 large layers or 3 small layers.

Caramel Icing

½ teaspoon nutmeg

1 cup milk

2 cups sugar

½ stick butter

Cook on low until thick. Spread on cake while cake is still warm.

Lemon Berry Cake
Dot Edmunds
(Published July 1, 2004)

"What is that?" asked 5-year-old grandson Garrison, looking at the glass baking dish of cake batter as I sprinkled on the blueberries.

"It's a recipe for the Courier," I explained. "I'm making this for the church supper tonight."

"Has somebody ever cooked this before?" he asked. I felt the same way when I poured the lemon gelatin over the batter and blueberries.

When the cake was baked, sprinkled with powdered sugar, topped with a dollop of dessert topping and then sampled, our doubts were gone. It was different and delicious.

Today's recipes are from Dot Edmunds and make use of fresh blueberries that are now available. I think everyone who has a little piece of land should have a couple or three blueberry bushes — and if you don't, then buy the berries. They are good eaten out-of-hand or in many recipes, and are good for you.

Dot and her husband, Alton, have been members of Hagood Avenue

Baptist Church in Barnwell for six years. In the past, she has taught Sunday school, and her husband helps with anything when asked but doesn't have a regular church job. Ken Catoe is the church pastor.

Dot was born in Lincolnton, Ga., and lived in Charlotte a while, but has made South Carolina home for 36 years — first in Spartanburg, then in Barnwell when Alton's job took them there. They have four children: Brooke White in Taylorsville, N.C.; Debbie Horton in Spartanburg; Jane Folk in Barnwell; and Terrell Edmunds in Hickory, N.C.

Dot has been a seamstress all her life, although she is trying to retire. People keep coming to her for projects, and she usually helps. She has just about decided to go back to the work full-time, though, because she misses seeing her customers. She likes all kinds of sewing, especially wedding clothes, and enjoyed making the wedding dresses and christening gowns for her daughters and granddaughters.

Some time ago, she and some of the women at Hagood Avenue Baptist made a 20-by-32-foot American flag for a patriotic program at the church. That was a big project.

Dot also enjoys cooking and, as many good cooks do, likes trying new recipes. She has a tendency, though, to "rearrange" them, as she calls it — either to improve the taste or because she lacks one of the ingredients. Sometimes she creates recipes. She remembers seeing a recipe similar to Lemon Berry Cake somewhere, but can't recall when or where, so she just put this one together.

Lemon Berry Cake can be served either warm or cold. Dot suggests adding whipped topping, but says it is also good with whipped cream or ice cream. However you top it, plan to make Lemon Berry Cake soon for ... *Sunday Dinner.*

Lemon Berry Cake

    1 1-pound, 2.25-ounce box yellow cake mix
    1 tablespoon grated lemon peel
    2 cups fresh blueberries
    1 6-ounce package lemon gelatin
    1½ cups boiling water
    Sifted confectioners' sugar
    2 8-ounce cartons frozen whipped topping, thawed

Wash, stem, and pat dry the blueberries. Set aside. Grease and flour a 9x13 baking pan or dish according to cake mix directions. Preheat oven to 350 degrees. Mix the cake according to package directions, adding the lemon peel during mixing. Pour into the prepared baking dish. Sprinkle the blueberries on the batter.

Stir the gelatin in the boiling water until dissolved, then pour over the batter and berries. Bake about 35 minutes. Cool slightly and dust with powdered sugar. With a spoon, scoop cake into a serving dish and top with the whipped topping. Serves 12 to 15.

Lemon Cheesecake
Permelia Creamer
(Published December 9, 2010)

Everyone loved her, and a year after her death, the women of Barker's Creek Baptist Church collected and printed her recipes.

    Permelia Creamer and her husband, the Rev. Randy Creamer, came to Barker's Creek in Honea Path in the early 1990s and were there until around 2005. The Creamers then moved to Atlanta, where he was (and still is) with the North American Mission Board. When they had been there three years or so, Permelia became ill and died in June 2008.

Most church members love their pastor and his family, and this was the case with the Creamers. They had two sons. Jason and his wife, Melesa, have a son Mack and live in Florence. David Creamer lives in Anderson.

Permelia loved to cook, recalls Kathy Kay, a member of Barker's Creek. Permelia would frequently host the youth and the Acteens and often carried food to people — not only to those who were ill, but to other groups also, Kathy remembers. She also loved flowers. Permelia was the daughter of Mack and Frances Mauldin.

The Rev. Wesley Taylor is currently pastor at Barker's Creek, which is in the Saluda Baptist Association. There are around 300 members, with about 200 active in the church's programs.

Both the Creamers, who always had a "servant heart" for missions, were involved with disaster relief — first in South Carolina, then with the North American Mission Board. Rev. Creamer is still with the program.

"The Favorite Recipes of Permelia Creamer" was printed last year, and the profits from it are given for cancer research.

The high regard the congregation had for Permelia Creamer should be an example for all of us here during the Christmas season. So when you make Permelia's recipe for lemon cheesecake, let it be a reminder to you to remember your pastor and his family.

You'll also like this pretty dessert, which, because of its lightness, is a good choice for all year. Its lightness is especially appreciated during the cake-and-pie season of the holidays. Near Christmas, garnish it with a green and a red maraschino cherry, a tiny triangle of lemon, etc. It can be easily doubled, made two or three days ahead, kept in the fridge, and be ready for you to enjoy any weekend after church for ... *Sunday Dinner.*

Lemon Cheesecake

    1 4-ounce package lemon gelatin

    3 tablespoons lemon juice

    1¼ cups sugar

    1 large 12-ounce can evaporated milk

    2 cups graham cracker crumbs

    1 cup boiling water

    1 8-ounce package cream cheese

    1 teaspoon vanilla

    1 stick margarine or butter

Mix together the gelatin, boiling water and lemon juice. Chill to syrupy stage. Put can of milk in freezer to get very cold. Cream together cheese, sugar and vanilla. Whip the can of milk, then beat with mixture of cheese and gelatin.

Melt butter or margarine and pour over cracker crumbs. Line a 13×9-inch pan with crumbs, reserving some of the crumbs, and pour in the cheese mixture. Sprinkle with the reserved crumbs. Refrigerate until serving time. Serves 6-8.

Eclair Cake
Earleen Kastner
(Published May 21, 2008)

Today's recipe is a great one for summer. It has three things going for it: 1) easy to prepare, 2) can be made ahead of the time you need it, and 3) good taste. This recipe has been around for a while, and I suspect it came from the Cool Whip test kitchen.

This eclair cake is just the thing for the outdoor meals you'll be serving with the warm weather's arrival, whether at a patio party at your house or at a family gathering.

The recipe is from Earleen Kastner of West Gantt First Baptist Church in Greenville, where Danny Burnley is pastor.

Earleen, retired from Allstate Insurance, and her husband, Ernest, retired from insulation work, have two children. Their son Jim has three children, and their son Ernest Jr. and his wife, Susan, have one son.

Earleen has been a member of West Gantt First Baptist for 51 years. Currently, she is in the choir and has held offices in her Sunday school class and in the Young at Heart group. Now that she is retired, she enjoys crafts — making quilts as well as crocheted and knitted items, which she shares as gifts.

The eclair cake recipe, which she has used for several years, came from her sister-in-law in California. The cake should be refrigerated, but will be all right at room temperature for a while if you are transporting it.

If you want an easy-to-prepare and good-to-eat dessert this weekend, make this on Saturday and you, your family, and guests will all say how good it is at … *Sunday Dinner*.

Eclair Cake

    2 small boxes French vanilla instant pudding mix

    3½ cups milk

    9 ounces thawed dessert topping

    Graham crackers, as many as needed

    3 tablespoons milk

    4 tablespoons butter or margarine

1½ cups powdered sugar
4 tablespoons cocoa
1 teaspoon vanilla extract

In a 9×13 pan, place a layer of graham crackers close together. Mix the instant pudding and milk, until thick, then fold in the thawed dessert topping. Spread half of this on the crackers, top with another layer of crackers and then the remaining pudding mix. Top with a final layer of crackers. Cool in fridge about 2 hours.

To make the glaze, heat the butter, milk and vanilla; then add the powdered sugar and cocoa. Heat until it boils, stirring until thickened. Pour on top of the "cake" and refrigerate until firm.

Honey Bun Cake
Sharon Tuttle
(Published March 31, 2011)

We have Sharon Tuttle of New Salem Baptist Church in Sumter to thank for this. New Salem was organized in the mid-1970s as an offshoot of Salem Avenue Baptist in Sumter and currently has 327 members.

Rev. Robert Rivers has pastored this Santee Baptist Association church for 12 years. New Salem has a full range of Southern Baptist programs: Sunday worship, Sunday school, church training, WMU, Brotherhood, etc.

Sharon has been part of this all her life. She and her husband, John, an employee of Unifirst Uniform Co., have been members a long time. Currently, Sharon teaches the 3-to-5-year-olds in Sunday school and the same age group in church training. She is in the mission prayer circle and a member of the church choir.

She retired some time ago after working with the Winn-Dixie supermarket chain for 35 years. Now she works part-time two days a week at one of Sumter's post office stations.

She and her husband have been enthusiastic NASCAR followers for a long time and often went to races. Now most of their NASCAR watching is not from the grandstand but from comfortable chairs in front of the TV.

Another project Sharon enjoys is cake-baking and decorating, and she is the official baker-of-the-cake for any family function. This honey bun cake doesn't require any decorating and is easily put together. She got this recipe from a friend years ago and makes it frequently. I think you will also.

The cake is easily assembled, so make it early Sunday morning. Let it bake while you study your Sunday school lesson, then have this warm, delicious honey bun cake for breakfast instead of … *Sunday Dinner*.

Honey Bun Cake

- 1 box yellow cake mix
- ⅔ cup oil (canola, corn, etc.)
- ½ cup sugar
- 4 eggs
- 1 cup sour cream
- 1 cup brown sugar
- 3 teaspoons cinnamon
- 2 cups 4x confectioners' sugar
- 2 teaspoons vanilla
- 4 tablespoons milk

Preheat oven to 325 degrees. Grease a 9×13-inch baking pan. In a large bowl, beat the eggs; then add the oil, sugar and sour cream, and mix well.

Add the cake mix; stir to mix well. Pour half the mixture into the prepared pan. Mix together the sugar and cinnamon and spread half over the batter in the pan.

Pour on the remaining cake batter, then cover with remaining sugar mix. Use a knife blade to make swirls in the batter. Bake 35 minutes in preheated oven. Cake will fall in middle when it is removed from oven. Mix the confectioners' sugar, vanilla and milk for a glaze. Pour over the warm cake. Serve warm. Makes 12-18 servings.

The Best Fruitcake

Barbara Massengale

(Published November 3, 2005)

Today's recipe is from Barbara Massengale of Mauldin. She has been a member of Cross Roads Baptist Church in Greer Association since she was saved at age 12. Mike Sheehan is the pastor. She sent the recipe last December, but I was too deep into December to use it then.

This week I received from our daughter Elizabeth in Greenville a funny note she sent following my last column about stocking the pantry. She had enclosed a copy of the comic strip "Cathy" about using leftovers in the fridge. I told Barbara about this, and we discovered we both keep stuff in the fridge perhaps longer than necessary. I think Elizabeth was suggesting that I be more specific and should have said to stock the pantry, fridge, and freezer with "new stuff."

Anyway, about the fruitcake. Barbara says it is easy and goooood. Barbara retired about four years ago from working 23 years in education at the Greenville Hospital System. She was in a near-fatal automobile accident, but after many surgeries, therapy, and being wheelchair-bound for a year, she is up and about now and active at Cross Roads Baptist.

One of her biggest jobs is program director for the seniors group, the Young at Heart. She is also on the outreach, public relations, and homebound ministry committees, and teaches the senior adult ladies Sunday school class.

Barbara and her late husband, Thomas, who died four years ago, have five sons: Randy, Ricky, Roger, Robbie and Rusty. They all have families and live nearby — except Rusty, who is in the Navy. He and his family live in Hawaii. Barbara visited them for two months this year and said they visited many churches, but her favorite was the military chapel at Waikiki, where she met Christians from all over the world.

Barbara says this is an old family recipe she has had for many years. Unlike many fruitcake recipes, which say to store for a while before using, this one can be sliced as soon as it is cool, and it usually doesn't last very long! It's good not only for Christmas, she says, but also for anytime and for any ... *Sunday Dinner.*

The Best Fruitcake

    1 jar (quart size) mincemeat
    1 14-ounce can sweetened condensed milk
    1 pound candied cherries (red and green mixed, or all one color)
    1 cup coarsely chopped pecans or walnuts
    2 eggs
    2½ cups self-rising flour

Heat oven to 300 degrees. Grease and flour a tube cake pan. Beat eggs slightly; add milk, then flour. Mix well. Add all other ingredients and stir well. Pour into the prepared cake pan and cook for 1 hour. Remove from oven and let cool in pan. Turn onto serving plate. Allow to cool thoroughly before slicing.

White Fruitcake
(Published December 13, 2007)

Fruitcakes, the traditional Christmas food, have been given a bad name unjustly.

People start with a poor recipe, don't do a very good job of baking it, then let the cake dry to the point that it is tasteless, hard, and crumbly. Well, you can see why the masses are not demanding fruitcake.

Bake this cake a few weeks before Christmas if you can. This is optional, but pour over it about a fourth-cup of orange or apple juice. Wrap the cake in waxed paper and put it in a tin or keep it tightly wrapped in aluminum foil until serving.

Today's recipe for white fruitcake was given to me way, way back when I first began housekeeping and home-cooking by Irene King, a neighbor and friend of my late mother in my hometown.

In addition to having a good taste, the cake is very pretty when served in slices on a glass plate. The bright colors of the cherries and pineapple don't get lost among raisins, figs, and other things the dark fruitcake recipes require.

A similar recipe I found in an old cookbook, even older than I am, suggested using a half-cup of white raisins and one cup of moist grated coconut. I haven't tried that, but I may.

Whatever recipe you use, make this white fruitcake for Christmas to serve a drop-in guest or for a great ending for any … *Sunday Dinner*.

White Fruitcake

    5 large eggs, well beaten
    ½ pound butter
    1 cup white sugar
    1 cup all-purpose flour
    ½ teaspoon baking powder
    ¾ pound glazed cherries
    1 pound glazed pineapple
    4 cups shelled pecans, coarsely broken
    ½ ounce bottle pure vanilla
    ½ ounce bottle pure lemon extract

Grease, flour, and line with waxed paper a tube pan or one or two loaf pans, depending on size. Cream butter, add sugar and cream thoroughly. Add the beaten eggs and blend. Sift together the flour and baking powder. Sprinkle ¾ cup of the flour over the fruit and nuts. Add these with the remaining 1 cup of flour to the butter mixture.

Add the lemon and vanilla flavoring and fold until well mixed. Pour mixture into the prepared pan. Place in a cold oven. Turn oven to 250 degree and bake for 3 hours. Cake will keep for two months.

Japanese Fruitcake
Requested by Jo Hammond
(Published March 14, 2008)

"Don't make that one," our daughter Gaye said. "No one likes it."

    We were discussing the dessert cake I would make for visitors to our house after we had eaten dinner at a restaurant.

"Mrs. Hammond likes it," I answered, "because she has asked for the recipe."

We were talking about a Japanese fruitcake, and I grant that Gaye is correct when, at Christmas time, it is sitting between a caramel cake and a fresh coconut cake, the Japanese Fruitcake is the third chosen. It's a good cake, though, but I don't know where it gets its name, because the only fruits in it are coconut and lemons — none of the candied cherries, citron, etc., usually associated with Christmastime fruitcake.

Mrs. Jo Hammond had written in November (yes, November), asking for the recipe, and her letter got lost in "the stack" — so here I am with apologies.

Jo is a member of Spring Branch Baptist Church in Nichols. Paul Alverson Jr. is the current transitional pastor, and the church is in Waccamaw Baptist Association. A small to medium church, they average around 88 in Sunday school, Jo said.

She has been a member of Spring Branch since she married in 1948. Her late husband, Thelbert Hammond, died in 1989, and since then Jo has lived alone.

She has always had a role in the church program. For about 10 years or so, she taught the junior class in Sunday school, then spent another 10 years with the nursery group. She also served on the church's social committee and enjoyed that.

Now, at 83, she doesn't do as much. She attends Sunday school and church, and she and a group of friends regularly go out for lunch or dinner. She formerly enjoyed doing various crafts, but doesn't do much of that now.

Her mother used to make a Japanese fruitcake, she said, but without a recipe. The times Jo tried to make the cake, her relatives were quick to say that "it doesn't taste like Mother's."

Maybe this one will, and she (and you) can bake this one Saturday and have it all ready and waiting for ... *Sunday Dinner.*

Japanese Fruitcake

- 1 cup butter, room temperature
- 2 cups sugar
- 3 cups all-purpose or cake flour
- 4 teaspoons baking powder
- ¾ teaspoon salt
- 4 eggs
- 1 cup milk
- 1 teaspoon vanilla flavoring
- 1 teaspoon each of ground allspice, ground cinnamon, ground cloves, cocoa

Grease and line with waxed paper three 9-inch cake pans. Preheat oven to 350 degrees. Sift flour. Measure, add baking powder and salt, and sift again. Set aside. Separate egg yolks and whites. Beat whites until soft peaks form. Set aside.

Cream butter until soft. Gradually add the sugar, beating until well creamed with the butter. Add the egg yolks and beat until well blended. Add vanilla flavoring and mix. The butter-sugar-egg beating should take about 8 to 10 minutes.

Gradually add the flour alternately with the milk. Remove mixer beaters and fold in the egg whites. (If you prefer, don't separate the eggs, but add them one at a time to the butter-sugar mixture.) Divide the batter into thirds, placing ⅓ in each of two of the prepared pans. To the remaining ⅓ batter, add the allspice, cinnamon, cloves and cocoa, and mix well. Add to the third prepared pan.

Bake about 30-35 minutes until the layers test done. Put together with the frosting below, placing the spice-cocoa layer in the middle.

This frosting is more of a glaze than a frosting. Spread it between the three layers and on top, letting it run down the sides, or use it to frost the sides also.

Frosting/Glaze:
1 fresh coconut, grated, or 2 6-oz. packages frozen coconut
2 whole lemons, grated (using both juice and rind)
2 cups sugar
3 tablespoons flour
1 cup boiling water

Combine in a saucepan and cook until thickened and clear.

Pie Crusts

(Published April 28, 2009)

Yes, I buy them and I use them and I love them. I'm talking about pie crusts, both those bought in a roll and those in the aluminum pie pans. But not always. Every cook should, I believe, know how to make a good pie crust or pastry.

Today we are looking at several pie crusts, depending on the kind of pie you are making.

The basic pie crust recipe includes flour, a fat, salt, and ice water. The usual ratio is ⅓ cup of fat to 1 cup of flour. Use the plain, all-purpose flour.

The fat can be butter, lard, vegetable shortening, cooking oil, or a mixture. I use lard, which makes a flaky crust.

The water should be icy cold, and one way to insure this is to put ice cubes in the cup with the water.

Handle the crust as little as you can to get it mixed. Have the solid fat cold; then, using a pastry blender, quickly cut it into the flour. Consider rolling the pastry on a flour-dusted cloth instead of directly on the kitchen counter. Your pie crust may be easier to handle if you wrap it in waxed paper and refrigerate it for a few hours. When placing the crust into the pie plate, let it fit loosely; don't stretch it. Roll the excess up or under the edges, and crimp it with your fingers to make a little wall to hold the filling.

Whether you need a pie crust for a meat, fruit, key lime, or chocolate cream pie, you'll be glad you chose the best pie crust for ... *Sunday Dinner*.

Plain Pastry

    1½ cups plain flour
    ½ teaspoon salt
    ½ cup shortening
    4 tablespoons cold water (about)

Sift together the flour and salt, and work in the shortening (lard, butter, etc.) Pour the cold water around edge of bowl, mixing to make a dough that just stays together. Chill (or not); then roll into shape. Makes a double crust.

For a single crust, use 1 cup flour, ¼ teaspoon salt, ⅓ cup shortening, 2 to 3 tablespoons water. (A similar recipe for a double crust suggests 3 cups all-purpose flour, 1 teaspoon salt, 1 teaspoon baking powder, 1 cup lard, ice water to mix.)

For cheese pastry, add 1 cup grated cheese to mix before adding the water.

Hot Water Pastry

- ¼ cup boiling water
- 1½ cups flour
- ¼ teaspoon baking powder
- ½ cup shortening
- ½ teaspoon salt

Stir together salt, flour and baking powder. Set aside. Pour the boiling water over the shortening (or lard, butter, etc.) and stir until fat is melted, smooth, and thick. Stir in the flour mixture. Chill before using.

Quick Coconut Crust

- ¼ cup melted butter
- 2 cups canned flaked coconut

Combine the butter and coconut and press evenly in an ungreased 8- or 9-inch pie plate. Bake at 300 degrees for 25-35 minutes until golden brown. Cool. Fill with ice cream; serve immediately. Can be used for chiffon or gelatin filling.

Graham Cracker Crust

- 1½ cups graham cracker crumbs
- 6 tablespoons melted butter

½ cup sifted confectioners' sugar
1 teaspoon cinnamon (optional)

Combine all ingredients. Press into pie plate and bake at 350 degrees for 10 minutes. Cool before filling. Makes one 9-inch crust.

Fresh Apple Pie
Joyce Tonroy
(Published February 16, 2012)

When we think of icons for America, we think of our beautiful flag, Girl Scout cookies, and apple pie.

Every cook has one of the latter, and most have more than one. These apple pies come in many forms. There are two-crust pies, pies with sprinkle-on topping, deep-dish pies, apple pie turnovers, etc. When you try today's recipe, you may decide to adopt it as the one you use all the time.

It is good, and it is from Joyce Tonroy of Crescent Hill Baptist Church in Columbia, where the Rev. Dr. Fred Miller Jr. is serving as interim pastor.

Joyce and her husband, Jerry, have been members of Crescent Hill around 15 years or so, following his coming here from Indiana to work at Fort Jackson. After his retirement, they stayed in the Columbia area, and their son Matthew and his wife, Stephanie, now live with them.

The Tonroys enjoy their retirement by visiting the zoo in Columbia, cooking, doing some work with flowers, etc. Their greatest interest, however, is Crescent Hill, where they attend Sunday school and both morning and evening services, and are part of the Young in Heart group.

Joyce doesn't know who Dee Stoughton is, but she remembers where she got the recipe. In October 1983, she was in a barber shop for young Matthew to get a haircut and she saw this recipe in a copy of the Indianapolis Monthly. She copied it, used it, later brought it with her to South Carolina, and has kept her original copy ever since.

This is a good pie, but it is somewhat different from the usual apple pie. It doesn't make smooth, even slices — and the apples are more crisp than in most pies. It is a good keeper, if there is any left!

One Saturday soon, make this pie. You will thank both Dee Stoughton, whoever and wherever she is, and Joyce as you enjoy one (or two) slices for … *Sunday Dinner*.

Dee Stoughton's Fresh Apple Pie

Crust:
1 cup plus 2 tablespoons flour
⅓ cup corn oil
½ teaspoon salt
2 tablespoons water

Preheat oven to 475 degrees. Mix flour, salt, oil and water. Form into a ball and roll between 2 sheets of waxed paper to form a circle. Put into the pie pan and bake 10 minutes.

Filling:
1 cup white sugar
½ teaspoon cinnamon
4-5 cups apples
¼ cup flour
1 cup milk

Combine flour, sugar, cinnamon and milk, and mix until smooth. Peel, core and slice apples. Arrange apples on cooked pie crust. Pour flour-sugar mixture over apples.

Topping:
½ **cup brown sugar**
½ **cup flour**
⅓ **stick butter**

In a small saucepan, melt the butter. Add sugar and flour, and stir until butter is melted and mixture is smooth (may need to add a teaspoon of water). Pour evenly over apples. Bake at 350 degrees for 30 minutes.

Fresh Strawberry Pie
Bessie Chamblee family cookbook, "Recipes & Memories," Providence Baptist Church, Anderson County
(Published August 25, 2005)

I found it!

Remember in the latest issue we talked about the unidentified writer who wanted recipes for lemon meringue, peanut butter, and strawberry pies? This is for her.

The recipe, Fresh Strawberry Pie, comes from the cookbook "Recipes & Memories," published by the Bessie Chamblee family of Providence Baptist Church in Saluda Baptist Association, Anderson County. The book, begun on Bessie Smith Chamblee's 100 birthday by her family and friends, took a year to complete. The family has given the book to the church, and all income from the book sales goes to the church. Mrs. Chamblee will celebrate her 102nd birthday in November.

She is the daughter of the late Steve and Minnie Smith of Fair Play in Oconee County, where she grew up. Mrs. Chamblee's late husband, Roger, died in the 1950s, and up until a few years ago, Mrs. Chamblee lived in their Anderson County home. She was an active member of Providence Baptist Church, enjoyed flower gardening and cooking, and was well loved in her community. She continued to drive until she was 91. She and Mr. Chamblee had three daughters: JoAnn McCaskill of Bishopville; Dorothy Powell of Knoxville, Tenn.; and the late Nancy Tooley of Greer.

For a while, as she got along in years, Mrs. Chamblee lived at Anderson Place in Anderson, but seven years ago she moved to Townsend Terrace Retirement Home in Bishopville to be near her daughter JoAnn and her husband, Laverne McCaskill. The McCaskills have three children: Nancy Lee Watson, Dr. Al McCaskill, and Clara Ann McIlhaney. Pastor Dale Warren of Bishopville First Baptist Church visits Townsend Terrace regularly for Mrs. Chamblee and others to participate in the ordinance of the Lord's Supper.

JoAnn said her mother always liked fresh fruits and vegetables, and all the recipes in the book are "tried and true." As she has gotten older, Mrs. Chamblee especially likes sweets, and this pie is one of her favorites. I, too, liked this pie.

The reason, I think, that one doesn't see as many recipes for baked strawberry pies as for peach, blueberry, etc., is that when the strawberries are baked, they become "smushy" — a non-dictionary word that we all understand.

This is a pretty pie with its flavorful crust, red filling, and white whipped cream topping. Make it on Saturday and have it chilled and ready for ... *Sunday Dinner*.

Fresh Strawberry Pie

Strawberry Filling
1 cup crushed strawberries
¾ cup water
1 cup sugar
2½ tablespoons cornstarch
1½ quarts fresh strawberries, sliced
Whipped cream

Crust
½ cup butter
1 cup all-purpose flour
¼ cup light brown sugar
⅓ cup chopped pecans

Heat oven to 375 degrees. Blend butter, flour and sugar until crumbs form. Stir in the chopped nuts and press mixture into a 9-inch pie plate. Bake about 15 minutes until golden brown. Cool.

Filling: Crush 1 cup strawberries. In small saucepan, combine berries, water, sugar and cornstarch. Cook stirring until mixture thickens and loses its cloudy color. Cool.

Slice the 1½ quarts of strawberries and arrange them in the baked pie shell. Pour over them the cooled strawberry glaze. Cover with waxed paper and chill. Serve topped with whipped cream. Makes 6 to 10 servings.

Coconut Pies
Susie Garrison
(Published March 25, 2004)

I found it!

Yea, diligently had I searched to and fro, hither and yon, up and down. The object of my search was a recipe for "old-fashioned" coconut pie. A few weeks ago, a reader wrote, asking for such a recipe, and I knew I had it … somewhere. The writer did not give her name, church, or town — but this column is for you, wherever you are.

I like cookbooks, especially old ones, and buy them whenever I come across them. I especially like those in which the previous owner has written her own recipes or included clippings from newspapers, magazines, etc.

Today I am offering three kinds of coconut pie: plain baked, cream, and custard. (I think the first recipe below is the one our reader wants.)

The recipe for Susie's Baked Coconut Pie was given to me by cousin-in-law, Susie Garrison, many years ago. Susie and her late husband, Paul, joined Welcome Baptist Church in Anderson County in 1932, moving to the community from Seneca. Paul was rejoining because he had attended Welcome when young.

Susie is from the Price family in Seneca, and during the 70 years that she has been active at Welcome, she has taught Sunday school, helped with VBS and training union, and served as secretary of her WMU Circle.

In more recent years, she has been a member of the Ethel Fred Bishop Sunday School Class. Susie is the oldest member of the church and is much loved by all who know her.

Susie has two, Jimmy Garrison and Betty Garrison McClellan.

Let us keep it our little secret that I used purchased pie shells, and you'll need the deep-dish ones to hold all the filling.

Both the coconut custard and the baked coconut pies can be served with a dollop of whipped cream, which, of course, improves everything. Let all the pies cool to room temperature, then refrigerate so they will be chilled and ready for … *Sunday Dinner*.

Baked Coconut Pie

　　3 eggs
　　1½ cups sugar
　　¼ cup buttermilk
　　1 cup or 1 3.5-ounce can flaked coconut
　　¼ pound butter, melted
　　1 teaspoon vanilla
　　1 unbaked pie shell

Preheat oven to 300 degrees. Combine all ingredients and pour into the pie shell. Bake for 1 hour.

Susie's Baked Coconut Pie

　　1¼ cups sugar
　　2 heaping tablespoons plain flour
　　Pinch of salt
　　1 egg, beaten
　　2 tablespoons butter, melted
　　1 teaspoon vanilla
　　1 3.5-ounce can flaked coconut
　　2 cups whole milk
　　1 unbaked pie shell

Preheat oven to 325 degrees. Combine all ingredients and pour into pie shell. Bake at 325 degrees for 25 minutes, then increase heat to 450 degrees and bake until brown.

Coconut Custard Pie

    4 eggs, slightly beaten
    ¼ teaspoon salt
    ½ cup sugar
    3 cups milk, scalded
    ½ teaspoon vanilla
    1 cup shredded coconut
    1 unbaked pastry shell
    Nutmeg

Preheat oven to 450 degrees. Scald the milk. Combine eggs, salt and sugar; add milk and vanilla slowly. Sprinkle the coconut on the pastry shell, then slowly pour over it the milk-egg mixture. Sprinkle lightly with nutmeg.

    Bake at 450 degrees for 10 minutes, then reduce temperature to 325 degrees and bake 30 to 40 minutes, or until a knife comes out clean when inserted into the filling.

Coconut Cream Pie

    1 baked pie shell
    2 cups scalded milk
    1 cup shredded coconut
    ⅞ cup granulated sugar
    ⅓ cup flour

⅛ teaspoon salt
2 eggs
1 teaspoon vanilla
½ teaspoon lemon extract
2 tablespoons powdered sugar
1-2 tablespoons coconut (optional)

Scald the milk in top of a double boiler, add coconut. Remove from heat. Mix together the flour, sugar and salt. Separate eggs and save whites for meringue. Beat yolks and add to the flour mixture. Then pour flour-egg mixture into the hot milk and replace top of double boiler over the hot water in the bottom of double boiler.

Cook about 15 minutes, stirring until thickened. Remove from heat and add the flavorings. Pour into the baked shell. (To make meringue, beat the egg whites until stiff, gradually adding the powdered sugar until all is used.) Cover pie with meringue and bake in slow oven (300 degrees) until light brown. If desired, sprinkle with coconut before browning.

Coconut Peach Pie
Mary Herman
(Published August 21, 2006)

The season for fresh South Carolina peaches is near its end, so we should enjoy them as long as we can. Peaches will still be available in stores, of course, but the almost tree-ripened ones from local orchards will be gone.

Today's recipe is a delicious use of fresh peaches. It is also a pretty dish, one that will cause your family and/or guests to say "ahhhhh" when they see it.

Mary Herman of Greer is sharing her recipe for coconut peach pie. She and her husband, John, are members of Mt. Lebanon Baptist Church in Greer Association. Their pastor is Mark Smith. Mary joined Mt. Lebanon 58 years ago, soon after she and John married.

They celebrated their 58th anniversary this past February, and last month they celebrated her 76th birthday with their family in Hilton Head. It was the first time in 34 years that almost all the family had vacationed together; two grandsons were unable to attend.

The Hermans' son, Keith, and his wife, Sandra, live in Greer, and their daughter, Denise, and her husband, Jim Campbell, live in Campobello.

Mary grew up in the Lake Bowen Community near Inman and worked for the Lucas company, makers of auto parts, in Greer up until her retirement. Mary enjoys reading, crocheting and cross-stitching. She started making cross-stitch seat covers for her eight dining room chairs, but finishing the project is "iffy," she admits, because she has put the two she completed in another room.

Mary found the recipe for coconut peach pie in a magazine and has been making it for about four years or so. She and I agreed that the sugar in the meringue shell could be decreased. She has had good results making the pie with strawberries, and says that using canned cherry pie filling instead of the peaches would probably work well, too.

She has also frozen the meringue shell and then thawed it only slightly before using.

This is a sweet dessert, so cut the pie into at least eight pieces for serving. A peach slice on top of each will make a pretty garnish.

This weekend, make the meringue shell on Saturday or on Sunday morning. After church, fill the shell with the fresh peaches, top with the whipped cream, and enjoy for … *Sunday Dinner*.

Coconut Peach Pie

- 3 egg whites
- Dash of salt
- ¾ cup plus 2 tablespoons sugar, divided
- 1¼ cups flaked coconut (3½-ounce can) toasted, divided
- ⅓ cup chopped and toasted pecans or almonds
- 2½ cups peeled, sliced fresh peaches (about 3)
- 1 cup heavy whipping cream or frozen dessert topping

Grease 9-inch glass pie plate. Toast coconut and nuts, and set aside. In mixing bowl, beat egg whites and salt on medium speed until foamy. Gradually add ¾ cup sugar, 1 tablespoon at a time, beating on high until stiff peaks form.

Reserve ¼ cup of coconut. Fold remaining 1 cup of coconut and nuts into beaten egg whites. Spread meringue on bottom and up sides of greased pie plate. Bake at 350 degrees for 30 minutes, until light golden brown. Cool completely on a wire rack.

Arrange peaches in meringue crust. In a chilled mixing bowl, beat the cream with the remaining 2 tablespoons of sugar until stiff peaks form. Spread over peaches and sprinkle with the remaining ¼ cup coconut. Refrigerate for 1 hour before slicing. Yields 8 servings.

Peanut Butter Pie
Marjorie Wilson and Deanna Myers
(Published March 19, 2007)

Perhaps you remember several months ago when I shared with you that someone had written asking for recipes for lemon, strawberry, and peanut butter pies? Several readers sent recipes, and I used some of them. Yesterday I found two recipes for peanut butter pie. They are identical, so I shall tell you something about both contributors.

The first is Marjorie Wilson, a member of Welcome Baptist Church in Saluda Baptist Association. William West Jr. is her pastor. Over the years, she has been active in many areas of the church: choir, president of WMU, ordinances committee, etc. Her husband, Ben, has been a deacon, member of the finance, cemetery, usher, and pulpit committees, and a trustee.

Marjorie was born in Scottsville, Ky., where her father owned a grocery on Wilson Square. Later, her family moved to Indianapolis, where she was working when a friend who was dating a soldier from Camp Atterbury introduced Marjorie to a young South Carolina soldier named Ben Wilson. Click! Ben was discharged in October, made some visits back to Indianapolis, then in April 1953 went back for a wedding and to bring Marjorie to South Carolina.

Marjorie worked for Milliken Research Corporation at the DeFore Plant as secretary to the vice president and general manager, then as planning coordinator — for a total of 49 years. During this time, she enrolled at Limestone College and graduated summa cum laude.

Ben has retired from his grading/contracting business. Marjorie enjoys her pets — both cats and dogs — and some time ago she participated in a cooking class and reading group.

The second peanut butter pie recipe is from Deanna Myers, a teacher at the Christian Learning Center in Williamston. This is something new with schools. This year, Deanna has about 350 students from Palmetto Middle School. They are in six classes which are off-campus, next door at Palmetto Baptist Association. The center provides the teacher, the classroom, and the transportation, all funded by donations; no state money is used. The curriculum includes Bible study and prayer, and serves as a support for any students with personal problems.

Deanna, a native of Greenville, and her husband, George, are members of Woodside Baptist Church in Greenville, where Ronnie Williams is pastor. She serves as VBS director, teaches a ladies Sunday school class, directs and sings in the young people's choir, and is church soloist. George serves on a couple of committees, and, like Deanna, is regular in attendance.

They have three children; Courtney, a student at USC; Wesley, 16; and Rebecca, 12.

This pie is rich but good, so serve small pieces. It's best made the day before. Be sure to chill it, and you will get a firmer product, Deanna says, if it goes in the freezer overnight. Garnish it with a dollop of the whipped topping, Marjorie suggests, and it will be a perfect dessert for … *Sunday Dinner*.

Peanut Butter Pie
- 1 cup powdered sugar, sifted
- 1 cup creamy peanut butter
- 1 8-ounce pack cream cheese
- 1 medium or large carton whipped dessert topping

Blend the cream cheese; add the peanut butter and mix well. Add the dessert topping mix, then the sifted powdered sugar. Beat until thoroughly blended and pour into a graham cracker pie shell. Chill at least 1 hour. Serves 6-8.

Apple Dumpling Bake
Mary McAlister
(Published February 24, 2005)

"There are places in Baghdad that look better than this," I said to our daughter Catherine, who was visiting briefly from Mt. Pleasant. It was time to start lunch, and my kitchen was upside down.

Earlier, I had made Mary McAlister's apple dumpling bake and I was telling Catherine how good it was.

Mary quickly gives credit for the recipe to a friend, Carolyn Boling. Mary has had the recipe only a few months, but says that each time she takes the dish to a gathering, everyone wants to know how it is made.

Mary and her husband, Arnold, who works for Glen Raven Mills in Anderson County, are members of Sierra Baptist Church, Anderson, and it was wonderful to hear someone talk as excitedly about her church as Mary does. The McAlisters were charter members of Sierra when it was organized about five years ago with only a few members meeting at Anderson College. They now have 106 members, and on the most recent Sunday had 150 for the morning worship service. Rex Simmons, who recently came to them from Airport Baptist Church, Greenville, is the new pastor.

Mary says she and Arnold have always been a church-going family — first to Six and Twenty, then to Corinth 2, both in Anderson County. They have one son, Steve, whose wife is the former Vickie Giles, and they have three children: Anna (Mrs. Eric) Harper, Beth (Mrs. John) Davis, and Alan McAlister and his wife, Angel. Beth's husband, John, is the choir director at Bishop Branch Church, Central. Anna and Beth are both nurses.

Over the years, Mary has had several jobs in the churches where she has attended, including teaching Sunday school. She also has several other interests. One is quilting, and she has made a cathedral quilt for each of the three grandchildren. Each quilt took about two and a half years to complete. She also gardens.

The apple dumpling bake recipe that Mary sent has two excellent characteristics for a recipe: It is easy to make, and the resulting dish is good. It is easily reheated. Not many recipes require soft drinks, and I don't know who created this one, but it's good. Mary says she pours a little more of the Mountain Dew in the pan before reheating, and then puts it into a hot oven for a few minutes.

So run to the grocery store, get your crescent rolls, apples, and Mountain Dew, and bake the dumplings that will be delicious for … *Sunday Dinner*.

Apple Dumpling Bake
- 2 tubes crescent rolls
- 2 medium Granny Smith or any baking apples
- 1 cup white sugar
- ⅓ cup soft butter or margarine
- ¾ cup Mountain Dew soft drink
- Ground cinnamon
- Vanilla ice cream

Preheat oven to 350 degrees. Peel and core apples. Cut each into 8 slices. Unwrap crescent rolls, separate each tube into 8 triangles. Wrap each triangle around 1 slice of apple and place in a 13x5x2 baking dish. Combine sugar and soft butter. Sprinkle or spread this over apples/rolls.

Pour the Mountain Dew around, not on, the rolls. Do not stir. Sprinkle on the cinnamon. Bake uncovered for 35-40 minutes or until golden brown. Serve warm with ice cream. Serves 16.

Warm Apple Crisp
Faye Faulkner Johnson
(Published May 26, 2011)

The late Roy and Gertrude Faulkner had to be pleased with the way their girls turned out.

Today we are writing about the delicious warm apple crisp, made from a recipe shared with us by Faye Faulkner Johnson of Troy. A couple of times ago, we had a recipe from her sister Mildred. The sisters married cousins: Warren Johnson and Charles Johnson.

Faye, like her sister, had been a member of Mountain Creek Church all her life. Her parents carried her to church regularly when she was a youngster, and she has been a member since that time. Organized in 1798, Mountain Creek celebrated its bicentennial in 1998 and is part of Edgefield Association. Rev. Robert Huffman is currently serving as interim pastor.

Faye's husband, Warren, is a deacon and the church treasurer. Faye teaches Sunday school and is active in WMU. She was formerly the church pianist, but now is the fill-in when needed.

She also has other interests. She likes gardening (both flower and vegetable), and her family maintains the grounds of Mountain Creek. She is also a member of the local volunteer fire department, helping mostly with fund-raising, etc.

Faye and Warren have two daughters. The younger is Lisa Johnson Murray. She and her late husband, Billy, had no children. She lives in Edgefield. Faye and Warren's older daughter, Diane, and her husband, Burt Wetzel, also live in Edgefield. As much as anything, Faye enjoys being near her only grandchild, Lucy Wetzel. Lucy is a busy girl, involved in the 4-H Club and other activities. She enters her goats in goat shows and her horse in horse shows.

This is an easy recipe with no crust to make, and you probably have most of the ingredients (except possibly the apples) on hand. She recommends using one of the crisp, cooking apples such as Granny Smith for the dish rather than one of the "out of hand" varieties. Faye doesn't remember where she got the recipe, but she has had it a long time. We thank her for sharing it with us. You can make this on Sunday morning, keep it warm, and serve it topped with a scoop of vanilla ice cream. Now wouldn't that be a great finish for any … *Sunday Dinner*!

Warm Apple Crisp

- **6 peeled and thinly sliced apples**
- **1 teaspoon cinnamon**
- **2 tablespoons butter, melted**
- **½ cup all-purpose flour**
- **⅓ cup sugar**
- **½ teaspoon salt**
- **¾ cup sugar**
- **⅓ cup butter**

Heat oven to 375 degrees. Mix together apples, ⅓ cup sugar, cinnamon, salt and 2 tablespoons melted butter. Place in a greased 8-inch square baking dish. Set aside.

Combine the ¾ cup sugar and the flour; cut in the ⅓ cup butter until crumbly. Sprinkle over apples. Bake at 375 degrees about 45 minutes, or until apples are tender. Serve warm. Makes 8 servings.

Applesauce Soufflé
Judy Holmes, as submitted to Edgefield First Baptist Church cookbook
(Published November 8, 2012)

When I saw this recipe contributed by Judy Holmes in the church-produced cookbook, I thought, "That is a strange thing" — but I tried it, and it is good. My test group here at our noon table all gave it a good mark, so I am sharing it with you today.

One of the good things about this applesauce soufflé is that you may have all the ingredients on hand to pluck from your pantry and refrigerator.

Judy and her husband, Hamp Holmes Jr., a semi-retired cattleman, are members of Sweetwater Baptist Church near North Augusta. Rev. Paul Noe is the pastor and has served for seven years at the church, which was organized in 1832. Sweetwater Baptist, with an average Sunday attendance of around 300, offers a full range of Baptist organizations.

When she shared this recipe with the cookbook committee, Judy was a member at First Baptist Church of Edgefield, where she and her husband were until about five years ago. That church, currently pastored by Rev. Stacy Williams, has a long history of growth and service from its founding 1823 and is a member of the Edgefield Association.

A medium-sized and growing church, Edgefield First is busy, as are many churches around the state, with the prisoner packet project. They also have praise bands for both youth and adults.

Retiring in April from Campbell Construction Company, Judy now has time for other interests, which include digital photography (with landscapes and nature as her favorite subjects), crocheting and reading. And time for making applesauce soufflé.

Judy and Hamp have two children — Connie and her husband, David Reynolds, who live in Lexington; and Hampton Holmes III and his wife,

Stephanie, of Trenton.

This recipe was given to Judy a long time ago by a friend, Janet Whitlock, and Judy makes it frequently. It is a favorite served with ham. Make it some Sunday soon and have it waiting when you and your family get home from church to enjoy for ... *Sunday Dinner*.

Applesauce Soufflé

- 1 large can (about 16-18 ounces) applesauce
- 1 cup sugar
- ¾ stick margarine, melted
- 2 eggs (or Egg Beaters)
- 1 cup vanilla wafer crumbs
- 1 cup milk (whole or evaporated)
- Sprinkle of cinnamon to taste

Have ready a large pie plate or baking dish. Preheat oven to 350 degrees. Beat eggs, then add other ingredients. I (Judy) usually melt the margarine in the preheating oven. Put the other ingredients on top of the melted margarine.

Bake 45-60 minutes or until lightly browned. Serves 5-6. (Double the recipe to fit a 9×12-inch baking dish. Triple the recipe for 16 servings. This is a good recipe to serve with ham.)

Peach (or Apple) Strudel
Cecil Salley
(Published May 15, 2007)

They traveled to every continental state, including Alaska, and also Canada. For years after Cecil Salley retired from his International Harvester dealership in 1978, he and his wife, Willa, traveled extensively, pulling their Airstream trailer all across our land. Cecil, who Willa calls her "co-pilot," died in 1978, but Willa has a fountain of memories of those wonderful trips.

Cecil's IH dealership was in Salley, and Willa helped him in the business. They had three daughters: Cecilia Salley, who lives in Salley; and Barbara Jean Cuve and Edith Moseley, both of Aiken. There are six grandchildren and 12 great-grandchildren.

Willa and Cecil began going to the Airstream park in Dade City, Fla., near Tampa many years ago. Since his death, she leaves the travel trailer there all the time and spends about half the year there, with a trip back to Salley for Christmas. She plays golf a lot while in Florida, but back home in Salley it is her large yard that keeps her busy.

Willa is a member of Salley Baptist Church, where Henry Cooper is pastor. The church is in the Edisto Association. She was a member of the choir for many years.

During their years of traveling, one of the places they especially liked was the Pennsylvania Dutch country, and especially their food! Willa says she doesn't remember seeing even one skinny Amish woman! While there, she bought several of their cookbooks, and it is from the book "Plain and Fancy" that she shares today's recipe.

If you are in a part of South Carolina where the peaches were not killed by our late cold weather, you will find good local peaches for this recipe. They should be firm. Or you can use apples. Both should be peeled and thinly sliced.

Strudel is a German dish, usually with pastry on the bottom and a thin crust on top. This dish is a bit different with the crumble top. The strudel can be made on Saturday and served cold, or reheated and topped with whipped cream, ice cream, or milk for a delicious dessert to end ... *Sunday Dinner.*

Peach (or Apple) Strudel
    1 cup sugar
    2 cups hot water
    1 cup flour
    1 teaspoon baking powder
    ½ teaspoon salt
    1 egg
    2 cups (or more) peeled, thinly sliced fresh peaches or apples
    ½ cup sugar
    ½ teaspoon cinnamon
    4 tablespoons (¼ cup) butter
    Whipped cream, ice cream, or milk

Preheat oven to 350 degrees. Butter the bottom and sides of a 2-quart baking dish. Combine the 1 cup of sugar and the 2 cups of hot water in a small pot. Bring to a boil to dissolve the sugar and make a light syrup. Set aside.

Combine the flour, baking powder, and salt. Add the egg and mix until crumbly. Set aside. Into the buttered baking dish, put the thinly sliced peaches. There should be a thick layer, so more fruit may be needed.

Mix the cup sugar and the cinnamon, and sprinkle this over the peaches. Dot with little lumps of the butter. Gently pour the sugar syrup over the peaches, then top with the crumbly flour mixture. Bake for 30-45 minutes, or until the crust is brown. Serve with whipped cream, ice cream, or a small amount of milk poured on top.

Denver Downs Delight
(Published December 17, 2009)

By now you are knee-deep in Christmas with church programs and dinners, Sunday school luncheons, charitable projects, etc., as you should be this time of year.

At our small church's nativity presentation, our daughter Lee was a "wise person," what with the congregation running short on guys who would serve. All was well until I discovered showing beneath her wise man robe her bright red, white-laced sneakers. Probably not the normal footwear for seers of 2,000 years ago.

There is no better time than Christmas to let people know that you care about them: Send cards, write notes of appreciation, invite them for a meal or for coffee and dessert, and especially remember your members who are in nursing homes.

That said, this is my Christmas present to you.

It is easily made, pretty in presentation, and a good-tasting cake. I don't normally use cake mixes, but for this recipe I do. Instead of the mix, you may make a white or yellow two-layer cake, using your favorite recipe.

I have read bios of people, mostly women, which say, "Creates her own recipes."

That may be true, but changing from shortening to butter or from ⅓ to ½ teaspoon of salt is not creating a recipe.

I claim to have "invented" this one and hope I am not fibbing because somewhere I may have seen, but don't remember, a similar recipe. Therefore, I'm claiming this one. You can alter it by using strawberry preserves instead of the apricot to make the cake colors in keeping with the season, but the sweet/tart taste of the apricot complements the sweet layers and whipped cream. You may want to use more preserves.

I hope each of you has a joyful holiday as we celebrate the birth of our Lord.

Denver Downs Delight

- 1 1¼-pound box white cake mix
- 1 pint heavy cream
- 2 tablespoons extra fine confectioners' sugar
- 1 18-ounce jar apricot preserves
- ½ teaspoon vanilla flavoring

Prepare cake mix according to directions, baking in 2 9-inch pans. Cool in pans for 2 minutes, then invert layers onto wire rack and cool. When completely cool, split layers in half horizontally to make 4 layers. Put a layer on cake serving plate cut side up. Spread on ⅓ of the preserves. Repeat with other 3 layers, leaving top layer without preserves. Cover and refrigerate.

A short time before serving, beat the cream, adding the vanilla and sugar. Frost sides and top layer generously with the whipped cream. Refrigerate until serving time. Serves 8-10.

(Optional: Place a canned apricot half on each serving plate beside cake slice. Also optional: Pat dry canned apricot halves, cut into pieces, and decorate top of cake.)

Chocolate Lust
Jo Hammond
(Published March 28, 2008)

"Yeaaaaay! I found it!"

Diligently had I searched, even as the woman looking for her lost coin. Because I don't throw away things, I knew it was someplace in my clutter corner, and after a half day I located it.

"It" is Jo Hammond's Chocolate Lust recipe. Last time we talked about Japanese fruitcake, which Jo, from Spring Branch Baptist Church, Nichols, had requested. During our telephone conversation, she told me about this recipe.

"Send it," I said, and she did. Then I immediately misplaced it. "Misplaced" is not the same as "lost," but sometimes it is quite close.

Jo and I aren't sure about the name. "Lust" doesn't seem appropriate, and "lush" means "green" or "growing" (and there's nothing green in the recipe), so you can make the call. Jo says she usually triples the recipe when carrying it to a church or family function.

Anyway, what was lost is now found, and here is the recipe for you to assemble on Saturday, refrigerate, and have waiting as a good dessert after … *Sunday Dinner*.

Chocolate Lust
- 1 cup plain flour, sifted
- 1 stick butter (½ cup), melted
- 1 cup chopped nuts
- 2 cups (1 pint) heavy whipping cream
    or whipped dessert topping

1 8-ounce package cream cheese, room temperature
1 cup sugar
1 small package instant vanilla pudding
1 small package instant chocolate pudding
2 cups cold milk
½ cup coconut or chopped nuts

(This is made in four layers.)
Preheat oven to 350 degrees.

Layer 1: Mix together the 1 cup of flour, butter, and 1 cup of nuts, and press into a 9×13 glass baking dish. Bake until golden brown and let cool completely.

Layer 2: Whip the heavy cream, adding about a tablespoon of sugar or to taste. Combine the softened cream cheese, the 1 cup sugar, and 1 cup of the whipped cream or dessert topping. Spread over the cooled pecan crust.

Layer 3: Combine the chocolate and vanilla puddings in a bowl, add the two cups of cold milk, and beat until thick. Spread over the cream cheese layer.

Layer 4: Top with remaining whipped cream or dessert topping, and sprinkle with the coconut or ½ cup chopped nuts. Chill a few hours or overnight. Serves 8-10.

(Note: Jo says she sometimes uses ⅓ less milk to make the pudding thicker.)

Sour Cream Banana Pudding
Carol Heissenbuttle
(Published March 17, 2011)

If a waiter in an upscale restaurant were suggesting this dish for your dining pleasure, he might describe it as "a delicious dish of small, delicate cookies carefully layered with fresh, slightly firm bananas combined with a delectable blancmange incorporating a touch of sour cream, topped with elegant peaks of sweetened cream whipped to perfection."

We would call it Carol Smith Heissenbuttle's Sour Cream Banana Pudding.

He, our waiter friend, should also tell you that if you have lost your sweet tooth, you may not like this. It is really good, and it is really sweet.

Carol has been a member of Ashley River Baptist Church all her life; her parents were married there. She serves as the church's resource manager. Rev. David W. Patterson is pastor, Rev. H.S. Yarborough is minister of music/minister to senior adults, and Rev. Ronald Shearer is minister of education. The large 2,500-member Ashley River Baptist Church, organized in 1943 as a "granddaughter" of Charleston First Baptist, has a contemporary service at 8:30 a.m. and a blended traditional and contemporary service at 11 a.m. on Sundays.

When it came school time for her daughter Jenna Leigh, Carol enrolled her in the kindergarten program at the First Baptist Church School in Charleston. Charleston First Baptist is a large church where Rev. Marshall Blalock is pastor. The church began its church school in 1949 with 39 students and four teachers. Now the enrollment is 450.

Tommy Mullins is the headmaster; Robin Riggs is the principal for K3-grade 6, and Betsy Fanning is the principal for grades 7-12. Jenna did all her school years there from K3-12th grade, then attended Trident

Technical College for a year. She is now taking the year off that many students do.

Carol works at the Medical University of South Carolina in the neuroscience department where research on addictions is done. In her away-from-work time, she enjoys sewing and crafts, especially making jewelry using Swarovski crystals. She often makes earrings, necklaces and bracelets for friends who want to give the pieces as gifts.

This recipe is another one of the "comfort foods" that everyone likes. The difference is the sour cream in Carol's recipe, which she got from a friend almost 30 years ago. You may have a favorite banana pudding recipe, but if not, do try this one with the sour cream from Carol. Make it on Saturday, put it in the fridge, and everybody will enjoy it for … *Sunday Dinner.*

Sour Cream Banana Pudding
- 1 8-ounce carton sour cream
- 2 cups milk (no less than 2 percent fat)
- 1 12-ounce container Cool Whip
- 4-6 medium bananas (not too ripe)
- 1 12-ounce box Nilla vanilla wafers
- 2 small boxes instant vanilla pudding
    (do not use French vanilla)

Whisk together the milk, pudding, sour cream and ⅔ of the Cool Whip until completely mixed and starting to thicken. In a large pan (lasagna or similar size, or deep rectangular plastic dish), put one layer of the vanilla wafers and then one layer of sliced bananas.

Repeat layering (all the wafers may not be needed) and then add pudding mixture.* Top with the remaining ⅓ carton of the topping. Keep refrigerated. Serves 10-12.

(*Carol suggests tapping the container on the counter a few times so the pudding mixture can fall down among the wafers and bananas. She says you may also layer the wafers, bananas and pudding, then repeat the layers and add topping.)

German Chocolate Brownies
Cindy Raines
(Published September 16, 2010)

"Are you a Baptist?"

"No," she said, "I used to go to ___," giving the name of another denomination.

"Were your parents Baptists?"

"No."

"Do you even know a Baptist?" I asked, trying to get a tie-in to the Courier.

I was talking with Cindy Raines, who, with her husband, Wayne, lives near Liberty in South Carolina's Upcountry. There is a Baptist connection. Her husband, she said, is a member of Laurel Baptist in Greenville, as are his parents, Melvin and Ione Raines. Cletus Lynch is currently serving as interim at Laurel.

Cindy had brought me a plate of 12 German chocolate brownies a few days earlier. Because I wasn't home, she had left them with our son-in-law, Joel Sprague, at his office near our house. She and Wayne are friends of Joel and our daughter Gaye. That was a mistake. Only four of the brownies made it to our house. They were good brownies, although I didn't understand the name. There was no German chocolate involved in the recipe. It was Cindy's mother-in-law, Ione Raines of Mauldin, who shared with us her recipe for Coffee Can Cake a few years ago. Cindy, who grew up in New England, graduated from Furman and for 27 years worked in Greenville as a legal secretary. When her employer retired, she did also.

Now she enjoys many activities. The major one is watercolor painting, and her favorite subject is flowers. The models for her floral paintings most often come from her yard, because her next favorite thing is gardening. Her entry was one of those in an exhibit at the Pickens County Museum, and her painting sold. She took a painting class at the museum four years ago and has been enjoying the hobby ever since.

Cindy explained that this is an old recipe. When Cindy was a child, the recipe was given to her mother by a neighbor in the New England community. It is an easy recipe to make. It has only seven ingredients and goes together quickly, and we thank Cindy for sharing the recipe with us. And for the cooked brownies she shared. All four of them.

You can make the whole thing from start to finish in less than an hour. Bake this over the weekend and enjoy it with coffee for dessert after this weekend's ... *Sunday Dinner*.

German Chocolate Brownies

    3 tablespoons all-purpose flour

    2 cups graham cracker crumbs

    1 14-ounce can sweetened condensed milk

    5 ounces chocolate chips

    ½ teaspoon baking powder

    1 stick butter, melted

    2 ounces chopped walnuts

Heat oven to 325 degrees. Grease and flour an 8-inch square pan. Mix together all the ingredients. Put into prepared pan, spreading and smoothing the batter with the bottom of a large spoon. Bake for about 30 minutes. Makes 16 pieces.

Lonesome Cowboy Bars
Sue Bogan
(Published October 6, 2014)

Don't you love the name of this church?

It's Pleasant Grove, and it's located in the Upstate near the Greenville-Spartanburg airport, although it has a Greer address. A member of the Three Rivers Baptist Association, where Randy Bradley serves as director of missions, the church has most of the Baptist programs and organizations. The Sunday evening service is called "Bible study."

One of Pleasant Grove's members is Sue Bogan, who has been attending church there since she was about 3 years old, but we aren't going to say for how many years! It is her recipe, published in the church's cookbook, that we are sharing with you today, and one you will want to try because (1) it is easy to make, (2) it is good to eat, and (3) it makes a large amount.

Sue and her late husband, Charles, had three children: Mike, Lisa and Cammy, who live in the area.

Sue worked for 35 years in the office of a local doctor as a lab technician. When her doctor sold his practice, Sue retired and was glad to have those later years with her husband until his death about four years ago.

Over the years, she has been busy in her church, teaching the 4-and-5-year-old Sunday school children for 25 years. When she ended that, she was asked to teach an adult class, which she was willing to do until another teacher could be found. That came about a year and a half later.

Sue enjoys gardening, which is a good thing because her three-acre yard contains flowers, shrubs and a vegetable garden. The latter is smaller than the vegetable gardens the family formerly grew, but there is enough for her to use and to share. Sue also enjoys sewing.

Sue, who collects cookbooks, doesn't remember where she got this recipe with the delightful name, but it's a good one. When shopping for Sue's recipe, I could not find butterscotch chips so I used chocolate chips instead. They were good, but I'm sure the taste was different. When you make it, try to find the butterscotch ones.

Because it makes a large amount, this is a good recipe for family reunions, church suppers, etc. A couple of Sue's Lonesome Cowboy Bars would make a good afternoon snack a couple of hours after you have enjoyed a light … *Sunday Dinner*.

Lonesome Cowboy Bars

1 cup sugar

1 cup corn syrup

1½ cups crunchy peanut butter

12 ounces butterscotch chips

6 cups corn flakes

Grease a 9×13 cake pan with butter or margarine. Set aside. Measure corn flakes into a large bowl; set aside. Over medium heat, bring the sugar and syrup to a boil. Stir in the peanut butter. Remove from heat and pour mixture over the corn flakes. Mix well, then press mixture firmly into the prepared pan.

In a double boiler over low heat, melt the butterscotch chips. Spread evenly on top of the cereal mixture. Cool completely and cut into bars. Makes 30 servings.

Baked Caramel Corn
Elleen Patience
(Published March 29, 2012)

I bet you're going to keep this recipe! It's one everybody will enjoy, and you will notice that they keep going back to the serving bowl for this caramel corn. The recipe is from Elleen Patience.

Elleen was baptized at Riverside Baptist Church in Anderson when she was about 7 years old and has been a member there since. After she married and moved from home, she still continued her membership there, following the Baptist practice of attending the church nearest one's home. The Rev. Wayne Adams is pastor of Riverside, which is in the Saluda Association — where the Rev. John Dill is director of missions.

Elleen and her husband, Sidney Patience, are both retired. They have a daughter, Melinda. A College of Charleston graduate, she is currently working in Charleston in a position involving computers. Elleen's son, Robert Hill, his wife, Kristi, and their children, Lewis and Tyler, live in the area.

Over the years, Elleen has served in many positions at Riverside, including being in the choir and being the choir director, and being an active member of the Young at Heart seniors. She has also served as the church's activities director, often planning church tours. She doesn't do so much now, and because of health sometimes misses a Sunday.

At home, she enjoys sewing and reading.

And making caramel corn.

She got this recipe from her mother-in-law in Belton and made it frequently when the children were young, but not so much now.

When I made this, I used a large pot for heating the butter, but when I tried to stir in the popped corn there wasn't much stirring space. I put the popped corn into a large roaster and poured the butter-caramel mix over it. It was easier to mix. Then I spread it onto the baking pans.

Watch this: You must keep it stirred every 10 or 15 minutes while it bakes (as the instructions say) or the caramel mixture will stick to the pan and scorch.

We thank Elleen for sharing the recipe. It is a good one for making on Saturday, then saved for a snack the next afternoon or evening after you have had a large … *Sunday Dinner*.

Baked Caramel Corn

- 1 cup (2 sticks) butter or margarine
- 2 cups brown sugar, firmly packed
- ½ cup light or dark corn syrup
- 1 teaspoon salt
- ½ teaspoon baking soda
- 1 teaspoon vanilla
- 6 quarts popped popcorn

Melt butter and stir in the brown sugar, corn syrup and salt. Bring to boil, stirring constantly. Then boil without stirring for 5 minutes. Remove pot from heat and stir in the baking soda and vanilla. Gradually stir in the popcorn, mixing well. Turn the mixture onto two large shallow baking pans.

Bake at 250 degrees for 1 hour, stirring every 15 minutes. Remove pans from the oven and cool completely. Break apart the corn. Yields about 5 quarts of Caramel Corn.

Pecan Candy and Sugar Peanuts
Mattie B. Evatt
(Published February 20, 2007)

Usually we have only one recipe, but today, because they are so good, we have two snacking recipes for you, with not one sweet tooth but a whole mouth full of them.

The recipes are from Mattie B. Evatt, who lives in the historic mill town of Newry in South Carolina's Upstate. The mill has been closed for several years, but for many people, employment there was almost a family relationship.

Mrs. Evatt and her late husband, Lawrence, who died in 1978, both worked at Newry. After it closed, she went to another plant, but it wasn't the same, she said. Mrs. Evatt, now 87, still lives there, and her son Marshall now lives with her. Another son, Rickey Evatt, lives in Oconee County, and daughter Sybil Reece and her husband, Stanley, live in Newry, not far from her.

Mrs. Evatt, who grew up in Georgia, has been a member of Lydia Baptist Church in Newry almost 60 years since she, her husband, and daughter Sybil were baptized at the same time. The current pastor is Glenn Kelly, and Lydia Baptist is part of Beaverdam Association.

Mrs Evatt is in good health and laughs when she tells the story that several months ago she had a problem that sent her to the hospital for the first time in her life.

"The nurse asked me if I had brought all my medicines with me, and I said, 'Oh, I forgot my Tylenol!' She couldn't believe I wasn't taking a bunch of stuff," Mrs. Evatt added. Since that little bout, she has had to drop out of the choir a few weeks, but hopes to get back soon. In the past, she has taught a Sunday school class and helped with the bereavement and benevolent service of the church. She enjoys crocheting — making caps, afghans, etc.

She has had both these recipes a long time. Her brother-in-law, who lives in the peanut country of south Georgia, gave her the recipe for the sugar peanuts. These are really good, and they won't last long.

The pecan candy is similar to pralines and would be, later in the day with a cup of coffee, a good mid-afternoon snack after … *Sunday Dinner*.

Pecan Candy

    1 cup buttermilk

    2 cups sugar

    1 teaspoon baking soda

    1 teaspoon butter or margarine

    1 teaspoon vanilla

    2 cups pecan halves

Put buttermilk, sugar and baking soda in a large pot, and stir to dissolve. Cook over medium heat until the mixture bubbles up, stirring constantly.

Continue to cook and stir until mixture turns medium brown and forms a soft ball when a drop is dropped into a cup of cold water. Remove from heat and add butter, vanilla and pecans, stirring the mixture until it becomes glossy and starts to crystallize. Spoon onto waxed paper to make 2-inch-wide patties. If mixture becomes too sticky, return to heat until of right consistency.

Sugar Peanuts

    1 cup sugar

    1½ cups water

    2 cups raw peanuts

Dissolve the sugar in the water in a saucepan over medium heat. Add the peanuts and continue to cook until the peanuts are completely coated and there is no sugar left in the pot. Pour peanuts onto an ungreased cookie sheet, spreading so that the peanuts are separated as much as possible. Bake at 300 degrees about 30 minutes, stirring every 5 minutes or so.

Miscellaneous Goodies

Pear Honey
Juanita Garrison/Lillie Wilson and Hassie Vaughn
(Published September 11, 2003)

"Are you putting all that sugar in there?" asked daughter Lee in amazement. She is the size of a No. 2 Eberhart pencil, and sugar and fat are her sworn enemies.

"This is what it says," I answered, having been conditioned to do what I am told and obey the rules.

I was making pear honey. A reader has asked for a recipe, and after searching diligently I had found one — but it didn't contain the pineapple that I remembered. Later, I found two recipes in the Mt. Bethel Baptist Church cookbook, and both contained pineapple.

When I was a child, a friend of my mother's made this, and I remember it being very good. It had been years since I made pear honey, and now I was making it again. We have two pear trees, so I was halfway there even before I started. But one of the problems with pear honey — with the exception of the large amount of sugar — is preparing the pears. Peeling a pear is somewhat like peeling a rock.

The pear honey with pineapple is from Lillie Wilson, a member of Mt. Bethel Baptist Church, Belton. She has been there, she says, since she was old enough to join the church, and her husband, Ben, and their three daughters — LaDonna, Janet and Cindy — also attend.

At one time, Lillie was the GA leader. She helped with the 4- and 5-year-olds in Sunday school for several years, and most recently has served as secretary for the 3- and 4-year-old nursery.

The recipe for pear honey with pineapple and coconut is from Hassie Vaughn, also of Mt. Bethel, where she and her husband, John, have been members since 1949. They have two sons, James and Robert. Hassie and

John work together with the homebound program, visiting those members who cannot attend church. She is also on the flower committee for her Sunday school class.

She got the recipe some years ago, Hassie says, from Sara Rogers, who was the guidance counselor at Palmetto High School.

The first recipe is for plain pear honey, the second requires pineapple, and the third both pineapple and coconut. One can only eat so many fresh pears, so having a recipe for preserving them for later use is good.

In all three of the different recipes, one should have the waiting jars hot and the lids and rings for sealing the jars simmering in hot water. All three recipes are good and easily made after you get the pears peeled — and, according to daughter Lee, if you eat enough pear honey for Sunday breakfast, you won't need … *Sunday Dinner*.

Pear Honey, Plain

12 cups pears (peeled, seeded and ground)
¾ of a lemon (seeded and ground)
9 cups of sugar

Mix all ingredients in a large pot. Cook over low heat until sugar dissolves. Bring to a boil, then reduce heat, and cook over low heat about 1 hour until transparent. Pour into hot, sterilized jars. Seal at once with lids and rings. Makes about 6 pints.

Pear Honey with Pineapple

3 pounds ripe pears (3 cups prepared)
1 large can (16 ounces or so) crushed pineapple

    1 lemon (seeded and ground)

    5 cups sugar

Wash pears; peel, core, grind pears, and measure. In a large container, combine pears, pineapple, lemon and sugar. Cook over low heat, stirring well. Cook about 20 minutes. Put into jars and seal.

Pear Honey with Pineapple and Coconut

    11 pounds pears (ground)

    6 pounds sugar

    1 large can (about 1 pound) crushed pineapple

    2 oranges (seeded and ground)

    1 7-ounce can flaked coconut

Peel and grind the pears, removing the seeds and hard cores. Grind oranges, taking out white sections and seeds. Combine all ingredients and cook slowly until very thick. Put into jars and seal.

Pear Relish

Frances Davis

(Published September 5, 2006)

You may feel about today's recipe as the doggie did when he chased the car: when he caught it, what would he do with it?

    I asked Frances that question about today's recipe. She says she serves it as a condiment with a meat-and-potatoes meal as one would do with chowchow.

    The Frances and the condiment I am referring to are Frances Davis and her pear relish. Way back, Frances was a member of Warrenville Baptist Church in Aiken County, but for the past 35 years or so has been a member of Good Hope Baptist Church in the Ridge Association at Ninety Six. Her pastor is Steve Justice. At different times, she has served as secretary of her Sunday school class and has worked on the church's hospitality committee, but she doesn't do as much now because of her health. In all the churches she attended — from the time she joined Central Baptist in Aiken County as a teen, until the present — Frances has been a faithful member and worker.

Since the death 10 years ago of her husband, James, who was also a member of Good Hope, Frances has continued to live alone and had done well until recently when she took a tumble, injuring her hip and spraining an ankle.

While she is recovering "in her chair," as she call it, she is spending the healing time crocheting. Frances also enjoys quilting and has made a quilt for each of her children, grandchildren, and great-grandchildren. She still lacks two but will get those done.

She and James had three children. The oldest, Sara English and her son James, live in Atlanta. Frances' son, Gary Davis, and his wife, Sondra, live in Charlotte, and Connie, the youngest, and her husband, Kenny Banks, live in Spartanburg.

Frances has used this recipe for years, she says, and doesn't remember where she got it, but has some suggestions for preparation: The relish is better if you chop or grind the vegetables, she says. You can use the "chop" setting on a blender, but make it quick or the veggies will be mushy. The amount of pears and peppers doesn't have to be exact, either. You can use all green peppers, but adding the red and maybe yellow ones to the relish makes it prettier, and the amount of red pepper you use can be adjusted to your taste.

Frances won a ribbon for her relish at one time so you know it must be good, but to be absolutely sure, make a batch, let it rest in its jar for a few weeks, then enjoy it with a roast, potatoes, etc., for … *Sunday Dinner*.

Pear Relish

- 1 peck fresh pears, peeled and cored
- 4 medium green bell peppers
- 8 red bell peppers
- 2 hot peppers (more if desired)
- 6 medium onions
- 4 cups vinegar
- 4 cups sugar
- 7 tablespoons salt

Using the coarse blade of a chopper, grind the pears, peppers and onions. Place in a large canning kettle. Mix together the vinegar, sugar and salt, and add to the pear-pepper mixture. Bring to a boil. Cook gently for 30 minutes or so.

Meanwhile, prepare 12 pint jars by washing in hot water and keeping hot. Put canning lids and rings in pot, cover with water, bring to a boil and keep hot.

After cooking about 30 minutes or a little more, spoon the relish into the jars, filling to within ½ inch of the top. Cover immediately with the lids and screw on tightly. Turn jars upside down and let stand overnight until cool. The jars will seal. Makes about 12 pints.

Pickled Peaches
Lana Major
(Published August 6, 2008)

Peach pickles are so-o-o Southern. I can't document this, but I suspect that the people in Montana and Maine don't make peach pickles. Too bad, because one of the pleasures of home is having a large glass bowl of peach pickles on the table or buffet at Thanksgiving, Christmas, and when the preacher comes to dinner.

Our recipe is from Lana Major, a member of Mt. Bethel Baptist Church in Belton, where Ron Culbertson is pastor. The church is part of Saluda Baptist Association.

Lana has been a member of Mt. Bethel for 40 years, growing up in the church. She and her husband, Ernie, have two children. Eleven-year-old Katherine is at Wright Elementary, and Ben, 15, is a student at Belton-Honea Path High School.

Lana knows about schools. She taught for 14 years, mostly third grade, and now works at the Anderson School District Two office. She helps with various children's activities at her church and also enjoys walking for exercise, reading and cooking.

Lana's recipe for peach pickles is from her grandmother, Hazel Ashley of Honea Path. Peach pickles are easy to make, but they do require a bit of time.

One of the challenges is finding the right size peach, which one can hardly do in the supermarket. If you have a few trees, then you'll be set for pickles. If not, visit a peach packing house or farmer's market to find the size peach you need.

Select uniform sized peaches; don't mix large and small fruit. The peaches should be small (about 6½ to 7 inches around) for three reasons:

If they are large, you won't be able to get them into the jars (well, maybe wide-mouth canning jars), and you can't get many in the jar; hence, fewer servings per jar. Another reason is that when you serve these, they are to be a condiment, an addition to your menu — not a big ol' pickled peach filling half the plate.

The peaches should be ripe but firm. Discard any that feel soft. You want them to hold their shape both while simmering and while in the jar. Lana prefers the clingstone varieties.

With any canning or freezing project, collect all the things you'll need before starting. Use quart canning jars with the two-part covers (the flat lids and rings).

Although Lana's recipe requires a half peck of peaches, she says that she and family members usually get together and do much larger amounts at one time.

The canned pickled peaches should sit for a few weeks before opening so they can develop the pickle flavor you want. They will be ready for a holiday table, a gift, or for you to enjoy any weekend this autumn for … *Sunday Dinner.*

Pickled Peaches

    ½ peck peaches (4 quarts), peeled
    3 cups vinegar
    3 pounds white sugar (2 cups sugar equals 1 pound)
    Spices to taste (about 2 tablespoons pickling spice or cloves)

Combine sugar and vinegar and simmer 20 minutes. Place the whole peeled peaches in the vinegar mix and cook about 15 minutes or until tender. Pack into hot sterilized jars. Pour the cooking syrup over the peaches, filling the jars; then add spices. Run a knife around the inside of the jar to remove any air pockets. Seal with the two-part rings and lids.

Chowchow
Jo Ann Sloan
(Published January 20, 2011)

You probably can't make this recipe now, but if you had the traditional Southern New Year's Day menu of peas and collards, you probably wished you had made some last year — so save this recipe so you can make it this summer.

We are talking about chowchow. I'm not stuttering, nor is that a typographical error. Chowchow is pleasing to the taste with many foods. It would be called a pickle, but "relish" best describes the concoction.

This recipe is from Jo Ann S. Sloan of Holly Springs Baptist Church, located centrally between Greer, Campobello and Inman. With a medium to large membership, Holly Springs averages around 400 on Sunday. Rev. Tim Clark has been the pastor there about 15 years, and Rev. Chris Jackson has been in his position of associate pastor eight years.

Jo Ann, a retired sixth-eighth grade school teacher, and her husband, Dan, a retired banker, have one child. Their daughter Danna, a CPA, and her husband, Dr. Jeff Brown, live not too far away in Greenville.

Jo Ann taught Sunday school for 50-plus years, but now is on a schedule with the Sanctuary Class to teach once every five weeks. She also set up the church's history room, and there's a lot of history because the church was organized in 1804 with 56 members. Meeting first in a brush arbor and later moving to the Hogan family cabin when winter came, the group looked for a place for a church building in the spring. What they found was a spring surrounded by holly trees — hence the name.

In 2004, Jo Ann wrote a history of the church, and the following year the publication was named "History of the Year" by the South Carolina Baptist Convention. Many of the historical facts were from her maternal grandmother, Mattie Caldwell Johnson, who also gave her this chowchow recipe.

This recipe, Jo Ann says, is like many others: It can be altered by availability of ingredients and "is made with what you have." Sometimes, she says, she uses "more tomatoes than pepper, sometimes more pepper." She always keeps the syrup mixture the same, but the amount of hot pepper can be varied according to taste.

She uses the food processor to prepare the vegetables because it saves time. My personal preference is to chop rather that grind the vegetables. One recipe suggests adding the salt to the mixture and letting it stand overnight — probably so the cook can rest from all that chopping.

The cooking time can vary with the recipe, from 15 minutes to an hour. Some recipes ask for celery, cucumbers, etc. It seems there are as many ways to make chowchow as there are to make vegetable soup. This is one way, and a good one, and we thank Jo Ann for sharing it with us. Jo Ann usually cooks two or three batches of the chowchow and makes preserves from her prolific fig trees, giving both as Christmas gifts.

Save this recipe, and next summer when the vegetables are available, take a day to make chowchow. If you do, this time next winter you'll be glad you have chowchow relish to add to your menu for ... *Sunday Dinner*.

Grandma Johnson's Chowchow
2 quarts cabbage
2 quarts firm green tomatoes

2 cups onion
2 tablespoons pickling spice
3 cups sugar
2 cups green sweet peppers
2 cups sweet red peppers
Hot pepper as desired
4 cups vinegar
3 tablespoons salt

(Note: The measurements for the vegetables are after they are ground or chopped.)

Grind (or chop) the cabbage, tomatoes, peppers and onions. Drain very well. Salt, let stand, and drain "dry" again. Place in large pan. Add vinegar and sugar. Remove the bay leaf, if any, from the pickling spice and tie spice in cheesecloth. Add spice bag to pan and boil well for approximately 15 minutes.

Mixture will change color when done. Remove spice bag. Pack hot chowchow into hot, sterilized jars and seal immediately. Chill to serve, and refrigerate jar after opening.

Crisp Pickle Slices
Elese Windham
(Published August 2, 2012)

If I were not a Christian (which I am) and if I believed in reincarnation (which I don't), I would want to come back as a rich woman's cat.

I would sleep most of the day on her bed if she weren't looking, eat the food and drink the water provided for me, look out the window at the birds, and not have to worry about the cold, rain and snow of bad weather. There would be no predators.

Because that is not going to be, this week I had to face the reality of the basket of cucumbers waiting to be turned into pickles. The recipe I used was from Elese Windham of St. Helena Baptist Church, located on the Sea Island Parkway on St. Helena Island.

The church dates back from its groundbreaking Feb. 20, 1966. It currently has a membership of around 300, with an average attendance of about 150, and is part of Savannah River Association. Rev. Richard Spearman has served as pastor since 2003.

The recipe was a good choice. It made a lot, about eight pints, and was easy. It could be completed in one day and didn't involve sitting for three or four days, although many of those recipes produce really good pickles.

Elese, retired from a banking career, and her husband, W.K., who retired after a 26-year career as postmaster at Fairfax, have lived in St. Helena for several years. They came to St. Helena with friends many years ago to visit and decided when the time came they would move there (which they did), and joined St. Helena Baptist Church. They are busy there.

They are both in the couples Sunday school class, "Growing with God," are part of the church choir, where W.K. frequently has solo parts, and are in the seniors group. They are also part of Land's End, a group of weekenders and retirees who have known each other for years.

The Windhams have two children. Their daughter, Rachelle, and her husband, Mike Googe, have a son, Michael, at Wade Hampton High School in Hampton — who, according to his grandmother, is "a great baseball player." The Windhams' son Walt is married to Jessica and they have three children. Their son Joshua is currently serving with the Army in Afghanistan; their daughter Brittany is a junior at Lander; and their son

Brandon, a recent graduate of USC-Aiken, works with a moving company in Augusta, Ga.

We thank Elese for sharing the recipe with us. Even if you don't normally make pickles or do other kinds of food preservation, try this. It's easy and it's good. In fact, you may want to open a jar one day soon to try them for ... *Sunday Dinner*.

Crisp Pickle Slices

- 4 quarts sliced cucumbers
- 6 medium onions, sliced
- 2 green peppers, chopped
- 3 cloves garlic
- ⅓ cup salt
- 1½ cups sugar
- 1½ teaspoons turmeric
- 1½ teaspoons celery seed
- 2 tablespoons mustard seed
- 3 cups vinegar

Wash and thinly slice cucumbers and place in large cooking container. Add the onions, peppers and whole garlic cloves. Add salt. Cover with cracked ice, mix and let stand three hours. Drain thoroughly.

Combine remaining ingredients and pour over the cucumber mixture. Heat just to boiling.

Have ready sterilized pint jars, lids and rings. Spoon cucumber mix into jars, cover with the vinegar mixture. Run a knife around inside jar to remove any air bubbles. Put on lids and rings, and screw tightly. Makes 6-8 pints.

About the Author

Juanita Bartlett Garrison was born on a farm near Perry, Georgia, but the family moved about thirty miles east to Cochran when she was 3 years old, and her growing up years were spent there. At age 16 she graduated from Cochran High School, then Middle Georgia College and the University of Georgia with a major in journalism.

Her first job was on the South Georgia weekly, the Sylvester Local. (When she first learned of the opening on the paper's news staff, she thought the Local was a train.) She then worked briefly on the news staff of the Albany Herald before coming to South Carolina with the Seneca Journal, which also published the Clemson Messenger.

She had been in South Carolina less than a year when she was introduced to a young Anderson County farmer, T. Ed Garrison. Later, when they had been married only three years, Ed became involved in politics, was elected and served in the state House of Representatives and then in the state Senate during a thirty-year career.

Over the years Juanita taught public school, journalism at Anderson College, and adults part-time in vocational training. While in that job she began writing a garden column, which she continues, in the Anderson Independent-Mail. A selection of those columns, *The Piedmont Garden*, was later published by USC Press.

Other writings include *Welcome Baptist Church History*, *Arrowood Family History*, *The Little Red Book of Good Manners*, *The Garden and Field Cookbook*, and editing a cookbook of family recipes.

She has been interested and active in many organizations, including garden club, Home Demonstration club, historical groups, writing groups, Girl Scouts, Camp Fire Girls, Cub Scouts, her church's GA group and

Woman's Missionary Union. An active member of her church, Welcome Baptist in Anderson County, she taught intermediate and young adult Sunday school classes for more than sixty years until she retired two years ago to join the women's class.

At the invitation of former Courier editor Don Kirkland and Butch Blume, who now serves as managing editor, Juanita began writing *Sunday Dinner* in 2002 — now going into its fourteenth year.

Juanita and Ed had six "perfect" children (although their spouses sometimes challenged the adjective): Gaye and her husband, Joel Sprague, Greenville; Tom Garrison and his wife, Angie, Anderson; Lee and her husband, Ron Smith, Anderson; Elizabeth and her husband, Jake Rasor, Greenville; and Catherine and her husband, Mark Davis, Mt. Pleasant. The Garrisons' son Bart died in a farm accident in 1990.

Ed died in 2013, and Juanita now lives alone and continues her writing, gardening and church involvement.

And cooking.

Index

DISHES AND RECIPES

Acorn/Butternut Squash Soup, 57
American Chop Suey, 189
Apple Dumpling Bake, 266
Applesauce Soufflé, 270
Bacon and Tomato Pie, 118
Baked Caramel Corn, 284
Baked Chicken that Makes Its Own Gravy, 161
Baked Onions, 120
Baked Savory Pork Chops, 170
Baptist Pound Cake, 219
Basic Chicken Pie, 159
Biscuits, 199
Blackberry Jam Cake with Caramel Icing, 233
Boiled Ham, 166
Broccoli, 126
Broccoli-Cheese Soup, 64
Brunch with Crabmeat Newberg, 45
Cabbage Casserole, 131
Cabbage, Collards and Kale, 133
Cabbage Slaw, 76
Catfish, 186
Catfish Stew, 59
Cheeseburger Pie, 175
Cherry Congealed Salad, 88
Chicken Rolls, 37
Chinese Slaw, 78
Chocolate Lust, 276
Chowchow, 298
$100 Coconut Cake, 229
Coconut Pies, 258
Coconut Peach Pie, 261
Collards and Cabbages, 137
Corn Casserole, 110

Corn Pie, 114
Cranberry Pork Chops, 173
Crisp Pickle Slices, 300
Crock Pot Macaroni, 96
Denver Downs Delight, 274
Easy Yeast Rolls, 205
Eclair Cake, 240
Eggs Benedict, 28
Eggs Mornay, 28
Ever Best Eggplant, 147
Fresh Apple Pie, 253
Fresh Corn Pudding, 112
Fresh Strawberry Pie, 255
Frozen Fruit Salad, 74
German Chocolate Brownies, 280
Glorified Squash, 142
Grated Sweet Potato Bake, 149
Green Bean Casserole, 122
Green Beans, 124
Gumbo Creole, 66
Hay and Straw with Pear Pie, 193
Hearty Potato Soup, 62
Honey Bun Cake, 242
Hot Crab Dip, 35
Iced Tea, 38
Infallible Rice Casserole, 101
Japanese Fruitcake, 247
Julie's Roast Beef, 157
Layered Lettuce Salad, 85
Lemon Berry Cake, 236
Lemon Cheesecake, 238
Lonesome Cowboy Bars, 282
Luncheon Veg. Dish/Squash Casserole, 139

Macaroni and Cheese, 93
Macaroni and Cheese My Way, 98
Mama's Scalloped Oysters, 181
Marinated Cukes and Onions, 80
Meatloaf and Veggies, 177
Neapolitan Casserole, 179
Okra Casserole, 129
One-Pot Potatoes, 102
Peach (or Apple) Strudel, 272
Peanut Butter Pie, 263
Pear Honey, 291
Pear Relish, 293
Pecan Candy and Sugar Peanuts, 286
Pickled Peaches, 296
Pie Crusts, 250
Pineapple Cake, 231
Pineapple Pound Cake, 224
Pork Chop Casserole, 168
Popovers, 212
Pound Cake, 221
Quiche, 47
Refrigerator Rolls, 207
Regal Chicken Salad, 83
Salads and Dressings, 71
Salmon Loaf, 184
Sandwiches, 214
Shrimp and Grits, 51
Sour Cream Banana Pudding, 278
Spoon Bread, 202
Squash Casserole, 145
Strawberry Bread, 209
Strawberry Pound Cake, 226
Stuffed Tomatoes with Yellow Rice, 116
Stuffings and Dressings, 104
Sunday Glazed Ham, 164
Sweet Potato Crunch, 151
The Best Fruitcake, 244
Toaster Oven Recipes, 191
Veggie Squares, 33

Warm Apple Crisp, 268
White Fruitcake, 246
Yum-Yum Chicken Soup with Cornbread, 68
Zesty Vegetable Casserole, 108

CHURCHES

Anderson First Baptist, 57
Ashley River Baptist, Charleston, 140-141, 278
Barker's Creek Baptist, Honea Path, 113, 238-239
Barnwell First Baptist, 115
Bel-Ridge Baptist, Belvedere, 179
Bishop Branch Baptist, Central, 266
Boiling Springs Baptist, Spartanburg, 75
Brandon Baptist, Greenville, 227
Brunson Baptist, 115
Calvary Baptist, Florence, 96-97
Calvary Baptist, Simpsonville, 152
Camp Creek Baptist, Taylors, 129
Canaan Baptist, Cope, 59
Central Baptist, Aiken, 294
Central Presbyterian, 37
Charleston First Baptist, 118-119, 278
Chestnut Ridge Baptist, Laurens, 147-148
Columbia Baptist, Honea Path/Princeton, 219, 234
Connector Church, Laurens, 68
Crescent Hill Baptist, Columbia, 210, 253
Crooked Run Baptist, Winnsboro, 224
Cross Roads Baptist, Greer, 244-245
Dalzell Baptist, Sumter, 157
Delta Church, 68
Dorchester Baptist, Saluda Association, 219
Eastlan Baptist, Greenville, 150-151
Edgefield First Baptist, 169, 212, 229, 270
Edisto Baptist, Cordova, 117
Edwards Road Baptist, Greenville, 140
Fairview Baptist, Spartanburg, 131

Florence First Baptist, 150
Georgetown First Baptist, 110
Glendale Baptist, Glendale, 191
Good Hope Baptist, Conway, 51, 77
Good Hope Baptist, Ridge Assoc., 294
Goucher Baptist, Gaffney, 101
Hagood Avenue Baptist, Barnwell, 236-237
Hampton First Baptist, 125
Happy Trails Cowboy Church, Pelzer, 68
Hardeeville First Baptist, 142
Harris Baptist, Greenwood, 221
Heights Baptist, Beech Island, 173
His Vineyard, Greer, 176
Holly Springs Baptist, Inman, 79, 93, 298-299
Homeland Park Baptist, Anderson, 57-58
Hopewell Baptist, Hampton, 125
Lake Wateree Baptist, 177
Langston Baptist, Conway, 52
Laurel Baptist, Greenville, 280
Laurens First Baptist, 74
Lexington Baptist, 207
Little Horse Creek Baptist, Graniteville, 179
Lowry's Baptist, Chester Assoc., 224-225
Lydia Baptist, Newry, 286
Millbrook Baptist, Aiken, 180
Mountain Creek Baptist, Anderson, 37
Mountain Creek Baptist, Edgefield Assoc., 268
Mountville Baptist, Laurens Assoc., 189
Mt. Bethel Baptist, Belton, 159, 291, 296
Mt. Calvary Baptist, Elko, 115
Mt. Lebanon Baptist, Greer, 262
New Salem Baptist, Sumter, 157, 242
North Augusta First Baptist, 173
Overbrook Baptist, Greenville, 145-146, 152
Pleasant Grove Baptist, Greer, 123, 175, 282
Pleasant View Baptist, Anderson, 57
Providence Baptist, Anderson, 255-256
Providence Baptist, Pageland, 81, 88
Riverside Baptist, Anderson, 171-172, 284

Rock Hill First Baptist, 64
Salem Avenue Baptist, Sumter, 242
Salley Baptist, Edisto Association, 272
Sierra Baptist, Anderson, 266
Simpsonville First Baptist, 68
Six and Twenty Baptist, Pendleton, 266
South Main Street Baptist, Greenwood, 137
Southside Baptist, Abbeville, 57
Southside Baptist, Sumter, 224
Spring Branch Baptist, Nichols, 248, 276
St. Helena Baptist, St. Helena Island, 33, 108-109, 301
Sweetwater Baptist, North Augusta, 270
Taylors First Baptist, 150
The Baptist Church of Beaufort, 108, 124-125, 205
Unity Baptist, Simpsonville, 85-86
Varnville First Baptist, 161-162
Wagener First Baptist, 150
Warrenville First Baptist, Aiken Assoc., 294
Welcome Baptist, Anderson, 150, 164, 231, 258, 264, 303-304
West Columbia First Baptist, 177
West Gantt First Baptist, Greenville, 241
Woodside Baptist, Greenville, 265